John and Alvin have a unique disarming ability to get leaders to speak about the most difficult issues and challenges of leadership and get them willing to go public on it. These conversations with leaders represent a peek into the psyche and emotions of leaders as they process through their journey in leadership. It is a priceless set of insights valuable to any student of leadership. A must read.

Mr. Sam Lam
President and Managing Partner of Linkage Asia

This volume is the result of John's relentless curiosity in learning from the successes and challenges of game changers in Asia. You will find honesty, humility and determination as the icons interviewed share their minds and hearts. A mandatory reading for those willing to learn from others.

Mr. Peter Chao
Founder, Eagles Communications

John, an evergreen human motivator, draws critical life lessons from several business and thought leaders who have gone through the feast and famine in their journeys. The easy prose style of the book makes it a warm book. I commend this book.

Judge (Ret) Richard Magnus
Expert (IBC) Member of UNESCO
Alumni of Network Agenda Council
World Economic Forum

If the earlier book was the Dim Sum, this is the entrée, the substantial meat. When the topmost leaders of brand name organizations speak and tell you the value of great leadership principles and beliefs in their corporate and personal lives, you will have much to chew on.

Professor Ang Peng Hwa
Wee Kim Wee School of Communication and Information
Nanyang Technological University, Singapore
President-Elect 2015/16
International Communication Association

This book provides the platform for readers to engage not just with leaders of their own country but also those from the nearby region. No leadership can escape trials. They say iron sharpens iron — what better way than to spend time learning from those who have triumphed!

Mdm. Hannah Yeoh
Madam Speaker of the Selangor State Legislative Assembly, Malaysia

The true stories of these great leaders are so powerful and enjoyable. Reading "Heart To Heart", I have learned so much from their experiences, wisdom and practical advice. I strongly recommend the book to everyone who wishes to be a great leader. Enjoy it, learn from it, and become a great leader.

Dr. Somjin Sornpaisarn
CEO of TMB Asset Management

I thoroughly enjoyed reading the interviews and the thought-provoking comments made by these Asian Leaders.

Mr. Lucas Chow
Chairman of Health Promotion Board Singapore
Member of Board of Trustees of the National University of Singapore

A must-have book for all leaders. Read and learn from those who have gone through tough times and made triumphant comebacks.

Mrs. Suwanna Eiampikul
CEO of Bertram Chemical (1982) Co. Ltd., Thailand
CEO and Founder of Peppermint Bike Park, Thailand

This book contains much wisdom that comes from the practical insights of leaders as they reflected on the choices they made, the struggles they went through, and the outcomes they achieved. I was touched by their humility, and inspired by their faith and deep convictions. This book is an invaluable resource for all leaders.

Professor Neo Boon Siong
Nanyang Business School
Nanyang Technological University, Singapore

In their intimate interviews with these 28 Asian leaders, John and Alvin have given us a portrait of authentic leadership. These leaders were never about power, prestige or position but principles, praxis and perseverance. Their stories inspire me to be a wiser person and a better leader.

Mr. Michael Tan
President of Eagles Communications, Singapore

PREFACE

The 21st century world is full of success stories, but is short on tales of facing up to failure and overcoming major setbacks. Social media posts and smartphone chat messages are fast-growing, but intimate face-to-face engagements are becoming increasingly rare.

It is in this new social climate that we set out to write this book: exclusive interviews with 28 illustrious Asian leaders. All 28 of them have been specially selected for the values they represent, their character as well as their ability to recover from crisis and mount comebacks. Great pain has been taken to choose leaders from a range of countries across different arenas — ranging from the corporate world to academia and politics, from those who inherited family businesses to those who built their careers from scratch.

Our interviews were conducted over a period of four years from 2012 to 2015. We have met and have spoken extensively and exclusively with each of the well-known personalities across Singapore, Malaysia, Indonesia and Thailand, at their homes and offices. We hope this book will give readers the feel that you are having an engaging and personal chat with each leader over a meal.

The questions posed to each leader were specially crafted and are intended to flesh out the challenges of modern leadership, as well as examine issues of personal adversity peculiar to certain leaders. A question-and-answer style was chosen to make the chapters more reader friendly and provide a more intimate feel. We have intentionally preserved each interviewee's cultural nuances and personality types, so that you can appreciate their different communication styles while maintaining editorial integrity in the language and grammar used.

Three central themes — ***crisis, comebacks and character*** — form the book's backbone.

The past decade has seen crisis come and go with increasing frequency. Many of the leaders have led through memorable events such as the 1997 Asian Financial

Crisis to the 2008 Global Financial Crisis and even the 2011 European debt crisis. Discover how they cope personally and galvanize their organizations and followers during these trying times. Most of them not only survived but also emerged stronger and wiser post-crisis.

The ability to recover from huge setbacks also differentiates leaders who thrive in the long haul from run-of-the-mill ones who swiftly fade away. We chat at length about how they bounce back from the tragic loss of a loved one, repay a mountain of financial debt or cope with the near-collapse of their businesses.

The strength of character can make or break a leader both in times of prosperity or adversity, and we examine the traits which make them tick. Ethics-related issues such as dealing with corruption and the challenges of upholding one's personal integrity are also addressed. Each interviewee shares his or her vulnerable side with us as well, speaking candidly and truthfully about his or her respective weaknesses while providing priceless practical advice for the next generation of leaders.

The next decade promises to be an eventful but also turbulent one for planet Earth, with natural disasters, political and social unrest and economic turmoil becoming more prevalent. The only certainty we have is uncertainty itself. However, eagles have been known to thrive in storms, as they are able to soar above the grey clouds by catching the extra wind that usually accompanies the bad weather. In contrast, almost all other birds go into hiding during these times of adversity.

We hope this book will serve as an invaluable tool for you in these tough times, enabling you to soar high above and overcome these difficult circumstances — a useful resource for both the board room and the living room; office or school.

May you glean many nuggets of practical leadership insights from the collective wisdom of these 28 individuals as you feel their pulse and hear their heart beats through the following pages.

John Ng and Alvin Foo

> The heart of education
> is the education of the heart.

AMNUAY
TAPINGKAE
The Educator
of the Heart Leader

The heart of education is the education of the heart." These wise words form the basis of Dr. Amnuay Tapingkae's core beliefs about education and leadership.

The academic is the Founder and Chairman of the Friends of Asia Foundation in Chiang Mai, Thailand, beginning in 2009. This foundation was established to:

1. Promote co-operation and cordiality among the peoples of Asia

2. Promote social development activities and a good quality of life, and to provide services to the community

3. Operate charitable activities

4. Avoid engaging in any political activities

These organizational goals truly encapsulate Dr. Amnuay's aspirations for our region and for education in our region — to teach our youth to reach out to their neighbors and help as best we can — to truly provide 'the education of the heart'.

Among his many previous leadership roles in institutions of higher education are serving as Dean of the Education Faculty at Chiang Mai University, as well as being the Director of the inter-government Regional Institute of Higher Education and Development based in Singapore.

His most prominent work, however, was serving as the founding President of Payap University in Chiang Mai from 1972 to 1993, leading the institution as it expanded from 200 students to more than 6,000. Established in 1974, Payap University is a private institution founded by the Church of Christ in Thailand. It became the first fully accredited private university in Thailand in 1984. It now offers 22 Thai language undergraduate degrees in 12 faculties, as well as four international undergraduate degrees in English. The university also runs several master's degree courses.

Dr. Amnuay studied for his undergraduate education at Illinois College in Jacksonville, Illinois, in the United States from 1956 to 1959. He was then awarded the prestigious Fulbright Scholarship in 1963 and obtained his graduate education from the University of Washington. Dr. Amnuay holds a Master's degree in Educational Psychology and a Doctoral degree in Educational Philosophy. He has also received a certificate in Educational Administration from the University of Pittsburgh, as well as one in Higher Education Management from Harvard University.

We catch up with the highly articulate and enlightening educator over coffee at a hotel in Chiang Mai.

 Who or what influenced you most in your leadership development? And why?

 President Vernon Caine. He was the President of Illinois College during my undergraduate days from 1956 to 1959. He was one of the main leaders who influenced me. He was not only an administrator, but also a warm person who knew you personally and was concerned for your future. He was an educator who touched the hearts of his students.

The second person was Dr. Malcolm Stewart, who was the Professor of Philosophy at Illinois College. Dr. Stewart was an excellent professor and at the same time he was a pastor of a small church in a rural area. Dr Stewart was also my mentor. He was not only a great intellectual, but more importantly, he was also a caring person. He did not exist in an 'ivory tower', rather, he had his feet firmly on the ground. He was warm and personable, and because he was so caring, his students responded well to him.

 What is one memorable life-changing experience that has impacted and shaped the way you lead?

 When I decided to accept Christ, it was the turning point of my life. In Buddhism a believer must work for his own salvation, to save his own soul. No one can save you except through your own effort. But I found this was not possible for me because I realized my own weaknesses.

I came down with typhoid fever when I was about 15. There was no medication then and when the fever became so high, my parents had to ice me to lower my fever. They came into my room when I was very drowsy and they thought I was asleep. My father thought I was going to die. He turned to my mother and said, "Let's go to the children's ward to see if we can adopt a son in place of Amnuay."

I was so saddened by the thought that even my own parents were so depressed that they had to succumb to the fears of the world, to the inevitable. Even before my life had ended, they were preparing to abandon me. I knew in my heart that there must be someone who cares for me, someone who would never abandon me, no matter what happens. Miraculously, I recovered. I knew then there is a God who cares for me.

I attended Prince Royal's College, a Christian high school, where chapel was a regular activity. As I listened to the Christian message, I began to be aware of my inner quest. The more I learned, the more I was touched by the wisdom and the meaning of the Christian message. I felt deep in my heart that the message was true and meaningful for me. During the "Religious Emphasis Week" at school, I was listening to the sermon, and when the preacher gave the invitation to accept Jesus, at that very moment I sensed God's calling and I accepted the call. That was the life-changing moment. From then on, I have prayed to Jesus, "Please lead me." He has been doing that all these years and has not let me go, even during times of doubt and confusion.

God has guided me throughout my life and He has been so real to me all these years. After high school, I attended Chulalongkorn University for one year. I studied science but it did not speak to my heart. Mathematics and science did not satisfy my inner quest.

In my classes, I would always ask serious questions about life. I recalled having many good discussions with a professor of physics, who was very interested in philosophy. During those times, I felt very lost and could not find the satisfactory answers to my questions.

I prayed to God, "Please lead me" and He opened the way by providing a scholarship to study at the Illinois College. I was accepted by the First Presbyterian Church in Jacksonville, Illinois as part of their mission outreach program. I was received into the community with open arms. I felt love. From then on, that made me want to follow Jesus to the best of my ability. He became my mentor.

I look up to Jesus all the time and He has never failed me. I have traveled many roads both peaceful and stormy. Through it all, He has given me the courage to move forward.

Another incident that demonstrated God's leading in my life happened in 1957, when I volunteered to serve as a counselor in several youth camps across the United States. I once served in a camp in Happy Valley, Pennsylvania. There were five counselors and on the last night, we were having a farewell dinner. One of the older counselors, Idabelle Riblet, who was very much like my mother, said to me, "Tap (my nickname), we are all going home tomorrow. Where are you going?" I said, "I will hop on a

Greyhound bus and God will lead me." She must have thought that this young man was crazy. After dinner, she asked me the same question and I gave her the same answer. She was not very happy with my answer, so she stepped out for a while. When she came back she said, "I called my husband, Henry, and he asked me to bring you home." So I said, "See, God has already answered my prayer."

The next morning, I hopped into her car and went to her home in Kensington, Maryland. Her husband embraced me and warmly greeted me, "Welcome home, son!' So, I spent the rest of my summer with them, helping my new 'dad' to plant trees and tend his orchids. I enjoyed my stay with them so much. I was even adopted into their family. Idabelle said, "We have three daughters but no son, you will become our son." They became my American parents. 'Dad' was a scientist at John Hopkins University. Even till today, I still keep in touch with my three American 'sisters'. These are just two examples of how God has been leading me in my life!

 What is one legacy you have left behind in your organization?

 All the people at Payap University are just like my family members, even though I have retired for so many years. Over the past 17 years, people still keep in touch with me and seek my advice on many issues, both personal and academic. We have a very close and personal relationship. I worship with them, I pray with them, and I pray for them. They are truly a part of my extended family.

A good leader is one that touches the heart of people. I learned this from the late president Vernon Caine. His lifestyle touched my heart and I always believed, "Should I become a president of a university in the future, I would follow his lifestyle to touch the hearts of my students and colleagues."

I have tried to help many students over the years. I pray that I have written something good on the hearts of the people I have been able to help.

When you are willing to give, people rally behind you because they know that you are working together with them for something that you both love. They know that you are working for the benefit of the people, not your own benefit. Payap University is very close to my heart. I have spent lots of time with colleagues and students even now.

Once, I received a letter from a lady who shared that she had difficulty paying her daughter's school fee at Payap University because her husband had passed away and she only had a small farm. I wrote back to her saying, "Don't worry, I will take care of your daughter." Without meeting her or knowing who she was, I made sure that the girl had enough scholarship to finish college.

Several years later, after I had left Payap, I was the interim President of Stamford University in Cha Am, Petchaburi, Thailand. A group of about 40 psychology students from Chiang Mai University came to visit our university and I met with them. In speaking to them, I encouraged them to listen to the heartbeat of the person they are working with when they become counselors. I then told them the story of this girl that I helped through Payap years ago. While I was speaking, one girl in the group began to cry. Everyone was concerned that she was not well or that there was some problem. She explained that she was the girl that I had mentioned.

You see, the heart of education is the education of the heart. I have helped guide several excellent tertiary institutions, but my greatest joy is my investment in the lives of people that I have been able to help along their path. I often tell my staff and students, "Remember the goodness that was done for you. Let it fill your heart so that you may pass on the goodness to others."

Give us a glimpse of your daily routine. And why do you keep these practices?

I rise with the sun, about 5 am. I wait for the sun to rise but I never wait for the sun to set. Let me explain what I mean: It is said that with the sunrise comes hope and encouragement — I have always found this to be true. The sunset is often seen as an end and associated with sadness. I have always looked to the sunrise and the opportunities that it brings rather than just waiting for the day to end. When working at a university, I was usually the first or the second to reach the campus. I would get there before 7 am. When you are there in those early hours, the campus is quiet and you can have quiet time with God. You can open your heart to Him and pray for the ministry of that day. I would ask God to bless me and shower me with grace and wisdom to touch the people I would encounter that day.

I look at problems as something that God gives you to solve, a way to help others. When I see a problem, I never panic and I don't let it grow out of hand. I try to make it smaller as best I can.

My belief is that when people come to see you and they are crying, you wipe their tears. When they come to you unhappy, they should walk out of your office happy or relieved of their burden in some way. You should not increase the burden of the person who comes to you. You must understand what their needs are. If you can't help them at that moment, you say, "give me time and I will try to help". So in that way, people go out encouraged and with hope. When people have hope, some problems will solve themselves. Some problems may persist but time will give you a new perspective to help solve the problem.

 What is the most crushing adversity you have ever faced in your leadership? How did you deal with it?

 Well, there are always those who struggle against you, those who want to work against you as a leader. In these cases, it is important to listen to them closely and ask them straight questions. In this way, you can try to get to the root of their difficulty.

I ask, "What is your motive in working here at Payap? Would you consider other places where you may be happier?" The answer usually comes gradually. After a few sessions, some would say, "Oh, Payap pays too low a salary." And I would say, "I know another place that pays better. Would you like me to write a recommendation letter for you?"

I try to encourage each one to find a place that fits him or her best. It is not to get rid of the person. If we can touch their heart and win them over, we would have their support. However, if the person is not able to be happy at your institution, it is better for them to find a different place.

Because Payap is a Christian institution, you cannot have many selfish people. That would drag the university down, so I try to find a better place for them. I hope they'll be happy elsewhere but sometimes after looking at other places, they come back because they realized that Payap is much better than anywhere else.

There is a tendency to become personal and introspective when asked to name our most 'crushing adversary'. In addition to the personnel challenges I faced as president of the university, there was institutional oppression that we had to meet.

In Thailand and throughout much of Asia, a private, Christian institution of higher education is not always considered a partner but rather a challenge or even an adversary in the overall higher educational enterprise. In official meetings, private colleges and universities were ignored.

The scales of justice are often tipped against us. We find it unfairly difficult to acquire research grants, access tax benefits for donors, and above all, equity with government institutions. In order to overcome the disadvantage of size we had to rely on combined strength. Together with other colleagues we have developed associations.

The two of which I am actively involved in are the Association of Private Higher Education Institutions in Thailand and the Association of Christian Universities and Colleges in Asia. As a Christian university we have unique perspectives and contributions to make not only to the education of individual students but also to the whole undertaking of higher education. I believe that leaders in other institutions can look at what we are doing at Payap and will be inspired. "If Payap can do it, we can do better." I feel challenged to strive for the improvement of higher education as a whole.

 What is the most intense tension between faith and academia that you have faced? How do you manage them?

 As a former Buddhist, I want to give respect to the Buddhist tradition. At the same time, as Christians, we must affirm our faith in God through both our word and deed.

When there is a difference of opinion, I don't try to win the argument. For example, some Christian faculty might say that Christianity is superior to Buddhism, but that is not fair even though you believe in your heart that Jesus is the answer, you have to be careful not to force that on another. Rather, it is through our actions, our empathy, our compassion, that people will see Jesus in our life and be moved by what they see.

One of my greatest challenges between faith and academia came in an encounter with the President of the Faculty Association at Payap. He came with a delegation and said, "Payap University is in Thailand under the Thai constitution, therefore we want to erect a Buddha statue on the campus."

I listened to them, and let them talk for half an hour. When they stopped, I said, "Ladies and gentlemen, this is a Christian university. There are only one or two Christian universities in Thailand. We are not trying to compete with the government universities or other institutions of higher learning. The constitution stipulates that Christians and Muslims can have their own institutions. Payap has a cross to display but nothing else because this is a Christian university. This doesn't mean that we live for Christians only. Payap exists for all faiths and we welcome them to our institution. However, you must understand our philosophy — we believe in a living God who is with us always. It is He that we honor here. I plead for your understanding and ask you not to press this issue."

They went away but they came back later, still insisting on erecting a Buddha statue on our campus so finally I said, "As a Christian I am strong in my faith, even unto death. My life is in God's hands and therefore, I cannot say yes to your proposal. How about you, are you willing to die for your faith? Go and think about that and come back again and we will set-tle the issue." They never came back. I am grateful to God for the courage He gave me that day.

 In your leadership within the university, what are some core values you want to inculcate in your students and why?

 As I said earlier, the heart of education is the education of the heart. It says in Proverbs, "Guard your heart above all else, for it determines the course of your life."

Examine yourself. If your heart is in the right place, good things will follow. If you put your head first, you could be misled. You'll listen to philoso-phies and other conflicting ideas, and you cannot come to a conclusion for yourself. If you educate your heart and begin there, you'll know what to believe, you will know which is the right philosophy and which values are best for you.

The second value is found in Ephesians, "Honor Christ and put others first". Think of others first, and not yourself. A person who lives for himself or herself is lost and is fighting a losing battle. If you live for others, life will be happier and more meaningful. Good will come from you and it will flow back to you.

When you think of others first, things will fall into place. But if you think of yourself first, things will fall into pieces.

If you think of others first, you'll have compassion for others and that's the life to live. A happy life is one that is lived for others.

 What keeps you going?

 I always look for a better tomorrow. A strong sense of hope and optimism keeps me going.

I never give up. If you give up, life is not worth living. God has given me this opportunity. I have only one life to live. When I have this life, I enjoy it fully and use it to glorify God.

 If you were to live your life all over again, what's one thing you would do differently? And why?

 I have made some mistakes where I was too quick to judge. I would try to love people more.

In the past, I have failed — as we all do. When a person is difficult and seemingly selfish, I have often tried to push the person away. Sadly, later on, it takes so much time to reconcile. I would like to have been more careful in those cases and would also have asked the Lord to guide me.

If I had another life to live, another university to lead, I would try to correct some of those mistakes and improve my actions with God's help.

What is one advice you would give to young, emerging leaders?

My advice is to stay humble. Humility is the most valuable asset a person can have. A person should have humility, honesty, and transparency. Do not try to win an argument. Instead, win the heart of the person you are dealing with. Get to know your colleagues very well and let them know that you care. Show them you want to work for the good of all in your organization and community.

I tell young leaders, don't jump to conclusions. Take your time, gather all the data available before you make a decision. If you move too fast, you will be sorry later. Before you make a decision affecting the lives of many people, make sure it is the wisest decision that you can make. Then trust that God will make all things right through His infinite wisdom and mercy.

> "Every person is not just a number.
> That person has a heart, a family,
> and a life ahead of him."

CHATREE DUANGNET
The Change Leader

r. Chatree Duangnet is a prominent Thai medical leader who is well-respected in the international arena.

The Chiang Rai native is the Chief Executive and Chairman of the Bangkok Hospital Medical Center, made up of Bangkok Hospital, Bangkok Heart Hospital and Wattanosoth Hospital — a cancer hospital. This group of hospitals is part of the Thai-listed Bangkok Dusit Medical Services (BDMS), which is among the largest private healthcare groups globally.

Dr. Chatree also sits on the board of BDMS, which has a market value of over US$3.8 billion. He is an American Board-certified paediatrician, having spent 21 years in the United States, both as a practicing physician and in senior management positions. The 50-year-old then returned to Thailand in 1995. Since then, he has been holding senior posts in key hospital groups there.

The all-rounder firmly believes in using both his left and right brain effectively. "I believe in balance. I might not be the best in anything, but I try to be good at everything," he said.

His passion for healthcare quality management led him to implement change at Bangkok Hospital, although that was not without heartache. His first attempt in 1995 to impose a quality standard there ended as a big flop. "I had everything right, and crossed the river. But when I reached the other side and stepped onto land, my followers were still on the other side of the river," he recalled.

Dr. Chatree then worked for another hospital before returning to Bangkok Hospital several years ago. This time, he succeeded in transforming his hospital into a regional healthcare icon, by putting people first and instilling a high standard of professionalism and quality healthcare. This led to Bangkok Hospital being a popular medical destination for Thais, and also for patients in the Middle East and other parts of Asia.

"I told my people 'saving lives is first, even if they don't have money'. There are no questions asked — this is the core job of the hospital."

We caught up with the compassionate and people-first doctor at his office in Bangkok.

Who or what influenced you most in your leadership development? And why?

 My father, Ajarn Tongdee, who was headmaster of a school in Chiang Rai.

He was a true leader in that community. He loved his people; he applied teachings from the Bible to his leadership. Unfortunately, he passed away when he was just 50 years old. Till now, people still remember him in Chiang Rai. He cultivated leadership principles in both the business and the Christian world into me. He taught me by example.

Two incidents stand out. Once when I was around 10th or 11th grade, I did so many things and did not see any returns. He said: "Son, time will prove you right — endure, don't quit. Wait and see, and things will come. Whatever you give will be returned to you."

Next, he taught me that there are things you have to say no to. When you are young, you say yes to everything in the world, and you end up with so many things to do. Sometimes, I cried because I had so many things to do. He told me to prioritize and learn to say no to certain things.

Because of that, I received the best all-round student award in 1963 at my high school, due to success in studies, sports and church. It taught me to excel in every way possible. Because of that, I believe in balance. I might not be the best in anything, but I try to be good at everything.

 How do you sustain these values?

 Every night before I go to bed, I'll spend some time to reflect on that day — certain things I've said or done, and see what I can do differently the next time. You can make mistakes, after all we are human. But how do you ensure you don't make the same mistake the next time?

If you preach, keep preaching what you believe. The more you say it, the more you'll believe it. Talk about it, practice it, do it with the people whom you love.

As doctors, we go to school with the left side of our brain, to pass exams and all. But when you go out there, you have to use the right side of your brain to survive, to make sure people love you. We flop in the world when we don't know how to communicate with people. So I try to balance the left and right side of my brain every day.

You have to teach people the importance of balance. To run a hospital, I use the right side of the brain, which I call the 'offensive team' — marketing, recruiting doctors, quality, making sure you look good and people know about that. You are using resources in this team.

But I also have another team — the left side of the brain which I call the 'defensive team' — the Chief Financial Officer and those in charge of managing costs to have a proper defensive margin.

When both sides balance, you grow and at the same time, you don't lose your pants.

 Give us a glimpse of your daily routine. And why do you keep these practices?

 As a leader, you have to lead the organization in a direction which everybody agrees on. I've to ensure there is a new line of people coming up — succession-planning.

I'm a people leader. I love people, and I want people to like me. Maybe it's my father's influence — people loved him so much. I became a pediatrician because everybody loves pediatricians — mothers, fathers, grandparents, even pets love pediatricians!

I want to be a family person, a personal leader for the people around me, so my daily life revolves around people.

For seven years, the leaders of the different hospitals meet every Wednesday in the early morning to discuss theories and readings which may not even be related to medical care. Because of this, they build a connection with me and with each other, and we don't fight among ourselves.

On Tuesdays, I meet with the offensive team to discuss marketing, growth, and to see which units need help.

On Fridays, I meet the defensive team and we talk about expense, margin and cost efficiency goals.

Good football teams usually win with a good defence.

Once a month, I have a town hall meeting to speak with 400 to 500 people. My people have my email. I try to connect with the bottom, so that people know the leadership tries to connect with the staff. At the town hall meeting, I communicate our vision for the next five years, and show them exactly where we are at now. I give them half-an-hour to ask questions and I reward them for doing so. At the end, they know that in order for them to love us, we must love them first.

Through these, we find out many issues that our people are not happy about. Usually, the biggest issue that they are not happy about is with their superiors, not money. The root problem is that we reduced the number of heads of departments (HODs), so communication is bad. Their assessment of KPIs (key performance indicators) is not accurate too, so people are not happy about that.

 How do you treat your staff, especially those who constantly underperform?

 I look at a person. If they don't perform well, is it beyond their control? Maybe you as their leader did not put them in the right place. I try to make my people feel like I'm their parent — if they stay here, they put their life under my responsibility, I make sure I do my my best to live up to that responsibility.

If we try our best to help them, and it still doesn't work out after the second time, they'll leave by themselves. We don't have to fire them.

In Thailand, you can't have a system based completely on merit. Otherwise, you won't have any loyalty left. It's about head, heart and guts. We only get rid of people who have defects in their heart — those who are unethical.

If a person doesn't perform even after they have been trained, it's still the fault of the superior. You just didn't give them the right job. If they give their heart to us, then we should be responsible for them.

If you have guts and perseverance, but you are not smart, don't worry we'll still keep you and find a job for you — that's my principle.

That sure sounds radical from a western perspective. Why do you do that?

Because I'm a personal leader. Each person is not just a number. That person has a heart, a family, and a life ahead of them.

In Japan, they have a strict selection process but they hire people forever. I try to bring both of these systems (America and Japan) together, so that there is strong continuity for the organization.

Backstabbers have a heart issue for sure. Anyone who disturbs the peace of the team has a heart issue. We don't promote them and they just leave us, because they know this issue is not tolerated. With close communication at the grassroots level, I know who has a heart issue.

For example, we had doctors who overcharge patients by doing some unnecessary procedures. Even if that doctor makes money for our hospitals, we ask him to resign, we don't tolerate it. We had three who have resigned, and income in those units dropped.

But you know what? We had good-hearted doctors who came in, and business has doubled and even tripled at those three units because people are no longer afraid. Everybody else is performing, and patients are happier.

'If you make this decision, the rest of the people will work harder for you, which will be better than just the effort of one person. Cooperation will be better, things will be smoother. The after-effects will be much better, when the superstar is not there anymore. Twenty non-superstars working together is better than one superstar. Others may come in to fill the gap, because they've been suppressed by the superstar.

How do you lead change effectively?

You have to be a committed, persevering leader. It takes at least three years or more. Don't change the script, even if you find a better script along the way. You still keep your old script, until everybody practices more than 8,000 hours of it and gets it into their culture.

After it gets into their culture, then your change process is complete.

Let's keep doing this until it gets into their blood. Don't keep changing. You need that one persevering leader to make sure they keep doing the same thing for at least three years.

 When do you know it's the wrong script?

 You have to find a script that has worked well already in the whole world. Don't do trial and error. Even if the script is 'half-good' and you practice it, it's better than a perfect script that you don't practice. You've to keep doing it until it becomes a habit, then the same habit will become a culture. You'll be unfair to your people if you keep changing.

 What is the greatest challenge in leading change and why?

 Communication. When people see change, there's a grief reaction — they'll fight it from Day One. They'll object, blame somebody, even go into depression. But you don't get mad at them, don't get rid of them — those are natural reactions. You just keep communicating the rationale and the benefits of the change.

Those who still keep doing the above after you have kept communicating will eventually just resign.

 What is one most crushing adversity you have ever faced in your leadership? How do you deal with it?

 There was one adversity which changed my thinking. I was in the US for 21 years as a paediatrician — the last 13 years there I was involved in quality and risk management. I was recruited by Bangkok Hospital in 1995 on a three-year contract — they wanted me to put quality into the system.

I tried to do so and I was personally successful. I came up with a quality standard but within three years, it fell apart because everybody was against it. They didn't understand what I was talking about. I flopped badly. It was a disaster. Doctors started rallying against me; nobody would accept anything I did.

Then I was recruited by Bumrungrad Hospital.

My lesson was this: When a leader leads, he has to know the people around him. What is the speed of your followers, their knowledge and how you communicate with them?

I had done everything right, and crossed the river. But when I reached the other side and stepped onto land, my followers had not even crossed the river yet! You have to know your followers well and try to communicate with them. A successful leader must have successful followers. I ended up with one person succeeding but the whole group failing.

So when I returned to Bangkok Hospital the second time, I took my time. Earlier, I flopped because I didn't know my followers. Now I've changed. I make sure I'm focused on them, that they are successful, then I'm successful.

Previously I used the same speed of the US hospital and applied it to the Thai hospital that had little idea about quality standards. I was so stupid. I felt very sad. After three years, they didn't even want to extend my contract. That was why I failed in the first attempt at change in the Bangkok hospital.

But I learned my lesson, and now I teach others. A leader succeeds only when his followers are successful.

 How do you balance between profitability and patient care?

 My medical career has always focused on quality and safety. I tell my people "saving lives is first, even if they don't have any money". There are no questions asked — this is the core job of the hospital. If somebody comes into the emergency room and my staff asks him or her "do you have any insurance", I will be mad at them.

If you save lives first, good will return to you. When they are discharged from the hospital, they'll tell their family members and relatives that this hospital saves lives without hesitation. That'll form our CSR (Corporate Social Responsibility) budget — this is better than putting up billboards. I teach my people — money is not your job as a doctor or nurse. It's my job.

What is the greatest challenge in succession planning and why?

We've been doing succession planning and ensuring there is a steady stream of leaders in the pipeline at the director level seriously for more than seven years now. We try to promote from within — 85% from the inside.

But when it goes beyond the director's level, such as the CEO level, we may have to recruit from outside. We have a medical fellowship program. We are in need of top-level leaders in Thailand right now. We need a separate succession planning for that level. The challenge is that we don't have enough top leaders, and a real good training for such leaders.

What is one weakness you have?

Not spending enough time with my family.

> If you are prepared to let go
> of the privileges of office,
> then you have little problem
> doing the right thing.

S. DHANABALAN
The Hold-All-Things Loosely Leader

r. S. Dhanabalan was a well-known politician in Singapore in the 1980s and early 1990s who served in various positions in the Cabinet. He stepped down in 2013 as the Chairman of Temasek Holdings, after serving for 17 years. He was also Chairman of DBS Bank. He is a Member of the Council of Presidential Advisers, a Member of Presidential Council for Minority Rights as well as Council Chairman Emeritus of Asia Business Council.

Singapore Prime Minister Lee Hsien Loong described Mr. Dhanabalan as "an exemplary Chairman, who provided strong leadership and steady support to the Board and management." He also praised him for instilling a "forward-looking culture, which has stood the organization in good stead in a rapidly changing world". PM Lee added: "Temasek has reviewed its charter to stay abreast of the evolving landscape, while holding the core principles of success: Emphasising long-term, sustainable investments over short-term bets, developing talent, and imbuing in your young officers a commitment to Singapore."

During his stint, Temasek's portfolio more than tripled from S$70 billion in 1997 to more than S$223 billion today, and he also steered it through the Asian Financial Crisis, the 9/11 attacks in the US and the global financial crisis.

Paying a glowing tribute, PM Lee extolled, "Temasek's high international standing reflects of you and the Board's hard work and adds to the Singapore brand."

Besides building up the financial strength of Temasek, under his chairmanship, the organization also established the Temasek Trust, committing S$1.5 billion to humanitarian causes, helping the under-privileged and educating the disadvantaged.

Prior to this appointment, he had served under Prime Ministers Lee Kuan Yew and Goh Chok Tong, and had different cabinet positions as Minister for the Ministry of National Development, Ministry of Foreign Affairs, Ministry of Culture, Ministry of Community Development, and Ministry of Trade and Industry. This has given him a wide perspective and deep understanding of leadership issues.

Yet, Mr. Dhanabalan will never forget his very humble background and beginning.

Born in 1937, he was raised as a Hindu by his father, A. Suppiah, but became a devout Christian. He went to Victoria School and later to the University of

Malaya, where he graduated with a Second Class Upper in Economics. He joined the Ministry of Finance as an Administrative Officer from 1960–1962. He was involved first in the establishment of the Economic Development Board (EDB) and later the Development Bank of Singapore (DBS Bank).

He left the Civil Service to join EDB and then left EDB to join DBS Bank as Vice-President from 1968–1970. He was promoted to Executive Vice-President and continued to serve from 1970–1978. He stood for elections in 1976 and joined the Cabinet in 1978. The rest, as they say, is history.

He is married to Christine Tan and they have a son and a daughter.

Even with such a distinctive service record, Mr. Dhanabalan is always known to be a self-effacing and private leader who shuns public limelight and seldom gives interviews. It is truly a great honor for us to interview him for this book.

 Who and what influenced you most in your leadership development? And why?

 The person who influenced me the most is Dr. Benjamin Chew. He was a medical doctor and father of my good friend Jimmy Chew. Dr. Chew was an elder of Bethesda Katong Church and a respected Christian leader here. He was a Bible-believing and most affirming person. He always tried to find something positive to say about the most unlikeable person.

Whenever I complained about someone, he taught me to see the positive things in the other person and try to see things from the other person's point of view. At times, it seemed frustrating to complain to him. He never tried to reinforce my negative view of the person. I believe it came from a consciousness of his own pride. He saw the 'demon pride' in himself and wanted to spare others from the grip of this demon.

 Could you share an experience of his influence with us?

 When I wanted to marry a Chinese lady, it became a big issue with my dad and mum. I sought Dr. Chew's view, hoping that he would support me. Being young and passionate, I was very upset with my dad for objecting to the marriage.

Speaking as a father, Dr. Chew explained kindly to me that my dad really loved me and wanted the best for me. He advised me lovingly that I should wait it out, be patient and not react instinctively until my father agreed to the marriage. I took his advice and my father finally gave his consent.

 How did that affect your leadership?

 I tend to be more forgiving. It has influenced me to be less judgmental. It is not that I am not judgmental at all. I am less so. I try to see things from the other person's perspective. If someone asks me for an opinion of another, I try to say something good about the person. If I have nothing good to say, I will not say anything to reinforce the negative views of that person. I am quite careful about what I say.

 This must be difficult in your job. How do you practice being forgiving, telling the truth and taking responsibility as Chairman?

 If I say it doesn't affect me, then I am naïve. If someone asks me for a candid opinion about a person, I have to be honest and give my opinion of the person, especially if it will affect the organization. If it is an issue of character or integrity, which can affect the organization, I have to speak frankly and make my stand clear. In my view, competence cannot trump moral defects in character. I will speak candidly and explain carefully my opinion to the inquirer. This is my responsibility as Chairman, even though it may mean that some people may find me too strong about this.

 You are prepared to be tough if you have to.

 Certainly. We have to be wise as a serpent but harmless as a dove.

 What is one memorable experience that has impacted and shaped your political views?

I was a politically alert person but not politically involved. I had strong political views about things, mostly left leaning, and I was not afraid to express them. In fact one good friend thought that I was a communist. The first time I exercised my right to vote was in 1959. At that time, the PAP was perceived by many to spell trouble for Singapore as it was seen as a communist front party. To win the Chinese votes, they had to attract the Chinese-educated and therefore the anti-establishment votes. To be anti-establishment was seen as being communist.

It became public that Mr. Chew Swee Kee, a Progressive Party member and a Minister in Lim Yew Hock's Government had taken a bribe, a huge sum. There was a commission of inquiry. He resigned. I was very incensed and angry with this. I wanted the whole bunch in the Legislative Assembly to be out. I was politically alert but did not necessarily want to be politically involved. I decided to vote for the PAP which upset some of my church friends. That experience galvanized and emboldened me to go with my instincts.

How did you finally get into politics?

When I was approached to join the PAP and contest in the 1976 elections, it was a surprise. I was recommended by the late Mr. Hon Sui Sen, who was the Chairman of DBS before he was elected to Parliament and appointed a Minister. However, the PAP leaders did not pursue the recommendation because one of their leaders, outside Parliament, told the then Prime Minister Lee Kuan Yew that I was not a man of principle because I became a Christian, not out of conviction but because I wanted to marry a Christian girl. That was not true because my future wife became a Christian after me and before we started courting. I was prepared to let it go, as it didn't bother me whether I was selected to run in the elections. But it was Mr. Howe Yoon Chong who having ascertained the truth rubbished the accusation, which had been circulated around in the Indian community. Finally, I was invited to join the party and stand for elections.

Since I graduated and started work, my philosophy has been that if I did not find any joy in the job or if it went against my personal convictions, even though it might be an important or honorable position, I must be prepared to let go and move on. Since I started work, I have always been prepared to step down anytime. If I am asked to do something against my convictions or values, I am prepared to let go. That approach of 'holding things loosely' has been my perspective. Don't let these things, positions or power, capture you.

The moment you cannot discharge your responsibilities in good conscience, you must be prepared to let it go.

 This is a very important leadership principle. Many leaders in business and politics find it difficult to let go of their power especially after they have tasted the sweetness of it all. How do you inculcate this value?

 Indeed, people have asked me, "Don't you miss what your position commanded? Or the prestige and privileges that come with it?" Frankly, I do not miss it. What I miss is the opportunity to make or contribute to policies that can shape the life of Singaporeans, to do what is good for Singapore. If I compromise on my principles, I feel that I have devalued my contribution.

 How do you deal with situations in your political career when you have to hold on to your convictions or principles as well as defend a cabinet decision which you disagree on?

 There are two views on this with regard to handling policy differences within the political leadership when you are part of the leadership.

One view is that in the rare instance of a position or decision being against some basic principle I hold dearly, I should leave the team. Not everyone will agree with me but I have to go with what I can live with.

The other view, which is more common, is that if you have strong views on a subject, you can moderate the outcome of the decision by continuing in the team. Being involved in the team, you can help tweak it to be different from what was initially envisaged. But as soon as the team makes the decision and you accept the consensus, you cannot speak in public against the decision even if it is not entirely in line with your view.

For example, on the casino issue, I remember that Dr. Tony Tan spoke against casinos being allowed in Singapore during the public discussion and explained why it was not a good idea.

He made his own position very clear that he did not support it. He never then tried to defend the decision. He just kept quiet.

My view is when the Cabinet has decided, you shouldn't speak against it. And if you took a position against the decision because in your judgment it is not good for the society or economy, you should not speak in favor of it in public discussion. You just keep quiet.

I remember a contentious issue that was discussed when I was in the Cabinet. PM Lee Kuan Yew told me, "You should not speak for it because you don't have the conviction."

 What if you were caught in a situation where a reporter came to you and asked you about your position on a matter that you don't support?

 Well, I will say, "I have already made my points clear. I don't need to say anymore."

 So, how do you hold things loosely in your life?

 It is the trappings of power that make you want to hold tightly to a position. That will make you compromise your position. But if these trappings of power do not hold you and you are prepared to let them go, you can quite easily hold and act in accordance with your principles. I have seen this again and again. People are so used to the trappings of power and position that they refuse to let them go. They continue to want to be the chairman or CEO or in a position of power and compromise their principles and lose their self-respect.

It requires a bit of effort. It's great to enjoy these things. But if they become very big in your life, then you are trapped. So, you have to be very careful. If you are prepared to let go of the privileges of office, then you have little problem doing the right thing.

But if you are focused on wanting to make progress in your office, looking for affirmations and promotions, and these become very important to you, you are more liable to get into trouble. When these things become a major consideration for you in making a decision, then you are in trouble.

When I was in the Cabinet, in considering an issue, I tried to take a position which I considered as the best for Singapore. That's all I was concerned about. In most cases when it is a matter of judgment and my view was different from the Prime Minister's, I will speak my mind strongly. He expected that of me and my colleagues. If my paramount consideration is to please him, then not only will I be going against my conscience, but I will also have no value to the PM in the decision-making process.

In any position, especially one with responsibility and power, you must strive to be totally honest with yourself. For me, only God knows my heart and I have to be transparent with Him. The way I communicate this to others I work with is whether I can wake up in the morning, look at the mirror and say that I am doing the right thing.

 A few things that stand out for me about you is that you are able to hold things loosely in your life and you have seen leaders who have done the opposite, and seen how destructive this attitude can be.

 They destroy themselves and their organization. I have to do the right things for the right reason. I obey a higher order. I need to obey God. In the Bible, 2 Corinthians 5:13,14 says, "If we are 'out of our mind,' as some say, it is for God; if we are in our right mind, it is for you. For Christ's love compels us…"

Some of the things I do may appear to be crazy. The so-called 'crazy thing' I do is because Christ's love compels me and it is because I love people.

When Dr. Moses Tay left the position of Chief Medical Officer of Tan Tock Seng Hospital to be an Anglican priest, some of my colleagues thought of him as doing a 'crazy thing'. The crazy thing was the right thing because he had a higher calling.

I hold things loosely because I heed a higher call. I must not give the impression that I don't struggle to follow a higher calling. I do have struggles.

But I try to be true to a higher calling.

 What is your chief struggle or your greatest weakness?

 Most of the time the trappings of holding high office are not attractive to me. In fact they embarrass me. Temptation only makes sense only if it is real. Temptation only becomes a temptation if we can be tempted.

However, at times I have to consciously be wary when I am treated with great deference, and am invited for this and that important function or event. I have to keep reminding myself, "Is this really something that I want?" Most of the time I am not tempted at all.

But I am tempted. My biggest struggle is pride or when I feel that I am not treated with respect. Pride comes when people treat you with great respect and you enjoy it so much that you refuse to let it go. The biggest difference being in office and not being in office is the privileges you enjoy, where you are treated special in many life situations.

There is a subtlety about pride. Being humble is relatively easy. But the ability to accept humiliation and not react to it is more difficult. I remember an instance. I, together with some others, used to have reserved parking lots in the Singapore Island Country Club (a prestigious golf club in Singapore).

When I stepped down from the Cabinet, an official told me I could not park at the special lot any more. I really felt slighted. I felt a little upset. Then I realized then that pride had crept in. It's so subtle.

Now, I have become more conscious about how I react when I am slighted. Humility is accepting humiliation and not being upset. Easy to say but difficult to do.

 What is one legacy you have left behind in your organization?

 The idea of a legacy was too ambitious for me. I can say that I am pleased that when I helmed the Ministry of National Development, I could lead a group of people in the upgrading program of old flats. This changed the physical landscape of Singapore

I like to encourage and listen to people at any level. I enjoy speaking directly to people. I support an open system of communication because I do not want to hear filtered views. For example, when I was serving in DBS, the people who knew the problems were in the frontline. I liked to talk to them directly. In DBS, I met with 10 different Vice Presidents or Assistant Vice Presidents every week. There were, I think, about 200 such officers. At times, you can get very watered down versions about what customers and the staff think. You got to be in touch with the front line and not only with those who report directly to you. I try to encourage people to speak up.

At Temasek, I also have an open line with people. I lunch with the Senior Managing Directors regularly even though they are not my direct reports. I try to create as many lines of communications into the system as possible. Some people are very comfortable to have only one line but they don't get the full view. Having said that, I have to make people feel comfortable with me.

 What is one advice you would give to emerging leaders?

 Be open.

Open lines of communication at many levels. Listen to different views, especially from the lower levels.

Don't put your own interest above others.

Difficulty is unavoidable but misery is optional.

EDWARD ONG
The Courageous Leader

dward Ong is the Singaporean Founder of Sutera Harbour Resort — an iconic tourism complex in Sabah, East Malaysia nestled on seashores facing the South China Sea with views of tropical islands and the majestic Mount Kinabalu.

Before going to Sabah, he was a property developer and main contractor for projects like the Orchard and Somerset MRT (Mass Rapid Transport) stations as well as the Singapore General Hospital buildings.

In 1993, he discontinued his construction business in Singapore and went to Sabah to develop 800 units of a medium-cost condominium. A year later, the opportunity came for him to start Sutera Harbour Resort project which transformed 384 acres of polluted tidal flats and degraded coastlines into a tourism complex. This development comprises two five-star hotels — the Pacific Sutera Hotel (500 rooms) and the Magellan Sutera Resort (456 rooms) — with 16 food and beverage outlets, a Graham Marsh-designed 27 hole golf course and a marina with 104 berths. He operated this complex so successfully that he was given the opportunity by the Sabah State Government to run two concessions — Kinabalu Park which is a UNESCO World Heritage Site, and the North Borneo Railway which runs a steam train.

However, it was far from smooth sailing for Edward when he went to Sabah to launch his business.

The first problem he faced when building the Resort was that he had to build his own power plant to have reliable electricity supply for the Resort. Although he had no experience in building power plants, he built it in 11 months and won the ASEAN Energy Award on Cutting Edge Technology because the plant provided by-products of steam for laundry and chilled water for air-conditioning the Resort.

To finance the Resort project, he had to borrow US$300 million at the exchange rate of RM2.5 to US$1. When the Asian stock market collapsed in 1997, the exchange rate went south and he faced RM450 million in currency losses in just one day. In September 1998, his marriage fell apart and he was estranged from his children. To add to the list of devastation, the tourism industry was badly affected by the severe acute respiratory syndrome (SARS) epidemic and the avian and swine flu, and the Resort was directly impacted by the Bali bombings. Edward had hit rock bottom.

In all the struggles he had to face, Edward knew what seemed to be the end for men is the beginning for God. He held on to make sure the Resort was well-managed so that it will eventually fetch a good price from investors and enable him to repay the bankers who had been so supportive of him and the Resort through all the difficulties.

In early 2014, he sold a 77.5% stake in Sutera Harbour Group to Singapore-listed property group GSH Corporation. GSH is related to Sam Goi, the Popiah King and Chairman of Tee Yih Jia Group, a global food and beverage conglomerate with operations in the United States, Europe, China, Malaysia, and Singapore.

It was through all these adversities that he came to live by the quote "difficulty is unavoidable, but misery is optional".

We caught up with Edward for tea in his beautiful resort where he told us his incredible story.

 Who and what influenced you most in your leadership development? And why?

 My late father, Ong Chwee Kou, was the most influential person in my life. Integrity was his lifelong commitment. His philosophy was, "One can lose money, but one cannot lose integrity." He would lend money to people without expecting them to pay back, but if he were to borrow from others, he would surely repay them. When we lend to someone, we must be prepared to lose it. If the person pays back, then it is a bonus.

My father was illiterate yet 'educated' while we are literate but 'uneducated'. He had much wisdom even without much formal education. In his life, he helped many friends. His workers became his sub-contractors and contractors.

I remembered an elderly supervisor, Soon Peh, who worked in my father's company. He stopped working when he became too frail. My father continued to pay his salary until he passed away. Soon Peh's children were very touched. That was the compassion and understanding of my father, he really took care of his workers.

There was another episode. There was a piece of land which belonged to Wee Thiam Siew. He had to develop it, failing which the government would take it away for other development. Mr. Wee had planned it for a hotel development and was desperate to mobilize the work. With just a handshake, my father mobilized his workforce the next day and completed the project. They remained good friends until they passed away.

Today, we build structures and systems to enforce agreements but I believe that agreements must come from the heart to be honored.

Another person who influenced me was Pastor Philip Lyn. Although I was a Christian and attended church, spiritually I didn't feel that I was progressing. I didn't find the services interesting enough and would make excuses not to attend. Unless you have guidance and mentoring, you will not learn much. Then Pastor Philip Lyn started the church in my hotel. To me, he gave apt sermons and I enjoyed them and looked forward to attending services each week.

The other person is Pastor Edmund Chan, former pastor of Covenant Evangelical Free Church in Singapore. He mentored me and taught me how to mediate on the Bible.

 What is one memorable life-changing experience that has impacted and shaped the way you lead?

 The Asian Financial Crisis of 1997 sent the ringgit on a dive, triggering hefty currency losses in one day as the Resort's borrowings were in US dollars. The debt ballooned from RM760 million to almost RM1.4 billion and coupled with the family crisis, I reached rock bottom with nothing to prove, nothing to show and nothing to hide. That's where I found God. I realise that at that stage, one can either deny God or come in total submission to Him.

 How did you get out of this devastating crisis?

 I believe it is the favor from God. We need to do what is right in the sight of God and God will do the rest. Technically, the Resort was broke with a huge debt. The syndicated loan did not come with debentures and personal guarantees and instead of walking away as advised by my peers, I decided to stay on and make sure that the Resort was well-run so that it could maintain its value for the lenders. Fortunately, the banks remained supportive and during this tough time, the Resort continued to win hospitality awards every year.

Another lesson I learned is knowing when to let go. I am not attached to my property. If I have to let go, I will. This is God's property and I am only His steward.

 Over the years, you have battled with corruption. How do you deal with it?

 Corruption doesn't come from the government. It comes from the business world. If there is no payment, there is no corruption. We cannot stop the solicitation but we can stop the manifestation. When there is no manifestation of corruption, there is no corruption. If you do not pay, corruption will not be crystalized.

Some people said to me "It is easier for you to refuse to pay as your company is big. Smaller companies do not have that luxury". I also started small when I started the Resort. But it is always the same, big or small. A friend once asked me whether to give in as he had two containers in the customs: the question is whether our salvation is worth more than the two containers.

The biggest challenge I have is to lead a prayerful life and spend time with God and the Bible. If we can do that we will always dwell in His presence as the Psalmist says in Psalm 27:4-6.

4 One thing I ask from the Lord,
   this only do I seek:
that I may dwell in the house of the Lord
   all the days of my life,
to gaze on the beauty of the Lord
   and to seek him in his temple.

5 For in the day of trouble
   he will keep me safe in his dwelling;
he will hide me in the shelter of his sacred tent
   and set me high upon a rock.

6 Then my head will be exalted
   above the enemies who surround me;
at his sacred tent I will sacrifice with shouts of joy;
   I will sing and make music to the Lord.

I had to remind myself that I am not here to maximize profit. If I did, I would be in trouble. I view my work as fulfilling God's calling and not just a job. Matthew 6:33-34 says "But seek first His kingdom and His righteousness, and all these things will be given to you as well. Therefore do not worry about tomorrow, for tomorrow will worry about itself. Each day has enough trouble of its own." We must not put the cart before the horse. We have to seek Him and His Kingdom first. In other words, live for Him, then God will take care of our worries.

In good times, we can thank God, enjoy His goodness and live well. But in bad times, we must continue to thank God and live within our means. "I learn to be content…I can do all things (survive good and bad times) through Christ who strengthens me." (Philippians 4:13)

Remember, difficulty is unavoidable but misery is optional. We can choose not to be overwhelmed or be discouraged and be miserable.

 Sutera Harbor Group is well known for good human resource practices. How do you deal with issue of integrity and fairness of the staff?

 Our core values are the moral compass of the organization. Embracing the core values is a journey, not an event. It must be our way of life, our lifestyle.

There are five basic core values that we uphold: integrity, passion and creativity, customer focus, professionalism and community service.

Integrity is No. 1. The world does not lack creativity, it lacks integrity. When we have integrity, the sky is the limit. Our walk and talk must be the same. When I moved into the hotel to stay, I made sure I did not practice double standards. The core values apply to me as much as the lowest rank in the organization. For example, if I do not uphold any of the core values, the bellhop has every right to confront me.

There was an incident whereby a staff who was an acting manager felt that he was unfairly treated because although he was doing the same duties as the other managers, he was not paid as much as they were. He could not make ends meet for his family. HR's perspective was that his salary was lower because it was commensurate with his education level. He came to see me to appeal his case. I found out that he was a very good staff and we did not want to lose him. I asked HR to consider and see if there was any way to pay him for his position despite his education level. We could progressively pay him up to the managerial level and, at the same time, help him to build up his educational level.

We emphasize a lot on training for the staff. We are not afraid that other hotels might poach them. On the contrary, we are delighted because we can train more people and send them out. This is the Kingdom principle. We train them for Kingdom employability and not just company loyalty. We cannot put people under our bondage. We employ 2,000 people, and if they have the potential for higher positions in other hotels, we bless them and let them go. Those who chose to stay on, we are grateful for them and it is also a blessing and bonus to us.

What are some weaknesses you have in your life?

I recognize that for the status and position that I hold, I have a lot of influence. It is so easy to become arrogant. My prayer each day is that God will give me a humble heart that I can hear Him, a pure heart that I can see Him, a heart of love that I can serve Him and a heart of faith that I can abide in Him.

Subconsciously, pride can take over. When people come to me with proposals, sometimes I will accept out of greed. It is easy to fall into temptations: the lust of the flesh, the lust of the eyes and the pride of life.

I might lose focus. I have the ability to do things but I have to remind myself why I am doing it. I want to do it out of compassion, to change lives and to transform people.

Another weakness I have is the fear of stepping out of my comfort zone. God is an equal opportunity employer. God's calling will come to us when we are in a most comfortable situation.

Spiritually, my weakness is not spending enough time in prayer. I am also ill-equipped with the Bible. I don't go deep into the Bible enough.

What is one advice you would give to emerging leaders?

 When God directs you, you have to move. God will prosper you and will even prosper your mistakes. Find solitude. Know the Bible and allow it to cleanse you every day. Let the principles and teachings of the Bible correct your values and transform your life.

 What is one legacy you have left behind in your organization?

 Learn to have faith in God. All my staff and associates who look at my whole project cannot but know that this is a faith project. How I turned an almost useless piece of land into an iconic tourism complex.

It's not about me. God's vision is a big vision; my vision is a small vision. Put your vision in God's perspective. There is no budget too big for God.

We need to do not only what is the right thing but also God's thing and find the peace of God.

> I was a 'Johnny-come-lately'
> leader and I am grateful that
> God has helped me through.

EDWIN
SOERYADJAYA
The Reluctant Leader

dwin Soeryadjaya is the founding partner of Saratoga Capital. He has led the company into one of Indonesia's top private equity firms with a strong track record of high returns on investments and governance. These results are attributed to a diverse investment portfolio, a seasoned and cohesive investment team, robust investment strategies, quality customers and partnerships across key sectors of the Indonesian economy. His investments span infrastructure projects, natural resources, agriculture and consumer products and services.

Edwin holds leadership positions across several companies in Indonesia and Singapore — in PT Adaro Energy Tbk, PT Tower Bersama Infrastruktur Tbk, PT Provident Agro Tbk, PT Mitra Pinashtika Mustika Tbk, PT Lintas Marga Sedaya, PT Tri Wahana Universal and Interra Resources Limited.

A long-time proponent of education, he remains active in the community through his roles as a founder of the Raffles International Christian School, co-founder of the William Soeryadjaya Foundation, and the Board of Trustees of the Ora Et Labora Foundation. He is also on the Capital Campaign Cabinet Board of Habitat for Humanity Indonesia.

Edwin graduated from the University of Southern California with a Bachelor of Business Administration in 1974. He was awarded Ernst & Young Entrepreneur of the Year in 2010 and is happily married with three children.

Mr. Kwik Kian Gie, former Indonesia Minister of National Development Planning noted that Mr. Soeryadjaya and his family are well known for their role and contributions in building Astra to become the largest listed company in Indonesia by market value.

"However, what impressed me most is not what they have done to Astra to make it successful, but rather what they did with Astra when the family's other investment in a financial institution was in need of funds to repay the creditors and depositors. The family's decision to voluntarily sell Astra to repay creditors and depositors in full, shows their integrity in business dealings," added Mr. Kwik.

Mr. Kwik also noted that Edwin Soeryadjaya has proven himself to be a "true entrepreneur", and has "risen above his family's loss of Astra to what he is now and what he will become in the future."

Edwin, tell us briefly about yourself. How did you get involved with the business?

 After graduating from USC in 1974, I took several MBA classes in USC and was involved in a few real estate projects as well as establishing a garment factory with some friends, both of which I did not take seriously. Hence I neither got my MBA degree nor made a success of my business.

My life at the time was without purpose except to enjoy the good things in life, which my parents' indulgence and wealth afforded me. With access to unlimited funds and minimal parental control, life was one big party and to this day I am convinced it was my parents' prayers that protected me from the deadly spiral of alcohol and substance abuse.

In 1978, after one of my father's brothers, the late Tjia Kian Tie, passed away unexpectedly, my father asked me to return to Indonesia and join the family business. Even at that time, Astra International was already a professionally well-run company so there was very little incentive for me to work hard. Even spearheading Astra's financial restructuring efforts in 1987, which culminated in its public listing on the Indonesian Stock Exchange in 1990 as the largest IPO in Indonesia, was not too difficult as I had so many professional people supporting me.

It was not until 1993, when our family got into trouble, that I started to take my work seriously. So you could say adverse circumstances forced me to step up and be a leader.

 Who or what influenced you most in your leadership development? And why?

 GOD and my father.

My father was a very generous, humble and gracious man. His biggest strength was his gift of being able to appoint the right person to do the right job. He was a great visionary and was able to sniff out good deals. He built the Astra Group from scratch with a compelling desire to create jobs, add value and be an asset to Indonesia. He is a devout Christian and has touched many people through his charitable works especially in education. He also instilled in me faith in the Lord.

God the Almighty saved me. So many times I made choices that could have ended tragically but God's faithfulness and love to those who believe and trust in Him is evident in all the good I have experienced in my life.

By 1990, I could see that our family was headed toward financial trouble. Astra was doing well but our other businesses were not. Our bank, Bank Summa, suffered a huge credit crunch due to excessive borrowing. Then in 1992 there was a run on the bank and we had to stop the bleeding. We tried very hard to find solutions for the family to keep Astra while trying to bail out Summa. We knocked on every door but none opened. Friends and family became strangers. I remember very clearly the day when I went to see a banker for help to do the restructuring and refinancing. At that time, admittedly my dossier was lacking. He didn't trust me and said to my face — "You are a playboy and do not know how to run the company."

It was the biggest slap to my face. It was also my wake up call. That was the turning point of my life. It was very humbling. I tried to save the family from losing Astra and failed. I felt like the prodigal son — unworthy. But while many turned their backs on us, God lifted me up. My wife Julie never lost her faith in me. I am forever grateful and blessed to have her love and support during one of the darkest and most frightening times in my life. She said selling Astra was the best thing that happened to us. She was right. It changed my perspective and priorities in life. Losing Astra highlighted who and what were important in my life. I thank God every day for His abundant grace and providence, and hope that every day I can become closer to the person He wants me to be.

 How did you rebuild yourself and your business?

 I left Astra as Vice President Director in 1993 and started my own business. My first successful undertaking was the establishment of PT AriaWest International in October 1994. At the time, under the World Bank-sanctioned process, Indonesia privatized the telecommunication industry by breaking the monopoly into six operators. Leading a consortium consisting of USWest (now AT&T) and AIF in 1995, AriaWest won the West Java region even though many people at that time thought of us as outcasts. I really saw God's hand at work in my life during this time as He gave me the opportunity to start afresh. Our power to survive challenges truly resides not in us but in God who dwells within us.

Many more business opportunities came our way and in 1998 during the political and financial crisis of Indonesia, Sandiaga Uno and I established Saratoga Capital. One of Saratoga's initial large deals was PT Adaro Indonesia — a coal mining company — in which we acquired a 51% stake in 2002. In 2004, Saratoga formed a consortium to buy the remainder of the shares from our Australian partner, Newhope. Thereafter, we took it public to its present PT Adaro Energy, built a vertically-integrated approach to coal mining from pit to port services and turned it into one of the biggest coal mining companies in Indonesia today.

Leaning on God's strength, I slowly built my reputation and learned how to lead. I had to earn the trust that was needed to cement business relationships. In Adaro, our borrowing cost is far below what other corporations are paying because we have built our credibility. Learning from my father, we found the right people to manage our company. I recruited a number of people with a proven track record from Astra.

When rebuilding a business, we have to be consistent in having good corporate governance, executing discipline, and being fair to people. Leaders have to set the example. As the saying goes: "A pendulum swings from the top". When my father was running Astra, we hired mostly professionals. We had nine directors and only three were related to me. My father even fired a close relative for misconduct. We were committed to excellence and rewarded people based on merit.

What is one legacy you have left behind in your organization?

To bring glory to God and be a blessing to others. God has given me so many chances to transform. I don't want to build a Tower of Babel for myself. Whatever I do, I do for His glory and for His kingdom. I am truly grateful to Him. He has blessed me abundantly.

Even finding my wife, Julie, was a miracle. For as far as I can remember, I have been praying for a good woman to share my life and build a family with. I know how important it is as I have seen too many broken marriages. I met Julie in May 1984 and fell in love with this fascinating woman. In August, I proposed to her, we got engaged in December that year and were married in February the following year. At the time, she had not been baptized as a Christian but was willing to be married to me in church. My wife is God's gift to me. I promised God that I will bring my family to faith.

For the first 15 years of our married life, I went to church alone 99% of the time. In 2000, we finally found International English Service led by Pastor Dave Kenney. We have been hosting a small group ministry and Bible study in our home regularly for the last 12 years. God is good. He has helped our family find Him. Last year was our 30th wedding anniversary and I thank God for Julie and our three children each day.

In 2001, our son Michael was very badly burnt while in school. At a school-sponsored BBQ event, a student threw a canister of lighter fluid into the BBQ grill and it became a fireball. Our son suffered 2nd to 3rd degree burns to his entire face, upper body and arms. We brought him to the Singapore General Hospital and he stayed at the Burn Unit for treatment. From the beginning, doctors prepared us for what might happen as a result of the burns — scarring, limited vision, partial use of his lungs and limited mobility of his hands and fingers. God again showed His steadfast love and poured His mercy upon us, put His hands upon our son and completely healed him. To this day, looking at Michael, many simply cannot believe that he did not go through a single skin graft or plastic surgery.

God always has His hand of blessing on me throughout my personal and corporate life. I thank Him for His everlasting faithfulness and pray that I am able to pay this debt of gratitude forward and be a blessing to others and bring glory to His name.

What is one advice you would give to emerging leaders?

Be agents of change. Always have a positive mindset. There are many opportunities out there and we should take them. Never give up and do not be afraid of failing. Be the best that you can be. Live with integrity. Respect others. Serve others like Jesus. But don't think you can do great things on your own.

Everything I do, I rely on God. I pray for His strength and wisdom to use whatever gifts and talents that God has given me to achieve success.

I pray for Him to surround me with a loving family and true friends to help and support me and bring out the best in me. God gives wisdom to those who pray and ask, and will help us to live our faith. If it's all Edwin, I will surely fail.

What is my greatest weakness now?

I was raised by indulgent parents and must admit I in turn indulge my children. I find it very hard to say no to them. I am fortunate to be blessed with a wonderful wife whom I love and enjoy being with, and who is a great mother to my children. She has no trouble saying no. We pray each day for God to show us the way to be good parents and raise our children to be good Christians. The good you sow in your children today you will reap tomorrow.

With success and wealth come temptations in all its varied forms. Even Jesus was tempted by the devil. Yielding to temptations ruins lives. The only solution is to know God's will by reading the Bible and through daily prayer. The Bible teaches and empowers us to know what priorities we need to have to sustain us from the challenges and temptations in life that threaten our stability and faith. I pray constantly and faithfully for God to guide me in all that I do so my family and I bring God the honor He deserves through the way we live. We can expect better tomorrows when we live right today.

> **If we look back at the growth of YTL's businesses, we not only see God's fingerprints everywhere but also His footprints! They are simply miraculous. I give God all the glory!**

FRANCIS YEOH
The God-honoring Leader

ention YTL and Francis Yeoh comes to mind. Managing Director of the YTL Group of Companies since 1988, Francis has helped transform his family construction business into a multi-disciplinary conglomerate. Comprising five listed entities, the YTL Group owns and manages regulated utilities and infrastructural assets in 3 continents. It has a combined market capitalization of over US$9 billion and total assets of US$17 billion.

Ranked as "one of Asia's most powerful and influential business personalities" by *Fortune* and *Business Week*, Francis is known for wearing his faith on his sleeves. He openly shares his beliefs both in public and in private. Having said this, Francis is not the pushy 'tele-evangelist' kind. He is immensely sensitive towards the complex multi-cultural realities of our world. Not least of Malaysia, where he calls home.

Francis is an advocate of environmental conservation and renewable energy initiatives. He serves on Nature Conservancy's Asia Pacific Council. He loves the Arts, having brought world-class vocalists like The Three Tenors and Andrea Bocelli to perform in public concerts in Bath and Singapore, as well as supporting initiatives like the Kuala Lumpur Performing Arts Centre. He is Regional Chairman of the International Friends of the Louvre.

In 2010, he was made "Primus Inter Pares Honouree" of the Oslo Business for Peace Award by a panel of Nobel Laureates, for actively advocating socially responsible business ethics and practices. He is also the recipient of the Corporate Social Responsibility Award at the 2010 CNBC's Asia Business Leaders Awards.

Francis is unassuming and modest. In this interview, he candidly shared details of his faith and highlighted Biblical truths to illustrate views on leadership, stewardship and family. He attributed all he has to God, as "coming from the hand of God".

He certainly did not hide his personal struggles as a believer. When asked what his one weakness is, his reply was telling. He admitted, "I have millions! I battle with them every day." His unflinching and courageous testimony is apparent, revealing a deep sense of dependency on God.

Francis is an avid reader, especially of the Bible. I once saw him on a flight from Kuala Lumpur to Singapore. He was studiously ploughing through the Bible with a Bible Commentary. He claimed that his wisdom comes from the Bible and from the daily habit of "consuming spiritual food first before all else."

Francis married the late Roseline Chan in 1982 and they have three sons and two daughters. We met up in his modestly-decorated office in Kuala Lumpur and he shared his story.

 Who or what influenced you most in your leadership development? And why?

 I would say, God! Quite simply, God is light and all learning comes from Him. Every intuition, every bright idea. This is what it means to be 'enlightened'. True enlightenment is only possible, when we know God, when He reveals Himself to us.

For example, after becoming a Christian at 16, it was quickly apparent to me that we give God very little credit for our bright ideas. We claim them for our own. Boast about them. Why is that? Thoroughly examine ourselves and we will be shocked by how motivated we are by greed, especially for wealth. Our desires are twisted, deeply entrenched in a need to have more than what will satisfy. The Bible calls this 'the way of mammon'. Even if we have a bright idea that is divinely inspired, it will be manipulated to serve greed, quite possibly towards evil intent. The way of mammon is so much a part of all of us. It takes a whole lifetime to break its grip.

I called myself a Christian back then. I knew that meant I had to be thinking quite differently — God centred, heavenly minded, not as how the world thinks. In reality, many of my ideas remained morally unsound, well-disguised.

Just like the children of Israel in the Biblical times of Moses. Moses took his people out of Egypt and out of slavery. But all throughout their journey in the wilderness, they could only moan and complain, showing little gratitude. They repeatedly spurned God's goodwill. They were no longer slaves, yet they spoke and behaved like slaves. Put simply, Egypt was still with them and in them — in their nature and psyche. So it was with me! Call it an epiphany.

Even as a young man, I felt my heart and mind had to change, and I went about working on my own greed. Very soon, I began to understand that if I could honestly credit God for everything, surrender to His will, I can be free from the shackles of greed. Now you see why I often publicly attribute every good thing to God, and why I do not like drawing attention to myself.

We also need to be practical. It takes a whole lifetime to root mammon out of us. I have learned that the best way is to trust God — 100%! When we trust God, there is little room for greed. God hates greed. Yes, He will remind us of that. Whenever I have trusted God, especially doing business, I discovered that the businesses that came our way were simply awesome.

It did not matter whether we were buying companies here in Malaysia or abroad, they were always 'one in a trillion' chances. Everything about them was perfect — place, timing, exchange rates, business climate, people. We concluded each of these deals knowing beyond doubt that God orchestrated everything.

Look at YTL's track record. Our market capitalization grew from US$10 million in 1968 to over US$9 billion today. Compounded 55%. Had you invested US$1 million with me in 1968, it would be worth US$160 million today. Only God can multiply in this way. My family and I cannot humanly fathom how we could have done all this. So we do not try. We have learned that humility teaches us to credit God for making all these opportunities possible. We merely take His bright ideas and capitalize on them. He gives the increase. He makes the impossible, possible. Always!

 Francis, how do you sustain yourself all these years, as you say, not to be sucked into the way of the mammon? How do you keep this value?

 I have said, trust God, attribute every good thing to Him. What this also means is that we must think long term. When we do, victories are never in doubt.

I painted a bleak picture of the way of mammon. It is bleak! Worshipping mammon is simply banking on a short-term mind-set. Has not our world suffered enough from a myopia of 'short-termism'? We like instant gratification, quick fixes, quick results and quick gains.

Ask CEOs and CFOs if they are not affected by the 'tyranny of quarterization'. Look at the global financial crash in 2008. Every level of the financial sector was compromised. Financial companies, regulators who gave credit ratings to these companies, bankers, insurers, shareholders, lawyers, governments, homeowners — too many got into the act of chasing hot money. Few wanted to ask the right questions. Can homeowners pay for their homes? Do banks have enough to lend?

The truth is, some people did speak up. They got people thinking and debating how unsustainable the asset bubbles were, or how 'hot' the housing loan markets had become. But instead of listening to them, they were shunned, labeled as 'prophets of doom'. Not surprisingly, their airtime was restricted. After all, who did not want to own homes and make quick money? Who wanted to say "no" to hot money? The entire system fed this temptation.

I am not against making money. Far from it. But we have to know what is real and what is not. We have to be able to tell the difference between the two. Just think! Had governments decided not to bail out the banks and financial companies in 2008, we would have had a complete global meltdown. Banks would have gone bankrupt. Savings completely wiped out. All your hard earned money, my hard earned money, lost! We were so close to an economic Armageddon!

Long-term thinking simply prevents us from making silly mistakes, chasing after the wrong priorities. In business as in life, all of us could ill afford to be short-sighted. Do not just think for the next month or year. Go beyond that! Be courageous. Think for the next 10 years, invest for the next 100. Do not gamble your companies' wealth away to look good on the books for one quarter and then lose all the next, like so many who did leading up to 2008. It defies common-sense and is highly irresponsible.

Let me add. Perhaps the greatest 'myopism' is assuming that our actions have little or no impact on others. I am always mindful that as Managing Director of YTL Group, my decisions affect not only my family, my staff, their families, their communities, but also every area our businesses operate in. This thought alone could keep me up every night.

I am equally conscious of the fact that when we get things right, many people will be blessed. The challenge then is to be good stewards of God and keep getting things right. That is why we can never ignore the wisdom of thinking long term. Of course, we also cannot do without God's help. Our lives are short-lived. He is eternal.

 How do you cultivate this discernment?

 I like the story about the Canadian Mounties. I read that to graduate as Mounties, they have to undergo training on how to detect counterfeit notes. You would assume they were taught everything about counterfeit notes. Not at all. For weeks, they were only shown genuine ones. The simple logic being: "if you know what is real, you could immediately tell the fake".

The trouble with all of us is that we cannot always tell apart the real from the fake. Only God can truly give us the discernment and knowledge on what is real. When we are sensitive to God's will, we will be able to tell whether a person is genuine, whether a deal is full-proof, or when the right timing is to strike a business deal.

If we look back at the growth of YTL's businesses, we not only see God's fingerprints everywhere but also His footprints! They are simply miraculous. I give God all the glory!

If we care to be still and to be discerning, we will see God's hands in what we do. Something that is not easy in the business world. Particularly when so many in business openly declare that there is "no room for God in business", which makes me even more determined to fight this mammon mind-set and avoid its temptations. That is why I must keep close to God. There is no room for complacency.

 How do you keep close to God? What are some personal habits that you keep?

 We easily forget that it is God who seeks to keep close to us first. God is far more interested in us, far more passionate about you and me, than we will ever be of Him. That makes me want to know more about Him, study the Bible, and find out what he is saying to me.

Back to the subject of 'discernment', it says in the Bible that we have eyes but do not see, we have ears but do not hear. I believe when we are influenced by the vagaries of mammon, our vision and hearing will be impaired. However, when we feed on the word of God, this problem will be overcome. Moses was certainly wise to have taught the Children of Israel that "man does not live on bread alone, but on every word that comes from the mouth of the Lord".

Quite literally, I need God's word as daily food for my soul. With it, my mind is renewed and my body is sustained. Think for a moment. We cannot survive without physical food daily. Yet, we regularly miss our spiritual food. Even for weeks, months! I know myself well enough. I need the guidance and nourishment of God's word.

His perspective of things orientates what I see and hear. And every morning, I meditate on God's word and let His truths sink in. I also try to read the whole Bible once through every year. These days, I use an audio Bible to help me along. Like those in ancient times who would have listened to the word of God than having read it themselves. I am using this really good Bible App on my iPhone called YouVersion.

Whenever I read the Bible, I always find that I have previously missed out on so many truths. The essence of God's teachings is really found in thoroughly combing through every detail in His word. We are so accustomed to saying that "the devil is in the detail". That is wrong. God is in the detail! He created the world, He designed the details. That is the only reason why the devil is into the details, in order to twist God's truth and trick us. He did that to Adam and Eve and got away with it. But when he tried it on Jesus, he was rebuked.

 What is the most crushing adversity you have ever faced in your leadership? How did you deal with it?

 If you choose to live life in a godly way and follow after God's wisdom, then you could expect all kinds of adversities in life. Do not expect them to get any easier. Expect more and more to come your way. Certainly this has been my personal experience! After all, the 'mammon spirit' has spawned an entire way of life, a kind of system based on greed.

Look around you, God created more than enough for all of us in this world. Yet, we have food shortages and over a billion people going to bed hungry. When there is surplus wheat, it is burned to control prices. When there are Tomato Mountains, farmers destroy them. It is immoral that millions of tonnes of food are thrown away every year that could easily feed the hungry. You would also assume it is common-sense to preserve the environment, which gives life and feeds us. Yet, someone living 10 houses away from you could be polluting the rivers, dumping toxic waste into them, and stripping forests bare for quick gains. All driven by a spirit of greed and a very short-term mind-set.

We cannot be naïve to assume we will never be affected. Greed follows us 24/7. It is literally like carrying a keg of gun powder on our backs. Someone lits the fuse and the sparks chase after us. But the question is: will I remain faithful and steadfast to God's ways in spite of whatever comes my way? And this answer is the only one that matters.

Invariably, the adversities that affect me most are usually a result of my own weaknesses and follies. Especially when I compromise and momentarily serve the spirit of mammon that I deplore so much. That is why God tells us to keep running the race He set for us until the very end. We must not give in and we sure cannot give up.

This said, we cannot sit idly and do nothing to put right what is wrong around us. God has also called us to be His witnesses, to reveal His glory by confronting the ways of mammon. When God instructed Moses to confront the Egyptian Pharaoh, He made it clear that when Pharaoh sees Moses, he will see God, not Moses. I take that to mean we are the face of God to our world, and we must be a force for good. I do hope that when people see me, they see the glory of God reflected through me.

I have crossed 1,000 Red Seas and have experienced big and small miracles in my business and family life. I have experienced His glory manifesting through my life and what I have done. Christians understand that this is very normal simply because we are His witnesses. In fact, if people do not see Him in our lives, we actually lose credibility. Of course, we do not Bible-bash. I certainly do not force my beliefs on others. Yet, people should be able to see God through our behavior, our character and also our integrity. Some will like what they see, some will hate it.

What you share seems so simplistic that your wealth and growth in the company is because of your faith in God. Where does business acumen come into play?

 God is not complicated. He is God. The clockmaker knows His clock. However intricate and unconventional some things are to us, they are pretty straightforward to God. God exudes simplicity! Similarly, our walk with Him is not meant to be complicated either. When we trust Him fully, we will be guided and led by a far greater wisdom.

Yes, God has given us acumen. He made sure of it when He created us. There is a stealthy, intelligent system within each one of us. Put simply, He made all of us naturally smart. But the wise chooses what is good. The real test then is using our acumen for good, instead of feeding the greed in us.

 How do you deal with corruption in your business dealings?

 Corruption is everywhere. It really does not matter which country you are in, what kind of government is in power. As long as there is greed, corruption exists. There is always going to be someone taking shortcuts, someone making someone else take shortcuts. It all emanates from what I said earlier about short-termism. This is the best example of it.

I hear people say that corruption is inevitable. I disagree! At the end of the day, corruption is a choice. We can choose not to participate. We do not have to bribe, cheat or fiddle accounts to get somewhere in business. It is always possible to do business on our own merit. Granted, in some cases, we pay the price for not participating and lose out on business opportunities. But is that not a price worth paying? Courage is needed to walk away from what is considered expedient.

All this means we have to work harder. As much as corruption is a choice, so is wanting to be transparent and be above water. At YTL, our responsibility is making business smarter and better. For this, we create niches or blue oceans, use 4G technology to power our digital economy, improve the value proposition of our products and services, and increase the portfolio of our investments.

We make every effort to offer the market leadership that others appreciate and want. And of course, we look to God for wisdom and patience. Wisdom to know where to grow and expand, and patience to avoid harming ourselves with knee-jerk decisions, especially rushing into industries we really should not be in. I keep emphasizing that when we trust God, He will make the impossible possible. In God's economy, there simply are no early birds or latecomers. It is all in His perfect timing.

Another practical note: find out who shares your values and work with them. There are people who like what YTL stands for and they genuinely prefer partnering with us. Some have been with us for as long as 20, 30 years — suppliers, sub-contractors, fund managers, lawyers. They do not wish to be molly coddled either. Everything goes by market rates and standards. Most importantly for us, we trust them. They are honest. And they have become good friends.

How do you translate these values into culture in your organization?

More often than not, we complicate how we articulate our values to people. Imagine trying to internalize values that we find difficult to explain in the first place and expect others to get them right. That is why years ago, we simplified what we wanted to say about who we are and what we are about.

Essentially, at YTL, we believe we are a force for good and that our purpose is to bring positive change through everything we do. You could be serving a customer in our restaurant, selling a bag of our finest cement or building the next bespoke home. The DNA is the same. The goal is the same. Everything else, culture, practice and procedures emanate out of this.

How do we internalize these values within YTL? In the first place, our leaders and non-leaders are aware that these values cannot be compromised. The fact that they work at YTL reflects their 'buy-in' of what the company holds dear and true. If somehow that had not been made clear enough in the initial stages of hiring, it would soon be.

So that everyone is on the same page, we encourage the mastering of 'The Three Languages'. First, the Language of God. We encourage you to have godly morals and to show integrity. No matter how brilliant you are, you are expected to do business transparently and uprightly. We also say, "Be a good steward of whatever you have been entrusted with, however big or small your responsibilities". This is one particular value I regularly emphasize to my own family. Needless to say, hard-work, loyalty and family matter a lot in our organization.

Of course, we have to make it easy for our people to get these values right. For example, 25 years ago, housing development was very lucrative, mainly because there was less supply. Customers actually paid under-the-counter money to secure a property. We were a small developer then but we did not like this practice. Going against the unwritten convention, we printed clearly in our promotion literature that our employees do not take under-the-counter money.

Today, our properties have become highly sought after. Folks actually queue 48 hours and camp-out to buy our homes. It is always reassuring to see that. And we continue to mitigate the risk of bribery by selling our homes through ballot. We recently sold RM350 million-worth of homes through this method. Every buyer has the same chance of getting our homes.

Second, there is the Language of Man. In this day and age, effective communication is absolutely essential. You cannot do business if you cannot communicate, and it's much worse when you communicate poorly and wrongly. Now that most things are online and on social media, so many of our mistakes can leave a trail and eventually haunt us. It is definitely not too much to expect YTL folks to have mastered the basics — languages like English and Malay, and perhaps Chinese and Tamil. And then, for them to focus on their ability to put into words clearly what they do day-to-day. After all, all of God's bright ideas have to be articulated. Otherwise, how can we turn vision into reality?

The third is the Language of Machines. If you join the company, we could safely assume you have basic skills to do the work you have been hired for. Or at least, you could be trained to do them. However, everyone at YTL must master the tools of their trade, whether operating a machinery or running a system. That invariably means being proficient in the language of Information Technology and the Internet. We now live in a digital economy, driven by 4G Mobile Internet. Businesses can thrive or be overtaken if they fail to grasp the power of the Internet.

The Three Languages must always follow in that order of priority. The Language of God, Man and Machines. That is why I know YTL has some of the best leaders and employees. They have mastered these languages and together, help us to remain as one of the more profitable companies in the world. And because we want this kind of culture in the company, we are very selective of who we hire. To start with, we do not over-hire. We carefully screen for those with values resembling ours, including those who prefer to build long-term careers with us, just as we invest in talents for the long-term.

It is very important that our people know that the company values them, and that we resist the 'quick hire and fire' methods preferred by some employers. When we hire employees, we do not think of them alone but we also consider the many other mouths they have to feed, and the communities they belong to. In any mass lay-off, thousands are always affected. This aspect alone dictates that we be very prudent in our hiring. What more, when we want folks to epitomize our values and work with us for the long-term?

 YTL is a family business and many family businesses have failed to preserve their values and businesses beyond the third generation. How do you deal with this issue and prepare for succession planning?

 Yes, I am well aware of this so-called 'curse'. The first generation sets up a business and works very hard to establish it. The second generation preserves it. Then, the third generation spends it all away. Sadly, family businesses are littered by horror stories of business empires breaking up, parents disowning children or brothers going against brothers. We do not deny that these stories affect our thinking and certainly influence our planning, purely because we all wrestle with human nature. Every generation has its own battles with short-termism. It is no different for my children's generation and that of my granddaughter's. It is reality.

All the more, we have to think long term! What we have done at YTL is to create business footprints that do not end in the 'tyranny of quarterization', in which every quarter we are expected to achieve unsustainable sales targets and results. Instead, we go after businesses that are concessions for perpetuity. For example, we own and manage Wessex Water in the UK and YTL PowerSeraya in Singapore — both businesses in perpetuity. One of our shortest concessions is 200 years — South Australia's ElectraNet. We also have other revenues and dividends from long-term concessions, so we do not worry about every quarter as if it is our last.

Let me avoid any misconception. Having long-term concessions do not absolve us of the responsibility of meeting short-term financial targets. On the contrary, we work very hard to meet these targets. We have investors' and shareholders' interests to fulfil. But when we are purely defined by the short-term, we can never run away from seeking instant results and satisfaction. Whereas God is eternal. He is not bothered by eternity. To me, a concession in perpetuity is like eternal life. When you plan and operate like that, you have room to build a solid foundation for your next generation. You also train them to think likewise — long term!

 So, how do you ensure this?

 It is reminding them to always put God first. I am thankful that my children, nieces and nephews know that for themselves now. They do love God and are rooted in His word.

Rose (Roselin) and I spent a lot of time with our own children when they were growing up. As you would guess, I was always busy. But no matter how packed each week was, we made it a practice to be with the kids on weekends. During dinners from Fridays to Sundays, we would talk about lots of stuff, and I would be teaching them about God. And every summer and winter, without fail, we spent three weeks together away. Add all that up, we spent half of their childhood together. Even nowadays, we still have these weekend dinners and holidays. Though with their work and own families, naturally, the time spent is less, but equally precious.

I can see that one of the problems for many children growing up today is that they do not know their parents, and their parents do not know them. It is as if they are estranged from each other. During the children's formative years, they need to be able to see and experience God's love, so they could learn and copy. As parents, we model that love to them, including everything else. If we are Christ-like, they are likely to be Christ-like. If we are not bearing the grace of God, chances are they would not be either. The emphasis for Rose and I was always to be godly parents. Rose was great at that.

Together, we also taught our children to value stewardship that "to whom much is given, much is expected." My children, and indeed their cousins, grew up tasting wealth. They could quite easily become spoilt. However, they have learned to appreciate that everything ultimately belongs to God, and is entrusted to them. They are pretty sensible and do take responsibility for their actions and choices. For example, my children and their cousins either have gone to or are currently at the likes of Cambridge, Oxford, Imperial, London School of Economics and Nottingham on their own merit, having achieved some of the highest pre-university grades. We could never fix it for them to go to these universities.

They have proven their stewardship and have made the best of their secondary schooling to enter these universities. More importantly, they have come to accept that there is a system of competition and meritocracy in the world. There are many business opportunities in YTL for the next generation. Nevertheless, they still have to work hard to find their own calling and the right fit for the right business. We could guide and support them. But like every leader at the company, they have to perform well and produce results, and do so without compromising godly values.

Another quality that we hope we have passed down is selflessness. All of us could push through something we are passionate about that could be non-beneficial to the Group. To be honest, very often it is for the purpose of serving our own selfish interests and personal goals and in the process, leaving a trail of destruction behind. When the next generation sees themselves as stewards, they will resist being self-serving and not get hung up on personal fancies. Instead, they will self-correct and learn to be united in purpose before God.

This is no different to how my siblings and I are. We each see ourselves as stewards of the company and we definitely want the company to do well. But we have our own opinions too. So we create an environment where everyone can speak out. We routinely have robust discussions and disagreements. But we are also like-minded people, who share the same values and goals. We learn by sharpening each other's ideas. If one of us has a better idea, then we learn together. Similarly, if we do not have consensus on something, we do not do it. But when we all agree, we push boldly ahead. And that is also often when the Lord blesses us. When we are united, we fly! It is amazing.

What is one weakness and how do you deal/cope with it?

Not one. Millions! I battle with them every day.

Our main human weakness is that we are not aware of our own weaknesses. I am not spared that problem. We all have battles in life, business and not least, family. The more successful we are, the more battles we have. Not less. That is why we must check our own motives — why we do what we do. For ourselves alone or for a greater purpose?

I must also keep on reminding myself that the devil is always out to tempt me with the lust of the flesh, the lust of the eye and the pride of life. He will never stop until he gets what he wants. And there is nothing good in him. He only comes to steal, kill and destroy. Therefore, I must guard myself against him and not give him one inch to work with. I must constantly keep myself in check. And by God's grace alone, I will overcome.

Of course, if the devil does not get us, he goes after our loved ones so that we are distracted, if not shaken. The more successful we are, the more he will try to divide our families and create anarchy. He knows family is where we can be hurt the most. The devil's schemes are predictable.

There really are no two ways about this: we are each other's keepers! We have to invest time with our families! We have to love each other, even if everything collapses around us. And we must be prepared to suffer for each other.

What is one advice you would give to emerging leaders?

I will give the same advice to every new, emerging or old leader — you must have passion! In the first place, you could only be a passionate leader if you know and understand your purpose for doing what you do, especially if your purpose aligns with a nobler cause or a higher calling. It is difficult to have a strong conviction if you are not clear about your purpose. And without conviction, it is difficult to have passion. One leads to another.

Earlier, I mentioned how our world has lost the sense of what is real and what is not. It is hardly surprising that we seem to see fewer leaders today who exemplify moral leadership and authority. I am not belittling our world leaders. But I do bemoan the absence of the kind of great leaders like Nelson Mandela and Winston Churchill. They were driven by moral convictions that, in time, fueled their passion to change their world.

And of course, if you have passion, you will naturally have stickability. I always remind my leaders that the YTL Group evolved out of our core business in construction. Construction is hard graft. It is backbreaking work. My father, my siblings and I went through those tough early years to achieve what we have today, because we all shared a passion to see the family business grow. Call it what you want — sustainable passion, lasting passion. The real measure of passion is how it survives everything thrown at it.

Ultimately, God is the source of all passion. When we have God, He will reveal to us our purpose and what better things to get excited about. And in time, we will grow to a place of maturity in our walk with Him, and then discover that our primary reason for existence, in fact, for everything we do, is to be passionate about Him. That is my story.

> Money is God's gift to us to give. It is not because I am good...When you loan money to help someone, don't expect it to be returned. If it's returned, thank God.

GEORGE TING
The Poor Man Leader

eorge Ting calls himself "the fast food guy in Malaysia". He is now the Chairman/Franchisee of Domino Pizza in Malaysia, Singapore and Brunei.

Starting with Kentucky Fried Chicken (KFC) and Pizza Hut, he grew the business from 17 stores to more than 300 stores in 20 years. During his tenure, KFC and Pizza Hut won numerous awards, including the "KFC Worldwide Operator of the Year Award".

He started out as a sales representative with a Japanese trading company, after he graduated from the University of Malaya with a Bachelor of Arts (Economics) and a marketing diploma from an Australian marketing institute.

His life has been a series of ups and downs. The son a fisherman and an uneducated rubber tapper, George says his rags-to-riches story is testament to God's grace and goodness. But two of the top things his parents did were to give him an education, and show him the imporatnce of God in his life.

His mother had experienced a miraculous healing from a terminal illness when George was about 11 years old. Her prognosis was so bad that the doctor wanted to send her home to Sitiawan so that she could see her children for the last time. But she was determined to go through with the operation after experiencing a vision asking her to go through with it, which saw her kidney and intestines being removed because they had rotted so badly. She recovered and went on to live for 50 more years. That experience transformed her life and George's perspective of life.

It is a deep sense of gratitude that propels George to treat people, especially the lowest rung of society, with kindness and compassion.

At one period of his life, he had chalked up a debt of RM100 million when he did a management buyout of KFC group of companies. But with the right timing and God's intervention, he was rescued. He was quick to emphasize that it was neither his ingenuity nor his smartness that turned things around. That is why George is one person who considers himself a steward. What he has does not belong to him. Rather, it is a gift that he has to discharge for the good of his staff and community.

For his work and many contributions to society, he was given the title of Dato' by the Sultan of Pahang. For him, caring for the poor and needy is not just part of any organization's Corporate Social Responsibility (CSR) duty, it is a lifestyle.

This is George's story, told over a cup of tea in his office in Kuala Lumpur, Malaysia.

 Who or what influenced you most in your leadership development? And why?

 I come from a Christian family. I am a third-generation Methodist, born in Sitiawan, Perak Malaysia. My basic principles are very simple — my people are my sheep. Like Jesus, we clothe and feed them. I have been in the fast food business for 30 years and I picked up a lot of ideas by attending conferences, learning the best practices from American and Asian operators.

In 1957, my mum was terminally ill in Johor Bahru. My sister was a nurse and my brother-in-law was an intern doctor in a hospital in Johor Bahru. The doctor told her to go home to Sitiawan. That way, she could at least see her children one more time. If she stayed on, she would die.

My mum cried to God, "I suffered as an orphan. I don't want my children to suffer as orphans too." I was only about 11 years old. That night, she had a dream where her pastor, Rev. Goh, told her to go for the operation or it would be too late.

The next morning, when my sister the nurse visited her, Mum asked, "Did Rev. Goh visit me yesterday?"

"Of course not, he is in Sitiawan, that's 14 hours away (at that time)," replied my sister.

Straightaway, my mum acknowledged that it was God speaking to her in a dream. When the doctor came on his rounds, she argued with him and wanted to be operated on. The doctor was very upset. My mum was very determined, "If I die on the operation table, that would be God's will."

So, they wheeled her in for the operation. When they operated on her, they were shocked. The kidney and intestine were so rotten that they could literally scoop them up. It was a good decision. She lived for another 50 years! That experience changed her life and she continued to share her testimony with many friends and relatives for the rest of her life — hundreds of times.

That had a profound influence on our family. From then, we realized the reality of God. He is in control. Although she was not educated, she would read the Bible to me in Hock Chew (a Chinese dialect). A lot of my management principles come from there. My mum was a strict disciplinarian and would tell us what to do and what not to do. That had great influence on my leadership style.

I have seen poverty and opportunity. More importantly, God always puts me in the right place at the right time.

 What a story! Tell us about your early days. Tell us how your upbringing have impacted the way you lead?

 My dad was a fisherman and my mum was a rubber tapper. We come from a very poor background in Sitiawan, Perak, in Malaysia.

That is why I can sympathize with the poor. For example, I treat my drivers like family members. I treat them well. Besides providing a basic salary, I help them when they are in financial need. My two drivers have been with me for 20 years.

Sometime, I advance their salary when they are in need. For us, RM200 may be just a meal. But to them, it is rent for a whole month. One of their most basic needs is a roof over their head. I will give them RM10,000 for the deposit to buy a low-cost house and another RM10,000 to buy furniture. I am very sensitive to their needs and sympathetic with their struggles.

I always tell my close friends: Don't loan money if you expect it to be returned. Such expectations can kill your friendship. You must be mentally prepared that it will not be returned and be prepared to write it off.

 I am sure there are times you have been cheated. How do you deal with that?

 Certainly, I have been cheated many times. God has to give me wisdom. People have taken advantage of and have exploited me. Recently, it was one of my old bosses. I loaned him some money a few times to clear his

RM200,000 debt. Finally, I realized that his story did not jive. I had to draw the line.

Actually from day one, I have to write it off. After it reaches a certain level, I know how to draw the line. I have written it off from the start. If I don't, I will never give or help people with genuine needs. If you don't clear that first hurdle, you will never give or help because you will always say, "Will I get it back? Will I get it back?" It will be very challenging for you to give. If you are prepared to lend, you must be mentally prepared to lose it. If it comes back, it is a bonus. And you recycle your loan and gift. There will be other people coming to you. I often receive letters of request for help.

It is God's gift to us to give. It is not because I am good.

 What is the most crushing adversity you have ever faced in your leadership? How did you deal with it?

 There are two parts to the KFC Story. One of the reasons I didn't want to list my current company is because it will involve too many shareholders. In the early days, there was a conflict between a minority group and my group. As a Christian, it was very challenging for me as I had to deal with this party, who did not share the same values, and went beyond the norms of corporate business.

To make the matter worse, I was the front-man and image for the group. My other partner was quite a character, who claimed to represent me and make decisions on my behalf with the other party. He would tell the other party that "George would not agree with this and he would not do this". I was portrayed as the bad guy when I didn't even know about the negotiation. As a result, it created a very deep rift between the other party and me. It endangered my life until my Deputy Chairman came to see me and told me what was going on. I told him my side of the story and he helped clear the air for me. He ensured my safety. That was the time when I had personal safety issues and was about RM100 million in debt.

My life was all messed up. I could not eat or sleep well. My temper became short, which was not very Christ–like. I was pressurized and stressed. I had to tell my church leadership. I was in the inner circle of my church leadership. They were the group of people who prayed for me and encouraged me. I appreciated their support and counsel. My church chairman, Daniel, told me that God impressed on him to ask me to sell my share. I told him it must be crazy because who would buy my share for over RM100 million with no management control?

Two weeks later, he told me that the impression to sell was even stronger this time round during our prayer session. He shared with me, "Don't get angry with me. If this impression is from God, He will provide. Just trust Him." I had no choice.

I had never heard of Singapore GIC (Government of Singapore Investment Corporation). I was not a financial person. I never got involved in fund management or went for road shows. I am strictly a marketing and operations person. They called me to arrange a meeting and told me that they were interested to buy into KFC. Within a short time frame, they bought my shares in KFC. After that, I thought I would be happy but I was not. My wife came to me and said, "What's wrong with you? When you were in debt, you were upset. Now you have cash, you are free and you are still upset." To me, I had sold something that was very close to my heart.

Two or three months later, the Asian Financial Crisis happened and the share price of KFC plummeted. I began to realize how great our God is. My tears started to come down. My corporate friends praised me for being so smart to sell at the right time as I had avoided the crisis. I realized that it is not how smart I am.

I always tell my children that we are only God's stewards of His money, so we cannot ignore the needs of other people. That episode had the strongest bearing on my life.

 How did you get into the RM100 million debt?

 Let me tell you about my career. I graduated in 1974 and started to apply for a job. I sent job applications everywhere. The first job offers were from Behn Meyer (chemical company) as an Assistant Administrative Manager and the other a sales representative with C. Itoh (Japanese trading company). I chose to be a salesperson which upset my mom as she would have preferred for me to be a manager. I told her that as a manager, I would be desk bound and a pen pusher. As a salesperson, I could go out, meet people and see opportunities.

As a salesperson, I had to indulge in some nocturnal activities like eating, drinking and clubbing to entertain clients and Japanese bosses. My life was in a mess. My manager would tell me that the driver would pick me as I had to drink with my customers. After one and a half years, I decided to quit as I told myself this lifestyle would not do. This was not my kind of lifestyle. I then applied for a Sales and Marketing position with Tan Chong Food Division, Instanco Food Packaging company.

I started selling sugar and creamer in sachets, packaged for the airlines, fast food chains and hotels. For six years, I was their marketing manager. That was how I was introduced to the fast food industry. When I joined Mr. Loo to run his KFC restaurant business, they were already 10 years in business with 19 restaurants. Although I did not know about the job, I learned quickly as the fast food business has to do with passion and common sense.

We expanded to 40 stores. Then, Mr. Loo went into the commodity business and got into trouble with the authorities on the commodity exchange. He had to sell KFC to Innovest Bhd. After Innovest bought over the company, they gave me a free hand to run the whole company. We expanded from 41 to more than 100 stores from 1986 to 1991.

Then, they went into trouble. They were unable to repay the money they borrowed to buy KFC. As a public company, they could only take dividends, which were not sufficient to pay the debt. They got jammed up in 1990. In 1991, they asked me to use my network to do a management buyout. I then bought over the shares. During 1991–1995, there were different crises. My reprieve came when GIC bought over my shares.

 From this episode, what did you learn?

 First, never borrow beyond what you can handle. To me, that's my biggest lesson. You must be a responsible borrower.

Second, good times do not last forever. Today, you may have very good cash flow. What happens if the market crashes? For example, let's say I have RM25 million cash, I can buy a RM40 million property. What happens when there is a crisis and your sales plunge? You will not be able to service your loans. You always have to be prudent in borrowing. I try to be prudent when it comes to borrowing.

Third, not going public is another lesson. Whatever you own stays intact and you are not under pressure to please somebody else because you want to enjoy doing what you are doing. My spiritual and family life is of paramount importance.

Finally, I realized that there are four key priorities: God, family, health, and work. You must put God first, then family, followed by health and then work, in that order. Mr. Loo taught me this. He said, "If you have God, at least I know you won't cheat me. Second, if you are a good family person, you will focus on the work. When you are healthy, you will perform." This is my mantra. With these four issues in place, your performance will be fine since you are qualified for the job you are employed for.

 How do you deal with corruption in your industry?

 Over the years, I have made it very clear to my people that the suppliers are our partners. They should not be abused; they should not be subjected to blackmail. But if you treat them fairly and they don't deliver, just release them and look for someone else. That principle worked very, very well over the years and we have developed a very healthy relationship with the suppliers. We have actually become very good friends, especially with those who have been faithfully supplying us for more than 20 years. In this way, we can ensure quality and reduce corrupt practices.

One of the ways I ensure internal accountability and transparency is that I pay my suppliers on time and better than others. I moved the normal payment terms from 150 days to 45–60 days, in order not to hold debt for too many days. In this way, the suppliers trust me. They give me the best price. This helps me bring the cost down. I have a fixed day for payment, so there is less chance for corruption. And I have put in place the whole process whereby my suppliers need not have to call for payment as it is paid once the payment date is due.

I also make it clear that we don't pay bribes in Domino's. If we pay to one department, the other departments will know and then it becomes a norm. Every department will come to you.

I tell my people, "Do everything to comply with the laws and regulations." If we don't, we remedy it. And if we have to pay the fine, we pay it. We have to be accountable.

We need licenses from different departments to operate a restaurant. We don't indulge in giving them bribes. And over the years, if you establish a reputation for that, they respect it. The general rules I have for my people are that you comply with all the laws. Then they have no reason not to give you a license. They can only delay the process, but they cannot stop it.

Just recently, one government department came and found that we were breeding mosquitos at one of the drains at the corner of our premise. They wanted to shut down my plant. They wanted me to come and meet them. I refused. I told them to speak to my lawyer. I told them that if I have to shut down because of the problem, we will and we will rectify it. But if they exceed their authority, then we will take them to court for the misuse of power. If we have to pay the fine for negligence, we will pay.

However, they did not come back to us with any summon as they had threatened.

We will follow the law. No bribes. Period.

 What is one legacy you want to leave behind in your organization?

 I want to leave behind a God-fearing organization.

Don't be arrogant. We can make it because God chose to bless us. When God gives, there is always a reason. We are His stewards. The issue of stewardship becomes very crucial. We must bless others and learn to provide for God's people and God's house.

Whatever we have is God's providence. We must use it wisely.

 What is one weakness that you have and how do you deal with it?

 I don't know how to say no. One day, my chairman and partner, Dato' Sarit, gave me a book on how to say no for my birthday. I asked him, "Why do you give me this book?" He replied, "You always get yourself into trouble because you don't know how to say, no. You are too soft. You say you will not do it but after the person speaks to you personally, you will do it."

Now, I have my church chairman, Daniel, to help me. He knows my problem. He tells me that I cannot say no because I tend to feel guilty that I am not compassionate enough, or I am not a loving person. He knows it is not true. So he told me, "Whenever people ask you for help or there is an appeal to give, pass the request to me. If you are not comfortable saying no, I will vet and explain to the person if you cannot help."

 What is one advice you would give to emerging leaders?

 Remember the four priorities of life: God, family, health and work, in that order.

Be open, don't be immersed in your own problems, wise up and move on.

HO PENG KEE
The Versatile Leader

olitics, church, school, soccer field, national sports association, welfare organizations — these are among the varied arenas in which Associate Professor Ho Peng Kee has served as a leader.

The versatile ex-Singapore Senior Minister of State for Law and Home Affairs has donned several leadership hats with success throughout his time as a student, academic, then politician.

Prof. Ho was a Member of Parliament between 1991 and 2011. After two years as a backbencher, he took leave from the University in 1993 and assumed full-time political office, first as Parliamentary Secretary at the Ministry of Law and the Ministry of Home Affairs, before he was promoted as Senior Parliamentary Secretary, Minister of State and Senior Minister of State at the two Ministries in 1996, 1997 and 2001 respectively.

Singaporeans may remember him fondly as the 'second-chance man', as the devout Christian who implemented several second-chance initiatives such as home detention, community mediation centres, community-based sentences, guidance and streetwise programs for youths, and the debt repayment scheme. For 15 years, he fought hard against loansharking, drug-abuse, youth crime and vice syndicates. He also oversaw the growth of more alternative dispute resolution processes like arbitration and mediation.

Former Singapore Deputy Prime Minister and Home Affairs Minister Wong Kan Seng, whom Prof. Ho worked closely with, described him as an "approachable, big-hearted and principled person", a "versatile player" who could take on various tasks such as tackling loansharks, mentoring younger civil servants or dealing with drug abuse.

Outside of the political arena, a passion for sports runs in the 61-year-old's veins.

The midfielder captained the Anglo-Chinese School (ACS), National Junior College and Singapore University football teams, and also represented ACS in athletics and rugby. Years later, he became the President of the Football Association of Singapore from 2004–2009.

He also fancies the occasional jog, swim or sports activity with his lawyer wife and three grown-up daughters. Together, his family of five has played seven sports competitively at school and university levels.

Since stepping down from politics, he continues to be actively involved in a wide range of community service as a volunteer in various capacities. These include chairing the Home Team Volunteer Network, being the advisor to the Football Association of Singapore and patron of the Children's Cancer Foundation.

Modest, approachable and forthcoming with his views, we chat about his leadership experience over tea.

 Who or what influenced you most in your leadership development? And why?

 I basically live my life fully, and am thankful for a family setting that was secure. My father was a good provider.

He must be an inspiration of sorts. He died from cancer when I was 19 years old, and was a self-made man who built up a successful watch business. He started from scratch after the war. He was innovative — learned English on his own, called himself Henry Ho to cultivate the British Airways and Qantas crews and developed a mail-order business, all these in the 60s.

He was hardworking and determined, and I picked up those traits.

Having five older sisters helped me to be a more sensitive person, more able to interact with the opposite sex in a natural way.

 How would you describe your leadership style and life philosophy?

 I would like to summarize it in four Ps.

Professionalism — you must know your stuff, you can't hide incompetence. You must be the best that you can be in your chosen field, in terms of domain knowledge and skills. If you are not good in what you are doing, it's very hard for people to respect you.

Second, Personal Touch. You must know the people you are working with, preferably by name. When I was a Master of the NUS Kent Ridge Hall of Residence, I tried hard to remember the students' names. All through my working life, I did this for people I worked or interacted with.

I see everybody as being unique, everybody is different and with different skills. There's good in everybody, and we should be more affirming with people to bring out the best in them. Their eyes light up when I address them by name!

Third, Pride and Passion. You must have pride in what you are doing. That pushes you to do it well. Without passion, you can do nothing. In politics, you need a lot of passion. When I was the President of the Football Association of Singapore, I brought that into the job. I'm a footballer, I epitomized football, so I was very passionate about what I did. For example, I initiated regular tea sessions so people could meet me. It provided a platform for those who wanted to talk to me.

Last P is the P in oPportunity — you must recognize openings. You need to seize them when they come your way. You must be willing to try and not be afraid to fail.

 What is most crushing adversity you have ever faced? How did you deal with it?

 During my Officer Cadet School course in 1973, my father died and my girlfriend left me, all within a month! I lost two persons who were very close to me. I was listless and was losing interest in my training.

But one day, my section commander pulled me aside and asked what was wrong. He spoke to me in a caring tone that touched me. That really woke me up. I figured that becoming a National Service (NS) officer was a once-in-a-lifetime experience. I learned to live up to my loss, make the best out of the worst, and seize the opportunity.

I learned that I must be open to the counsel of people who know you, and who mean well, and not be immersed in my own problems. I need to wise up and move on.

 What are the principles which you live and work by?

 For working life, I've got three guiding Bible verses. The first is Colossians 3:23 — work heartily in all things, as serving God and not man.

The second one is Matthew 10:16, to be wise as a serpent and yet as innocent as a dove. How do we strike a balance? You can't be naïve, and you also cannot be scheming and devious! But you do need some guile and to be street smart.

For politics, Micah 6:8 was very real to me — to act justly, to show mercy, and to be humble before your God. That verse is something which I try to live out every day, even now.

 A lot of Christians think that politics is dirty, so they would rather not be involved. What advice do you have for Christians who aspire to be politicians?

 Christians should enter politics if they are given an opportunity and provided he or she has the right motivation, because they can be salt and light, and influence the shaping of public policy.

Your foundation and values must be strong. The first thing is you must know God's word — that's very important. Second, you must have godly people who will come alongside you to pray for you, and also rebuke you if need be, to provide accountability. Third, your motivation for going in must be correct. Go in because you want to do something good for Singapore, not to be somebody.

 What are the two most intense tensions between faith and politics that you have faced? How do you manage them?

 One area of discomfort is style. For example, in Parliament you have to win arguments, and once in a while you slip up.

On one occasion, in an exchange with an MP in Parliament, I retorted that he must have forgotten to put on his hearing aid. I received quite a bit of criticism online as being too personal and hitting below the belt. After that, I apologized personally to the Member who assured me he did not take offence at my remark! But still, I felt bad as I had appeared ungentlemanly. It was a lesson learned. Other times, I think I was more cutting in my remarks than I should have been.

In retrospect, it was a good thing that when I was introduced as a candidate in 1991, the media highlighted that I was a committed Christian, an elder in church. In what I did as MP and office-holder, people then knew where I was coming from. In other words, I shared God's love and my testimony by doing good. Looking back, that was the best approach.

 Give us a glimpse of your daily routine and habits which enable you to excel and succeed as a leader, and why you keep these practices?

 First, you must love God, and always affirm your personal relationship with Him, to live out what the Bible teaches, and to glorify Him in everything that you do.

Next is family. My wife and three girls are all quite independent. I am very grateful for them and draw strength from them. My best and most honest critics are my wife and kids, and I listen to them. I make it a point to have at least a longish holiday of about 10–14 days with them once a year. In this way, we have self-driven in many countries with strong abiding memories.

Third, exercise. Sports have been a big part of my life, imparting values that underlie my upbringing and leadership skills. These include teamwork, complementing strengths and weaknesses, experiencing both wins and losses, bouncing back from defeat, being patient when the chips are down, analyzing evolving play in the course of a match etc. Now I jog three times a week, at the Botanic Gardens and running track, to recharge and also do strategic thinking whilst exercising. It's amazing how somethings fall into place when you're running! My wife still plays badminton twice a week, without fail! My girls who are now between 21 and 30 years old still play competitive sports such as soccer, netball and basketball.

 How do you strike a balance between your busy schedule as a politician and your family time?

 I thank God for an able and supportive wife. I think she wears half the pants in the family! She recently retired as a lawyer. When both of us were holding full-time jobs, we worked as a team. When my kids were young, I was the one changing the nappies, and that's something my wife still talks about because she appreciates it.

I make it a point to attend key events in my children's lives. For example, when they went on stage to receive any prize in school, I'll be there to videotape them, to meet the teachers. When I travel, I'll try to buy something back for them. In this way, over the years, we amassed an array of small musical instruments and mind-boggling games from different local cultures and settings.

It's not about the quantum of time, but being there at the right time and being always available. For example, when my children want to talk about which school to go to or which course to choose, I'm always there. When my youngest daughter wanted to learn how to throw the javelin or shot put, I said let's go and try, and she appreciated that.

 During your term as FAS president, we had the Goal 2010 target for Singapore to reach the World Cup Finals in 2010, why didn't we achieve it? Will we ever make it?

 I inherited Goal 2010 from my predecessor, Mr. Mah Bow Tan. Goal 2010 sounded quite sexy; 2014 doesn't sound as nice. So we said let's go for Goal 2010. And that was in 1999! It jolted everybody up, at least initially.

My first task as FAS president in 2004 was to slowly distance ourselves from Goal 2010 without it sounding like a defeat. 2010 was put there not really as a fixed target, but as a milestone to reach the finals, someday. We want to go to the World Cup Finals, but 2010 was not that realistic.

But I kept that mission. When you inherit the ship, you don't do things which will put your predecessor in a bad light.

I still think we can make it to the World Cup Finals, maybe in 2018 or 2022. But, personally, I think we need more flexibility with NS. NS is important and doing basic training is correct, but after that we should have more flexibility. If you can play games and bring glory to Singapore, then that's your NS!

 What is one advice you would give to emerging leaders?

 I use another framework — The four Cs. I like to have a framework because it helps me in my own development. I've shared this on many occasions, especially in schools. The first C is Competence. Competence reflects professionalism — that's one thing you have to be, whether you are an adult or a student. As a student, you may say you are good at your CCA (Co-Curricular Activities), but the first thing is that you must study hard — you are there basically to acquire academic knowledge and skills.

Second is Confidence, not the bragging, strutting kind of confidence. You must be quietly confident of yourself. Sometimes, our students are not self-assured enough, maybe because they compare themselves to others. Maybe you are not very articulate or your academic results may not be as good, but you must be quietly confident that you have gifts and talents.

Compassion — this is something which I feel for. Over my 20 years in public office, people know me as someone who pushes very hard for rehabilitation — the 'second-chance man'. Every person is unique and has some good in him. Give him or her a chance if he or she truly cherishes it.

Character — this has to do with one's values: integrity and reputation are very important. Strive to be somebody people can trust as a leader. As a politician, people may scold you because of their unhappiness with government policies, but at least they trust that you have their interests at heart, that you mean well. They know you are not dishonest or insincere and will always do your best for them.

 What is one weakness that you have and struggle with constantly? And how do you manage it?

 In my passion and enthusiasm, there are times when I may come across as being overly-assertive and dominating; for example, by sending off a series of emails, firing from the hip. This is not my intention. I have to be more sensitive as to how those who are less gregarious may respond better to a lower-key approach.

> "Leaders should lead from the front during tumultuous times, and resist the urge to play the blame game.

HSIEH FU HUA
The Lead-from-the-front Leader

r. Hsieh Fu Hua is no stranger to dealing with crisis. The 63-year-old Singaporean has weathered several maelstroms in his corporate career, from the Pan-Electric crisis in 1985 to the Asian Financial Crisis in the late 1990s and the Global Financial Crisis.

As the Singapore Exchange (SGX) chief executive from March 2003 to November 2009, Mr. Hsieh steadily helmed the bourse through the 2008 Global Financial Crisis — an event thought by many experts as the worst worldwide slump since the Great Depression in the 1930s.

Leaders should lead from the front during tumultuous times and resist the urge to play the 'blame game', he says.

Mr. Hsieh has had extensive experience in the financial services sector, ranging from stockbroking, investment banking to fund management.

He began his career at British investment bank Morgan Grenfell Asia in 1974, rising to the rank of managing director by 1985. In 1993, Mr. Hsieh co-founded Prime Partners, a corporate advisory firm based in Singapore.

He has also served on the boards of major government investment agencies Temasek Holdings (2010–2012) and the Government of Singapore Investment Corporation (2003–2010).

One of his more recent appointments is non-executive chairman of United Overseas Bank, a position he took up in April 2013.

Outside of the corporate world, Mr. Hsieh is also active in the charity arena.

He was appointed president of the National Council of Social Service (NCSS), the umbrella body for about 400 member voluntary welfare organizations in Singapore, since August 2012. He also founded BinjaiTree, a privately-run charity that gives out grants to various organizations.

Mr. Hsieh is married with two children.

To Mr. Hsieh, leadership means being able to live up to the highest professional and moral standards. Whatever position he takes, he is always true to himself.

We catch up with Mr. Hsieh over tea in his office.

Who or what influenced you most in your leadership development? And why?

 A play, which I read at school called *A Man for All Seasons*[1], captured my imagination and resonated deeply with me. The protagonist Sir Thomas More was known to be an accomplished man and chancellor.

Amid all the complexity in his practice of state craft, he held a 'constant'. As a leader, you have to be clear what that constant is. There is also a definite part of you, core values which you cannot compromise. There will be many times and situations that you have to be true to yourself and to those 'very core' values. That was what I found most significant about the play and its lead character.

 In your leadership, what are some core values which you will never compromise on?

 Integrity and listening to the inner voice that tells you to do what is right.

But it's never easy. Even defining integrity is not easy.

As a leader, whether of a large organization or one fellow, you make hard and significant decisions at different stages.

To me, as a leader, it is not about enforcing rules or holding to unyielding doctrines. There has to be a balance of listening, deep reflection and accommodation. And yet at which point do you say "it's inviolable"? Where you say "no matter what it costs, I will not agree"? Even when the price is extremely high, you choose not to consent. Are you prepared to give up all? That, to me, is the most challenging part. There is a worldly

---

[1] The play portrays Sir Thomas More, the 16th-century Chancellor of England, who refused to affirm the Act of Supremacy making King Henry VIII the supreme head of the Church of England. Sir More is a principled man with a conscience, who chooses to remain true to himself and his beliefs while accommodating the complicated circumstances throughout. More represents "a man for all seasons," whose conviction remains constant even in the face of external pressures.

saying: "Every man has his price". If you subscribe to that, then it is a lost cause.

 Have you ever been in a situation where you were prepared to give up everything and not compromise on your core values?

 As a leader, we have a duty to uphold the rules of the game and the rules call for fairness and transparency. These rules must apply to you, even if it is hugely embarrassing. That is the right thing to do.

Earlier on in my career, I made an erroneous investment decision which I could have hidden. Nobody would have known. I didn't know what the price would be. But could I have lived with it?

I owned up to it and paid my dues. Till today, I am still reminded of it.

In short, you must live up to the highest standards expected of you as a leader.

 What is one memorable life-changing experience that has impacted and shaped the way you lead?

 In leadership, there are times when you have to confront people far more important, far more powerful than you. "Confront" meaning you disagree on the point of fundamental principle because of what you know and understand. To choose not to voice your disagreement is a cop-out. It can make one feel very uncomfortable and be very unpopular. There are definitely such times that one should make a stand.

You have to say this is wrong when it is wrong. As leaders or board directors, we should not allow nor encourage willful blindness. Don't just look the other way to stay popular.

My conscience must work.

 What is your impression of corporate governance here and how do you see it in the next few years?

 Singapore is widely recognized to have a higher level of corporate governance, and that is because we have a robust and strong enforcement structure. The compliance nature of corporates in Singapore is attributable to having an effective enforcement system. However, compliance and governance are not the same thing at all.

Corporate governance is more than just the Board monitoring compliance.

Some CEOs may not fully understand or have taken on their responsibilities in governance. Some Boards may not appreciate the role they can play, the advantage which they can actually confer.

As a personal view, good corporate governance is realized when a Board and their CEO are able to engage in a transparent, open and trusting relationship to ensure that their company delivers sustainable performance in the long-run.

When the Board is focused on helping a CEO achieve higher standards all around, it becomes more of a mentoring relationship, like that of having a coach. It is like helping the CEO build an open relationship with the Board, in which he or she is not afraid to share vulnerabilities. Having said that, the Board has to be wise, and the CEO has to be transparent.

The best athletes are physically and mentally very strong and they do not achieve this on their own. Their coaches are there to assist them in harnessing their strengths and to identify their weaknesses. Their achievement is based on trust. And this is the highest level of governance, where the relationship is based on openness and transparency.

To ensure openness and transparency, both must share and embrace a common purpose, which is to build the organization, not your own ego. As chairman of the Board, you have to understand your role. You help the CEO by scanning the environment and situations, and providing useful information to the CEO. You must not direct. That's the job of the CEO.

You can also help the CEO by showing understanding and listening well to the ground, not micro-managing or interfering. If both have any major disagreements, the issues must be raised directly and not through a third party. The CEO must be given the opportunity to execute and let him/her deliver the goals in his/her own way.

One of the main themes of this book is about dealing with uncertainty. What advice do you have for business and investment leaders dealing with turbulent times?

 One key lesson is not to play the 'blame game' during tumultuous times.

In a crisis, leaders should take on the responsibility of leading at the front. During such tough times, a leader should confront the problems head-on rather than confronting his/her people. Be more proactive and outward facing, and at the same time, maintain your sense of perspective. When your people know that you are with them and demonstrate control, the team becomes stronger to deal with the issues at hand. Without a doubt, a leader takes on the most pressure and makes the final call.

 How do you prepare for crisis management?

 Besides having a robust crisis management plan and going through various simulation exercises, be prepared to be up front when those moments arrive.

Being open and honest will take a leader a long way.

In any crisis situation, no one should play the 'blame game'. The organization should not unnecessarily sacrifice its leader or staff. When the leader takes up such responsibility, the Board should stand with and behind the leader and see through the crisis together.

 What do you consider to be your greatest weakness?

 I would say managing one's ego.

We are used to having our voice heard and we end up not listening.

It is important for leaders to remember that it is about projecting what the organization does, not about the personal agenda.

 Any word of advice to current and future leaders?

 I believe a leader is not a boss who bosses people around and has an entitlement mentality. It is a huge responsibility. The leader has to lead by example. It is also important to have the right mentors: people in one's life who throw light on how you should think of yourself and matters around you.

A leader is someone who is able to do the right thing despite the challenges, pressure and circumstances pressing down on you.

> Dream the impossible. Create an adventure that you cannot do yourself. You will become better from it. If you want to be the change, act the change.

IDRIS JALA

The Impossible Dreamer Leader

Idris Jala is the Minister without Portfolio in the Prime Minister office in Malaysia. He is the Chief Executive Officer of PEMANDU (Performance Management and Delivery Unit), whose main role is ensuring the successful implementation of programmes which will transform Malaysia into a high-income nation by 2020, and provide all Malaysians access to improved public services.

Before PEMANDU, Idris used to work for energy giant Shell. In 2005, the Malaysian government selected him to be the CEO of Malaysia Airlines (MAS) because of the massive losses in the company. The state-owned airline had booked a loss of RM1.3 billion in that year alone. It had cash to last only 3½ months, which means if it was not turned around, there would be no money to pay salaries or fuel!

He had to choose between taking up the position of Chairman of Shell Malaysia, which would have been given him more security and a higher pay, or taking up the position of CEO of MAS, which meant taking a big challenge to turn around the company. Against the counsel of his family members and close friends, he chose the latter because he believed in the impossible. In his own words, he saw his involvement as "a calling, not just a job."[1]

In February 2006, he announced the airline's Business Turnaround Plan (BTP) to improve the company from a 9-month loss of US$400 million in 2005 to an ambitious profitable level of US$260 million. The BTP was successfully implemented and the company achieved the targeted profit ahead of schedule by one year.

Idris' story was important, says a senior analyst from a Kuala Lumpur think tank. "Firstly, Idris Jala is a Kelabit from Sarawak and a Christian. He was the first non-Malay non-Muslim to be appointed to head a Government-Linked company. Secondly, Idris Jala only had experience in a multi-national company setting and had no experience working in a Government-Linked company, so there was skepticism that he can transplant Shell methods to MAS. In the end, Idris proved the pundits wrong when he managed to improve MAS both operationally and financially."[2]

Idris' story is truly one of dreaming the impossible. He started life in a small village in Bario, in the inner part of Sarawak, Borneo.

---

[1] Deepa Iyer, Princeton Case Study. Innovations for Successful Societies. Civil Service Series. Interview: ZB1. March 2011. Princeton University

[2] Jed Yoong, In Malaysia, Signs of Government Reform. Asia Sentinel Consulting. 29 May, 2008.

He became the Managing Director of Shell in Sri Lanka (1998–2000), where he had to handle the explosive situation of an industrial strike. He went on to become the Vice President for retail marketing for Shell International (2000–2002) before becoming the Managing Director for Shell MDS (Malaysia) and Vice-President of Shell Malaysia Gas & Power from 2002–2005.

We got together with Idris over tea for this interview.

 Who or what influenced you most in your leadership development? And why?

 It was certainly my stint with Shell in Sri Lanka. I learned about unconventional leadership. I had to reinvent myself despite the fact that I had been with Shell for 10 years.

When I arrived in Sri Lanka, my first challenge was a union strike in my depot. We had just completed a manpower downsizing exercise, during which the staff strength was reduced by 30%. Around 200 workers were angry and went on strike. Within the depot, there was a storage tank that holds 800 metric tonnes of flammable gas. To make it worse, they were holding Mr. Surin, the plant manager, hostage. Anything could happen!

When my staff called me and told me about the situation, I immediately rushed to the depot. My first priority was to rescue Surin. I requested for police assistance and they sent two truckloads of police. It took me one hour to get to the place and I had no chance to think. I had to act very quickly in this crisis.

When I ran inside, I ordered the people to come out. They refused and asked, "Why did you bring the police?" as they feared being arrested. I identified who the ring-leaders were and negotiated with them. After some hard bargaining, I negotiated for the release of Surin after promising them that I would organize a domestic inquiry to be conducted by an independent tribunal headed by an ex-judge, even though at that time I had not arranged for any like that before.

Without the luxury of time to think, I decided to promise them first and then sort out the details later. I just felt intuitively that it was the right thing to do to give them a fair trial with an independent tribunal.

To cut the long story short, the judge found them guilty. However, if all the staff were sent to the jail, there would be no one to work in the depot, and that meant that the only source of cooking gas in the country would have been disrupted, which would lead to a crisis situation in Sri Lanka.

The Sri Lankan President called and asked me to drop all the charges and release the workers. I felt I could not do that because that would lead to lawlessness in the country. People would be more daring to go on strike regularly. I stood my ground. I told the President I had no power to discharge them from jail, as the independent tribunal had already given the verdict and had sentenced them.

 So, what did you learn about leadership?

 I have learned very important leadership lessons from this experience, which now forms the foundation of my leadership principles.

The over-arching leadership lesson is you need to have the courage to make tough decisions and to act. Sometimes in leadership, you do not have time to analyze, so you have to trust your judgment. You have to make the decision and figure out the details later.

 We have heard a lot about your famous 6 principles of leadership. Can you kindly elaborate?

 Over the years in my career, I have developed six principles of leadership which I also call my own 'Experiential Truths'. Let me clarify that these 'Experiential Truths' are unique to me and they are different from the universal truths on leadership which everyone reads in books and hears at seminars. Of course, everyone is welcome to learn and adapt my experiential truths to suit their own situations.

The first is 'Going for the Impossible'. A leader must start with the impossible. I cannot use the old ways. I have to search for new ways.

During my time in Sri Lanka, I came across Tracy Goss' book, *The Last Word on Power*, which talks about reinventing executives to make the impossible happen. Jim Collins uses a different term, BHAG (Big Hairy Audacious Goals).

An impossible dream is something that even your wife, your boss, your children and your friends think is impossible to achieve. It's important to make sure everyone agrees or confirms with you that the task is impossible and that it is ok to fail, because only then would you have overcome the fear of failure. If you are a salesperson and you target a 10–20% increment in sales, then you will not change.

If you want to transform, you must set an impossible target. In my case, I was charged with an impossible situation in Sri Lanka, I had to think and act differently.

Second, a leader must always 'Anchor on the True North'. In the corporate setting, the true north is the profit and loss statement and not the cash flow or balance sheet, although the latter is important.

From there, you set your KPIs (Key Performance Indicators) to achieve this. The typical situation is that we have too many KPIs. We have to bring it down to a very core set of KPIs that you are actually going to measure, that is critical and that everyone agrees on.

Third, a leader needs to demonstrate 'Discipline of Action'. Many people want to take action but have no discipline to execute them. They keep postponing their actions. If you say you are going to do it on the 16th of next month, then you really need to do it on the 16th of next month.

Discipline must be coupled with detailed action plans and activities to execute the strategy. After you have set your true north, you have to work out all the activities to achieve this. You have to specify and quantify the activities from step 1 to 10. And then ruthlessly monitor the implementation of the activities.

Fourth, a leader must practice 'Situational Leadership'. You may have heard of the Ken Blanchard model. According to Blanchard, when one starts a journey on transformation, the leadership style must be quite directive. Whilst you obtain views and input from your subordinates, as the leader, you must be quite directive in making the final decision, even if sometimes it means making a decision that is unpopular or based on limited information at hand.[3]

I like to use the story of Moses who brought Jewish slaves out of Egypt. At the start of the journey, after crossing the Red Sea, I don't think Moses really knew which direction to go since there was no GPS back then. But as the leader, Moses was directive — he pointed to one direction and told the rest to follow him. I suspect they were lost in the deserts for decades before Joshua led them to the promised land. On hindsight, Moses had no choice. If he wasn't directive, he would not have gotten those people out of Egypt.

However, a leader cannot be directive forever. As the team becomes more experienced and competent, the leader should start to empower.

This is the essence of situational leadership. A leader must be prepared to change his/her style of leadership (between directive and empowering) depending on the team's development.

Fifth, it is imperative to forge 'Winning Coalitions' all the time. No man is an island. I mentioned earlier about putting key people together in a lab setting to come up with the best solutions to a problem. Once the solutions are in place, it is always important to engage everyone that matters. In the case of the Government Transformation Program (GTP), we engaged the public through town halls so that everyone can come together to criticize and/or improve the solutions. This was how we forged a winning coalition.

Lastly, and also importantly, is 'Divine Intervention'. Even if you could do all the first five things I had described earlier, you could still fail because in reality many things happen outside of our control, for example tsunami or floods. This last one is important because it counterbalances the first principle of 'Going for the Impossible'. It makes us feel vulnerable and

---

[3] Ken Blanchard is an American author and management expert. His book *The One Minute Manager* (co-authored with Spencer Johnson) has sold over 13 million copies and has been translated into 37 languages. Blanchard is the Chief Spiritual Officer of The Ken Blanchard Companies, an international management training and consulting firm that he and his wife, Marjorie Blanchard, cofounded in 1979 in San Diego, California.

humble, which are good virtues. If you feel vulnerable, you know that the world is not at your feet. We can have the best troops running at their best but we still do not get the desired results. But we should not shoot the troops

Whether you are a Muslim, Buddhist or Christian, we recognize that there is a divine element. Some people say it is God, some people say it is fate, some people call it luck.

This is why I believe that if one is a religious or spiritual individual, he or she should pray. It is a path to becoming a good human being. I always advise my team, "We must always do the right things and not be tempted by corruptive behaviors. If you do a job based on what is right, God will reward you somehow, one way or the other."

In your opinion, what is your role in the Government?

My role in the cabinet is akin to an architect of transformation who is hired by the Prime Minister to help him implement his vision and goal. As the architect, I design the architecture framework which drives commitment, accountability and transparency in the government.

When I took on the job at PEMANDU, the first thing I did was to run six labs involving 200 people from various government ministries and agencies. In each lab, we got the people to dream the impossible and set very high targets.

For example, crime rates have been on the rise in Malaysia since 2006. During the first year of the GTP, the government set a target to reduce the street crime in the first year by 20%. Everyone in the lab and also the public said it was impossible.

If we had come up with an incremental target to reduce street crime by 1%, there would be no need for transformation since the existing way of doing things would suffice. The police would just have to run a little harder, and they would achieve it. But if we were to tell them to bring street crime down by 20% in one year, the police would conclude that the existing way of doing things would not work; they would need to come up with a radical and out-of-the-box approach.

I generally believe that people know the solutions. Like all large organizations, the common problem is always the existence of roadblocks: political, administrative, technical and process hurdles, which prevent people from implementing the solutions. By setting impossible targets, everyone from top to bottom is forced to radically change their method and also remove any roadblocks that have prevented good ideas and solutions from being implemented.

Now, I do these for all government ministries, departments and agencies. We put them in labs that last 6–8 weeks which set impossible targets and force them to come out with radical and out-of-the-box approaches.

We then produce a 'roadmap' i.e. book that tells everyone in the public that this is what we are going to do and we are committed to implementing it. Every single government ministry, department and agency has a role to play in this roadmap. You see, when you put it out in such detail to the public, you have no choice but to deliver it.

At the end of each year, we will write a report to assess how we perform and we share that with the public.

 What is one memorable life-changing experience that has impacted and shaped the way you lead?

 When I first became the CEO of Malaysian Airlines, to help turn it around, I had a town hall meeting with the employees. I laid out my vision and plans for the future. When we had a Q & A session, one Muslim employee raised his hand and asked me a question, "Sir, I want to ask you about serving liquor on our airline. We are a Muslim country. Why do we need to sell liquor? I don't want a business answer. I want an answer from the Koran."

It stumped me for a while. I said to him, "Before I answer you, I would like to ask you two questions."

"Do you believe that God is all-powerful?" He replied, "Yes."

"Do you believe that God can eradicate evil since He is all-powerful if he wanted to?"

"Of course!" he shot back.

"Do you believe that liquor is evil?"

"Yes"

"Why doesn't God stop all the liquor?"

He could not reply.

"You see," I shared, "God is all-powerful and yet He allows people to choose. So, in the same way, we should be like that. We should allow people to choose whether they want to drink or not."

My answer satisfied him and later, he became one of my best leaders and we are now very good friends.

From this experience, I realized that leaders must win the hearts of their people and if we can do that, we will have their loyalty and they will do their best for you.

 Give us a glimpse of your daily routine. And why do you keep these practices?

 I spend much time reflecting in solitude. There is a difference between loneliness and solitude. Loneliness is when you are alone and you don't want to be alone. Solitude is when you choose to be alone so that you can reflect and refocus your mind on what you are trying to accomplish in life.

I take both short and long moments of solitude. For example, when I am in the car alone, I reflect. At night, when I am at home, I spend time alone, reflecting and refocusing. At times, I take longer breaks to do the same.

What is one weakness that you have and how do you deal with it?

My biggest weakness is my inability to make the trade-offs. Should I be directive or empowering? At times, it is difficult to make the judgment call. In the public sector, which part of the public are you listening to? The majority of the public are silent. The loudest, noisiest group may not actually represent the majority.

Another weakness that I have is when I make a mistake, I am slow to identify it and make the corrections. This is why I always surround myself with capable and trusted people. Having a solid team that is comfortable enough to speak freely with you (as a leader) is important: you need people who tell you the truth and point out your mistakes so that you can make the necessary corrections quickly.

What is one legacy you have left behind in your organization?

Make a difference to society. John Ruskin said, "The highest reward for a person's toil is not what they get for it, but what they become by it." Nothing makes me happier than to see that I have managed to change the mindset of the people and organization which I have led. This is the legacy that I would like to leave behind.

What is one advice you would give to emerging leaders?

Dream the impossible. In reality, most people do normal things. Create an adventure that you cannot do yourself using the existing way. If you want to be the change, act the change. You will become better at it over time.

活到老，学到老。**As long as you live, Learn**

JAMES CHIA
The Life-Long Learner Leader

ames Chia is one of the founding directors and the Group President of Pico Group, one of the world's leading corporate event management and planning companies. They have a staff strength of around 2,000 in more than 30 cities globally, with production facilities in Asia and the Middle East.

Pico Far East Holdings Limited is listed on the Hong Kong Stock Exchange. Its associate company, Pico (Thailand) Public Company Limited is also listed on the Market for Alternative Investment (MAI), a stock exchange of Thailand.

Pico Far East Holdings Limited posted a turnover of US$494 million and had a market capitalization of US$275 million in its financial year 2014.

With a track record of more than 40 years in the exhibition industry, Pico brings brands to life through powerful and engaging experiences — from strategy to execution — for many Fortune 500 enterprises. It is ranked second in 2014 CEI Asia magazine's Industry Survey of Asia's Top Business Event Companies. In 2012, Pico won the Event Marketing Agency of the Year Gold Award from Marketing Magazine and was ranked second in America's Special Events Magazine's Top Event Company listings in 2012–2013.

With a younger generation of professional managers as well as family members in leadership roles, James is able to devote more time to his pet projects, which is to develop new business lines. We were able to catch up with James over coffee to find out what makes the man tick.

 Who or what influenced you most in your leadership development? And why?

 At different phases of my life, I was blessed to work with very capable people who became my mentors. I also had the opportunity to work under systems from which I was able to learn and then apply in my line of business. You can say that my repertoire of leadership styles is a distillation of the gems gleamed from my growing up years and working experience. I am still learning as the business environment is never static and today's challenges require both experiential wisdom and new skills.

Learning while serving National Service

I had invaluable learning opportunities while serving National Service. By the time I completed two-and-a-half years of service, I seemed to have graduated from management school! As an army officer, I was privileged to be trained in strategic thinking and organizational and leadership development. The way the army is structured is a key component of its success. When I joined Pico, I applied the same principles and created strategic business units (SBU). Each SBU is a functional unit accountable for its own profit and loss. Depending on the size of a project, one or more SBUs can be involved. This arrangement gives us the flexibility to pool resources whenever necessary.

Besides management skills, problem-solving skills were also developed which I was able to apply very effectively in my business. I learned to break down problems into bite-size. As an example, Pico was tasked to complete the set up for a motor show in two days. This had never been done before and many of my team leaders said that it was impossible to achieve. I took up the challenge and delivered the result on time by dividing the huge exhibition area into manageable smaller units, with each team responsible for a unit. We were complimented for a job well done!

Learning from my Brother

At the start of my working life in the events business in 1973, my brother, SL Chia, the founder of Pico, was the key person instrumental in teaching me the ropes of the business. I daresay the foundation for the success of Pico — creativity and quality of service — was laid by him. As an artist, and a very exacting one, he was uncompromising on the best offering to our customers in terms of creative content and quality. I learned to serve my customers with excellence, pay attention to details and to look for the best creative solution.

Learning from Cultural Heritage

Some people may consider being Chinese-educated to be a disadvantage in the English-speaking business environment. On the contrary, principles and truths learned from Chinese history and expressed in rich Chinese proverbs and teachings still influence the way I live life as well as my leadership. For example, "活到老, 学到老", can be translated to "As long as you live, learn". That's the reason I will never stop learning.

Learning from Customers

There are many lessons to be learned from customers. They are experts in their own fields and many have existed long before Pico came into the picture. From their experience, I can learn what I should or should not do in business in order to thrive.

 What impresses us most about you is your deep sense of curiosity, and your willingness to learn. You are always buying books to read and purchasing audio tracks/CDs to download onto your iPod. What sustains your curiosity?

 I have my carefree childhood to thank for. In those days, the school bag was opened only in school! After school, we were free to roam around, catching spiders, playing in the fields or river, or whatever caught our fancy for the day. There were many learning opportunities in all these fun ways.

There was also a season of my life that impacted me greatly. After completing my secondary school education in a predominantly Chinese learning environment, I chose to be in the pioneer batch at National Junior College where subjects were taught in English. Those two years in college were very tough for me as I was not able to follow the lessons in class. There was a deep sense of inadequacy and help was limited. I had to resort to self-learning. Thank God that I was able to pass my A-level examinations. But those two years taught me that no matter how tough the journey, success can be achieved if I work hard and have the right attitude.

I am also grateful to my wife who's a voracious reader. Together, we encourage each other to continue learning. Now we are learning to be grandparents!

 How have you changed as a leader after all these years?

 I have matured as a leader over the years. I confess that I was a perfectionist in my younger days. I must have terrorized my secretary and colleagues then. As I moved up the management ladder, I had to delegate and I learned to be influential instead of being directive. I am now a servant leader. My job is to make others successful. The more successful they become, the more successful I will be. I don't need to be the champion. I help my people to become champions in their own team and in their own right.

 What is one most crushing adversity you have ever faced in your leadership? How did you deal with it?

 The periods when SARS (Severe Acute Respiratory Syndrome) and the Asian Financial Crises hit were the greatest tests of my leadership. By then, Pico had already grown to a sizeable organization, and it was not easy to sustain the business without taking some drastic measures. Thankfully, the management and staff were united in seeing us through the rough patch by accepting salary cuts without resorting to retrenchment.

 What did you learn from this experience?

 It was Zig Ziglar, a well-known motivational speaker and author, who rightly pointed out that "Sometimes adversity is what you need to face in order to become successful." I have learned a few invaluable lessons from such adversities. Firstly, I realized that the company should concentrate on its core business. It is alright to break new ground, but this should be done after careful evaluation and testing of the ground. Secondly, we have to take care of our most important asset — our people.

 James, one of the hallmarks in your life is your family. Tell us how do you keep your priorities?

 I view life as a 'four-legged stool' comprising key components of Faith, Family, Self and Career. At different seasons of life, one may place more emphasis on each area but ultimately, we need to do well in all four areas in order to be truly satisfied and happy. The difficult part is making right choices, as often, time spent in one area may result in neglect of the others. Career is important, and I do my best to contribute towards the success of the company. However, as a married man, I have to ensure that my career advancement does not compromise the needs of my family. Neither should it be at the expense of my health or my commitment to God.

At the beginning of every year, I pen down some important dates, such as birthdays, anniversaries, family vacations, special occasions, seminars, conferences and mission trips that I would like to participate in. As far as possible, I would keep to these commitments. I also do regular reviews with my wife and make adjustments wherever necessary.

Setting my priorities and working purposefully to fulfill them keep me balanced. Sometimes, one 'leg' of the 'stool' gets longer than the other. I then have to see what can be done to 'shorten that leg' or lengthen the other three.

 Succession planning is one of the most difficult challenges in a family business. Tell us how it should be done well?

 There are six of us from the first generation in the business. Presently, we have eight from the second generation with us, in different locations and with different responsibilities. For succession planning, there are some guiding principles that we abide by.

Firstly, all our children are encouraged to get the best possible education. After graduation, they are also expected to gain some working experience to broaden their perspectives. There's no iron-clad guarantee that they will be accepted into the business, as they are recruited based on the same criteria as the other professional staff, namely, attitude and competence.

Secondly, each one of them has to prove his or her worth not only to us, but also to their colleagues. Those who excel, we will empower and provide them with opportunities to grow, just as for other staff members. We play a consultative role and try not to interfere in their decision-making. When mistakes are made, which they invariably will, they will be coached so that invaluable lessons can be learned.

Thirdly, we recognize that older staff do not always accept younger family members to be their leader. On one hand, we value the contribution from our experienced staff but on the other hand, we also want our children to have a free hand to develop their own teams. We try to create a win-win situation by reorganizing portfolios.

Last but not least, we try not to practice favoritism. We maintain a professional approach to their assessment and they are subjected to the company's human resource practices. The Bible teaches us to act justly, love mercy and to walk humbly with God. The practice of these principles helps us to maintain the right balance in forging healthy working relationships amongst our staff and family members.

What is your greatest weakness?

Ironically some of my strengths can also be my weaknesses. I have mentioned that I was a perfectionist. I still am, to some degree. I am also a very determined person. Whatever I set my heart to do, I will make sure that it happens. This competitive spirit and never-say-die attitude is both a positive and negative attribute. I find that it's not easy to relax my mind. I am thinking and planning all the time. I have to learn to focus and enjoy the present and not let my mind be too preoccupied with the future.

What is one legacy you want to leave behind in your organization?

Pico started as a family business. The first generation pioneer family members and committed staff worked hard to build the business. Unity is a key factor for our success. Those of us in the leadership of the company are intentional in ensuring that unity continues to be a key pillar of our growth. The people, market and organization will change over time. However, with unity, I believe that we will be able to face whatever challenges ahead of us and grow from strength to strength.

What is one advice you would give to emerging leaders?

Be self-disciplined. We will never get anywhere in life without discipline. We are made up of soul, body and spirit, and we need to exercise self-discipline in all these areas in order to be the best that we can be. Discipline required in these areas include taking care of our physical and emotional health, and cultivating routines that help us know God and make Him known. Then there's work discipline. Making effort to spend quality time with your family requires discipline too.

Remember that money isn't everything.
I had very good chances to get rich easily,
but if I had taken the money, I would be
in jail now and would have had my
reputation ruined. And if that happens,
how can my children face society?

JARUVAN MAINTAKA
The Anti-Corruption Leader

hunying Jaruvan Maintaka was at the forefront of the fight against corruption in Thailand from 2001–2006.

The mother of three is the first woman Auditor-General of Thailand, well-known for being one who is independent, and who stood for integrity and uncovered corrupt practices among high-level government officials.

The eldest daughter from a family of eight children, Jaruvan studied commerce and accountancy at Thailand's Chulalongkorn University before obtaining an MBA from Michigan State University in America on a government scholarship.

"When I went home (after getting the scholarship) I told my mother the good news, and she asked which bus route goes to USA. She had never heard of America before," said the feisty 64-year-old.

She started out as an auditor in the private sector before becoming a government auditor. In 2001, she was appointed Auditor-General in a process which was fraught with controversy, as she did not receive the majority vote among eight candidates. Instead, she was appointed only after the Senate had voted to select her from a shortlist of three.

A year later, she made headlines after revealing that corruption in state projects cost Thailand some 100 billion baht in 2002. However, it was her work in uncovering evidence of corruption involving a top Thai politician which made her a controversial but also well-loved figure in Thailand.

Her fight against corruption resulted in her and her family receiving daily death threats for nearly a year in 2007.

"These people tried to scare me — every morning and night I would receive death threats concerning me and my family. After a while, I just refused to take any phone calls for about a year, I had five soldiers come over to my home to transport me around in a van. The five of them had M-16s, revolvers, bulletproof vests — they came with me every morning and night."

In the last election for senators, she garnered the highest number of votes among all the candidates. Recently, she also obtained her PhD from the Chulalongkorn University.

We caught up with the unwavering and witty woman in Bangkok on a warm afternoon.

 Who or what influenced you most in your leadership development? And why?

 My father — he's Cantonese, and he always had something good to teach me. He owned restaurants and had rooms to rent out.

My father's family was very rich in Canton but because my grandfather was afraid the communists would take him away, he paid some people to bring him to Thailand.

Once, my father brought me to a rice field and told me to bring a rice stalk to him. He said this rice stalk is very humble — even though it's full of rice grains, it bows to everyone who walks by when the wind blows. He told my brother who's very spoilt to go to that rice field and bring him a rice stalk. He brought one that was empty. My father said when you are empty you tend to be very arrogant because you don't bend to anyone.

He also told us to eat with our own money rather than from other people's money — to earn your own keep.

 What were your growing up years like and how did they shape your future?

 From a young age, I liked to challenge those who are wrong. In secondary school, I raised my hand and told my teacher: "If there's a God, you tell that God to stand in front of me." I was very rude. The teacher told me to go home and ask God to present himself to you. So I asked God if you are real, help me to go to the United States to study.

God answered my prayer. In 1962 the American Field Service Scholarship was offered to Thailand and I was one of nine students who got it. I was just 16 years old. It took me two days to fly there — I had to stop over at Japan, Guam Island, and stay a night before flying to Los Angeles.

What is one memorable life-changing experience that has impacted and shaped the way you lead?

 I came from a rather wealthy family. I was lucky. Even my husband is very kind and generous to me, I'm the one who's rude to him.

During my time as Auditor-General of Thailand, I was tempted many times through bribery but I said no. When I had problems with the former Thai Prime Minister, I kneeled down and asked God what to do and He spoke to me from the Bible.

On behalf of the Assets Scrutiny Committee, I investigated the case of the Ratchada Land for which he was sentenced to jail for two years — that's why he can't enter the country. At that time, the land belonged to a bankrupt company, so the government decided to put the land into the Bank of Thailand. A lady wanted to buy the land, and the Cabinet even declared Dec 31 not to be a public holiday for the first time in Thailand so the lady could get one more day to change the name of the title deed.

The land was bought really cheaply — at 772 million baht — and it was then sold for 2,000 million baht.

There were other cases, such as the CTX involving the purchase of airport detection machines. It cost more than 1,000 million baht. That's why some political leaders hated me so much.

 Was there any fear and apprehension when you uncovered these things? Where do you draw your moral courage from?

 My courage comes from God. I was absent from my job for one year and seven months before the King appointed me again to the job.

One day, I was ordered to see one of the top ministers. On the day I was going to see him, I was at home and opened my Bible. I read a verse which told me not to go. I decided not to go to see him — I hid myself and just stayed quiet in my bedroom the whole day. Later, I found out that if I had gone there he would have had me sign on a paper that said I didn't want to stay on in the job. It was a trap.

Are there people or your own values which keep you going?

I think it's my family. Anytime I want to take a bribe, I look at my children and I say I cannot let them down. I'm also the eldest sister in the family so I've to set a good example.

Family plays an important part. My husband also tells me not to take anything — we don't want to be too rich. We have enough — we have our own house and our own car.

We are building a new house — they thought I was too rich but it took me 40 years to save up for it. Actually, the land belongs to my husband — he bought it 50 years ago when he graduated from school, and I took a bank loan for 5 million baht. The objective was to have a home for my own family.

Was there any time you felt you were under great threat?

When we were in the AEC (Assets Examination Committee) group after the coup in 2007, I was threatened over the telephone every day. I used to drive home late at night after teaching night classes, and there would be some people following me.

These people tried to scare me — every morning and night I would receive death threats concerning me and my family. After a while, I just refused to take any phone calls and I would tell my husband to take those calls.

For about a year, I had five soldiers who would come to my home to transport me around in a van. The five of them had M-16s, revolvers, bulletproof vests — they came with me every morning and night. They put me through a training course and taught me not to sit at the same position every morning and also to take a different route each time. At that time, I was very scared so I listened to whatever they told me — I just wanted to live, to spend time with my children until they were older.

The soldiers told me these people will come on a motorcycle and there will be two persons and they usually wear black clothes with visors. If they came, I would have to lie down on the floor of the van and put my head near them. It was very serious at that time. I didn't want my son or husband to go anywhere with me during that time so I traveled alone.

I also wrote down details of my bank and assets, and passed it to my son in case something happens to me. I didn't pass them to my husband, in case he remarries after I'm gone.

One early morning, traffic was bad because it was the first day of school. We were stuck in traffic and we saw two guys on a motorcycle in black shirts, and they looked like they had something under their shirts which they were going to take out. I thought: "Oh no I still haven't told my children what they should study next time." The soldiers who were protecting me were getting their guns ready.

In the end, the two guys took out their mobile phones. The whole van was quiet for a minute then everyone burst out laughing. I was so scared.

After a while, I grew sick of this arrangement of having bodyguards, and I didn't want to grow over-dependent on them going with me everywhere. Everywhere I ate or drank in public, there would be someone staring at me because of all the body guards. So, I decided to give them up.

 How do you respond when people openly offer you bribes?

 I have had offers of 100 million baht to drop certain cases.

It's very difficult to respond without appearing arrogant. When they bring the money, I tell my security to stop them. There are lots of people who come with many offers. Some offered to construct my house. Others offered to purchase the adjacent piece of land next to my house and give it to me. Then, there were others who wanted to provide me cement for me to construct my house. I had to say "no" and paid them for the cement. There were also offers to pay for my children's overseas education. I refused all these to preserve my integrity. Whenever I think of my family, I am able to say "no".

How do you cultivate integrity and good character among leaders?

Alexander the Great won many wars and at that time everyone thought the Greeks were the greatest people. But he told his soldiers: You have to understand other people, even your enemies. You have to know your environment and sociology. You have to bend down and not be too proud of yourself. Thats how so he won all the battles.

You have to take care of all your subordinates. When their loved ones pass away, I go and provide support during the funeral. Everybody needs to eat and to have their own house. So, during my term of office, I increased the salaries of my auditors to 4,000-6,000 baht per person per month so that they would not become corrupt. I reminded them that the money came from the King of Thailand so they won't become arrogant.

What if you find out that your employees are corrupt?

I'll fire them — I've to be very strict about this.

There was an employee who had just gotten divorced and she had to take care of her two children and her mother, so she took a bribe of 100,000 baht. When this was discovered, I signed the papers to dismiss her. I did help her find a new job though.

We have to uphold the reputation of our organization. We cannot lose that, otherwise nobody will be afraid and everyone will take bribes.

My son always says that if his mother took bribes we would own Mercedes Benz and Volvo cars instead of Toyota.

How do you feel when people you have nurtured betray you?

At first, it really hurts. I rest in the Lord and my children. My son encouraged me to ignore these people and reminded me that I still have him. I believe God will avenge me.

You have been criticized for nepotism, hiring your own son as a personal secretary using the state budget. How do you respond to that?

 My son was my personal assistant and he had to take a pay cut to do so. He's very intelligent. He's overqualified. Normally, a secretary is just a graduate from college but my son has a Bachelor in Engineering and a Master's in Economics. He helps me with auditing and is not just a secretary.

Even senators appoint their relatives to be their secretaries. After all, who else can you trust better than your own son? It's a pattern of Thai officials to have their own relatives to be their secretaries. It's safer.

 What do you want people to remember you for?

 I want them to remember me for this: that I have dedicated my life to my job for the country. I think people remember me in a good way. Sometimes when I'm out having dinner with my family, people approach me to take pictures and to ask for my signature. Sometimes I feel embarrassed — I'm not a movie star. I also get a lot of notes and calls to bless me.

 What's one main weakness which you have?

 Maybe I'm too demanding — when I order my people to do something, they have to be fast and right. When they don't do it right, I'd rather do it myself.

 What's one advice you would give to young leaders?

 You have to be yourself, and remember that money isn't everything. I had very good chances to get rich easily, but I tell myself if I had taken the money, I would be in jail now and would have had my reputation ruined. And if that happens, how can my children face society?

> Crisis to me is always a stepping stone or platform for us to move further. Whenever there are challenges or adversity in business, it is always an opportunity for me to do better.

JOCELYN CHNG
The Resilient Entrepreneur Leader

ocelyn Chng took over Sin Hwa Dee Foodstuff, a soy sauce business, at the age of 21 after her father passed away in 1988. At the time, she was still studying at the National University of Singapore.

When she was 37 years old, her beloved grandma died and eight months later, her 42-year-old husband, Richard Wong, passed away leaving three young sons. The deaths were a huge blow as they were "the twin pillars in her life."

At that time, while running Sin Hwa Dee and JR Foods, she had to almost single-handedly raise her three young children — Noel, 8, Joel, 5, and Emmanuel, 1.

She faced an uphill battle, straddled with the stigma that came with being of the fairer sex in a male-dominated food industry. Opportunities to prove herself, build trust and her credibility amongst potential suppliers and customers were extremely challenging. Nobody expected her to last long.

Jocelyn not only survived but is also still the driving force behind the success of Sin Hwa Dee Foodstuff. Her story is one of a woman who overcame immense adversity while maintaining her poise and the dauntless spirit of an entrepreneur.

With a strong passion and a clear vision, she transformed the traditional family-run business into a modern, global company, with a strong commitment to technology and innovation. Her success is well recognized by the many awards she has received. She was the NUS Winner of Best Entrepreneur in 2005, and was named the Mont Blanc Woman of the Year in 2003.

But success did not come easy. It was a tough, emotional roller coaster ride for her as she endured not only personal tragedies but also intense business crises. We met Jocelyn over tea in her office as she recounted her incredible story of comebacks.

 Who or what influenced you most in your leadership development? And why?

 There are two people who influenced me greatly in my life. My grandma, Kee Siok Cheng, was the most influential. She had come from China and was a strong woman. She brought me up with deep Christian values and principles that formed the cornerstone of my life.

She would always tell me stories of her struggles in life: We have to be strong, independent, wise, and able to cope with crisis. She was a source of constant encouragement for me.

Despite her tough realities that prevented her from receiving traditional forms of education, she taught herself by reading the newspaper and the Bible. She was the one who urged and encouraged me to make it to university even though it seemed like an impossible feat in that time.

Despite the tremendous odds stacked against her, she did possess an entrepreneurial spirit. We used to stay at Tai Seng Kampong and would plant fruits like papaya and bananas. She would gather all these fruits and sell them. With the little money she made and accumulated, she started a facility business. Her first major contract was for facility management at Paya Lebar Airport (Singapore's first international airport).

When I went to kindergarten, my grandma would first learn the alphabet from my aunt just so she could teach me ABCs. When I was young, she taught me how to read the clock. Every morning, I had to wake up very early to help her prepare breakfast. She was a firm believer of 'teaching me how to fish' rather than spoiling me by just giving me the fish.

Beyond this, she taught me to love others — and share what I have with the neighbors' children, not because we had abundance but because it was the right thing to do. Most of all, she loved life. I found life worth living because of her love for me. She taught me how to be positive and how to persevere and press on despite difficulties. She taught me how to have a heart of gratitude; it has now become a habit for me to count my blessings every morning.

The other person, who made the greatest impact in my life, is my late husband, Richard Wong. He had also given me a lot of love. Even when he was sick, he was still able to keep a positive attitude. He was my soul mate.

I used to be a very shy person. Richard was the one who trained me to speak in public and give talks. For example, he would tell me to focus on one person when I am speaking. He was an economics and accounts teacher, who started his own learning center. Besides running his center, he was also helping me with my business.

In 2001, he saw a business opportunity and together, we founded JR Foods (Jocelyn & Richard). He was full of ideas and was extremely personable in nature. He was able to motivate and influence people positively. When he went out with me for exhibitions, he would help me close sales too. He was a diligent listener and always was able to know clearly what the clients really wanted. Whenever he spoke, he was able to understand the clients' needs and made the right proposals to customers to close the deal.

He came from a humble family, but made it to the university. I sometimes feel sad because I believe he has the potential to impact many more people with his wisdom, especially his children, if he had lived longer.

He firmly believed in contributing back to the community. He has helped so many people. The life he lived was he postured outwards and is clearly seen in how he has impacted so many lives.

My husband had a creative disposition. He loved to write poems. He would write a poem or drop me a note next to my bed. I remember his poems fondly. They were really beautiful.

 What did you learn from Richard?

 One thing I learned from my husband was the way he impacted others. He always put other-people first. He always had his employees in his mind. He would never fail to buy food back for them every time he returned from his meetings.

He would also pamper my mother and me with food. Whenever he knew that I had not taken my lunch, he would drive out just to buy my favorite pineapple fried rice for us. Whenever he discovered a new restaurant, he would take the whole family there.

He was also very filial to his parents. He remembered all his parents' medical appointments. Both his parents would simply rely on him to remember these things. Even before he passed on, he reminded each of his siblings to remember their parents' appointments.

 How did both of you meet?

 We met at the university. When I was studying there, I couldn't attend lectures because of my business priorities. He would attend lectures on my behalf. He would tape and take notes of all the lectures I missed. He would tell others jokingly later on, "Although I studied for two degrees, I only passed out with one certificate!"

Richard had so many friends. Friends and business associates loved him so much that they even flew in from the Philippines, Indonesia, Taiwan and other countries to pay their last respects to him during the funeral.

 What is the most crushing adversity you have ever faced in your leadership? How did you deal with it?

 My most crushing adversity was when the two closest people in my life passed away. In that year alone, I lost the two pillars of my life.

You see, my grandma was very close and dear to me as I spent almost my whole life with her. After staying with her for 11 years, she came to stay with me. Whenever I would travel or get into difficulties in my business, I would talk to her and she would always pray for me. Her death was a crushing blow to me.

Eight months later, I lost my husband. He suffered from lymphoma. When he passed away, I thought I could not carry on. It felt like the whole world had just collapsed. I was despairing, "How can I live one day without him? I have so many responsibilities and so many problems. There is no one to share my burden or my worries. How can I live? I can't live."

Thankfully, I managed to pull through, but it was a daily struggle. When I look back on these past 12 years, first, I realize that I have grown stronger. Second, I have become a better mother, because when Richard was around, I relied on him for family matters. Every day, I was just thinking about my business. I left all the family matters and chores to my husband. That's why he was very close to the kids. He took care of everything. When he died, I didn't know anything. I didn't even know how to register my son for Primary One.

My husband passing away was really a wake-up call that life is unpredictable and we cannot take it lightly. I learned to approach life differently.

Despite these tragedies, God has blessed me in so many other ways. For example, I have three wonderful children.

The boys have given me great comfort and God has also taken care of them all these years.

I remember when my husband passed away, Noel was only eight years old. On the day my husband died, Noel challenged God, "I want you to resurrect my father now. If you can resurrect Lazarus, you can also resurrect my dad!" He was trying desperately to revive his dad and kept yelling away, "Wake up now." He was most hurt and angry at that moment.

However, over the years, Noel is the one who has overcome his grief and anger and recovered most remarkably. He is the one who is comforting me now. He is always there to remind me that everything happens for a purpose.

It was so very difficult when grandma and Richard died. I remember telling my sister Kathleen, "God just took away two pillars from me." But my sister said, "God has made you the pillar for your three boys. You must press on as you are now the pillar for them."

 How were you supported during those times of crises?

 God has sent me so many good people not just in my business but also in my life, and in my family to support and help me.

I have to learn to lean on other people. When my husband was around, we were able to handle a lot of things on our own. I didn't need my mother-in-law or my sister to do things for me, like sending my kids to school.

But, after he passed on, I really had no choice. My mother-in-law and sister-in-law came to live with me to support and help me. My mother and sisters literally camped at my home for a period of time. My youngest brother, Tony, who was working in a bank at that time, quit his job to help me when my husband was in the hospital. He told me that he will help me till my husband recovered. Because he didn't recover, he stuck on.

God has sent many people to help us recover from adversity. They didn't need to say fantastic words. The fact that they were willing to sit with me, to shed tears with me, to keep silent with me and be there with me was sufficient to help me through the pain and grief. They prayed with me.

Sometimes, we see leaders as being very strong and think that they don't need close friends, but inside each of us, we have a softer side. We need family and friends to see us through our crises.

On reflection, what did you learn from this most crushing adversity?

In life, there are always ups and downs. Whenever there's a barrier, you always think that it is the worst case. But when you cross that barrier, we learn, grow and we come out stronger.

I remember some years ago, after my husband passed on, there was this father-son adventure camp organized by the school, Anglo-Chinese School. So, I called the school and enquired, "Can a mother attend the camp because I want to be with my sons?" They replied, "Yes, mothers can go."

So I went with my two sons. After I went through all the adventures with my sons, I felt a deep sense of achievement and satisfaction.

The camp was held in a very 'ulu' (remote) area in Malaysia. We had to cross the river, jump through valleys and climb mountains. It was quite a difficult camp for me. It was like living in a bunk just like the army days. On top of that, there were so many mosquitoes as we had to sleep outside.

When I was climbing the mountains, I was very exhausted. As I looked up to the mountain top, I saw it was still a long way to go. I wanted to give up so many times.

But I told myself I cannot give up and I have to do it. I must press on for the sake of my sons. I want to show them by example.

So it is the same in life. Very often, our own minds tell us that we cannot do it. Only our positive mindset helps us to overcome the obstacles that we face. But it is the faith that we have that will help us.

Because I have been through so much, I know that God will make all things beautiful in His time. Now, every time I come to a dead end, I see it as a turning point, a turning junction for me. Once I have this perspective, then I see how I can get over it, how to cross it, and how to make it better. Comparing my life from 10 years ago, I am probably a much better person now, not in terms of my achievements but more in terms of my inner self. I have learned to be wiser in life.

There are always different seasons in life: Different things that we need to face. There are always challenges. Crisis to me is always a stepping stone or platform for us to move further. Whenever there are challenges or adversity in business, it is always an opportunity for me to do better. Otherwise, I am always in the comfort zone, in an unchanged zone.

 Jocelyn, let's talk about business adversity. What is the most challenging or crushing business adversity you have faced so far?

 When we first started, it was very difficult. We did not have enough capital and resources. All we had were people: myself, my bare hands, my mom, and my siblings. We just worked our way through. We didn't know where our business was leading us. Even my relatives encouraged us to give up when my dad died, saying, "You are a graduate. You can go out and work in a bank. Maybe you can strike bigger and you should give up this business." They were well-meaning but very discouraging.

When our business started to expand, we bought a bigger factory. At that time, I had two small factories (1,500 sq ft each). I was planning to sell both to fund the bigger factory that I had committed to buy.

Unknown to us, the government had plans to relocate all the factories there and build a wafer fab, which the authority did not announce. Somebody had already committed to buying the two factories and we had put in the deposit for the bigger unit. We were stuck. They did not approve our sale of the two units. We had already committed to buying a bigger factory for $1.6 million.

We managed to secure a loan and we went ahead with the purchase eventually.

To be an entrepreneur, is about understanding the business. If you want to be in the food industry, you must have an understanding of it. You need to know the demands and have a strong pulse on the context in the industry.

 What have you learned from your various business challenges?

 We have to more careful before we make any business decision. Nowadays, I learn to cut my losses very fast. In the past, I would still try and persevere. But now, I give myself a deadline. If the business does not turn around after a certain time frame, I will cut my losses immediately. The decision must be made fast. We must take calculated risks.

In life, there are bound to be ups and downs. Sometimes, we make the right decisions and also the wrong decisions.

 Let's talk about women in leadership. When you started in the industry, what were some of the challenges you faced?

 There were a lot of challenges. When I first took over the business, people were not willing to accept me. The trust was not there. They thought I would not stay in the business long. The suppliers were not willing to support us by giving us credit facility. On the other hand, customers were requesting for long credit terms. It was not uncommon for them to say to me, "I want to see your father or I will only talk to your husband." The banks didn't want to extend credit because we had little collateral, thinking that we would not survive.

It was difficult to recruit and retain talent and it was not easy to find the right people. My management approach is to lead by example and to have a listening ear. I like to hear different opinions and ideas before we make a decision. This is to make sure that we look at all angles of risks. Even when I have new ideas, I prefer to talk it out so that I can hear my team out. I prefer to let the team take ownership.

I have always believed in teamwork. I accept my limitations and appreciate my strengths. I am not good at numbers and operations, but I am good at negotiation and business. Of course, there are times I have to make the call and make the decision, and they have to follow. Most of the time, I am willing to listen to them as they are the experts.

 Let me ask you about being a leader in the company and yet having family obligations as a mother, raising three kids. How do you do that?

I spend quality time with them. I stay connected with them via mobile phone, Facebook, Instagram and social media. I try to think their age to understand them. I enjoy taking to them and sharing with them what I learn.

I know that my presence with them is very important. I want them to know that if there is any problem, mommy will be there for them. I want my kids to take me as a friend.

On Mothers' Day, my youngest boy wrote me a card and told me, "After reading the card, you mustn't cry." I replied, "Why would I cry?" "I wrote something so touching that you will cry," he replied. True enough, I cried.

When my second son was sick, my youngest son wanted to accompany me to the hospital. I told him not to. He said, "I will go with brother to do the admission at the hospital, while you sleep in the car so that you can get some rest!"

I always take them along to different events. If I need to go to a restaurant during the weekend, I bring them along. I have also learn to love them equally without any favoritism.

We have to make that personal connection with each one, always pushing them to do better in that they are passionate in.

Finally, with regard to family, we may have all the successes and great academic results, the most important is the need to have the right values. You need to inculcate the right values so that the will have a strong foundation as they are growing up.

 What is one weakness that you have and how do you deal with it?

 In leadership, I am very soft hearted. I always empathize with people. Sometimes, they would abuse and exploit my weakness. People will come asking for help. Some of them may play me out. But there are times that I just have to stop and realize that I have done my part.

 What is one advice you would give to emerging leaders, especially women leaders?

 Passion. In whatever you are doing, being passionate is very important. Whether at work or with family, you must be passionate. If you do it with passion, with love and the right attitude, you can do so well!

I have this expansion for PASSIONATE.

Persevere: You must not give up.
Attitude-positive: You must be willing to learn.
Sacrifice: You need to work hard and sacrifice and spend time in your work.
Set Vision and Goals in life: You need to have the right vision.
Impact others: Your business must make a difference to others.
Opportunities: You need to identify and look out for opportunities in business.
Never give up: You must never say die.
Action: You must take action and execute.
Think out of the box: You must be creative.
Encourage and motivate (family and staff): You must be an inspiration.

> **When we lead knowing our own failures, we lead with humility. That's the legacy I wish to leave behind.**

KIM TAN
The Failed Again Leader

ato Dr. Kim Tan is the Founder and Chairman of SpringHill Management Ltd, a private equity fund management company specializing in biotech and social venture capital investments. He sits on the boards of several companies in Malaysia, India, the UK, South Africa and the USA, and is also an advisor to a number of Asian government agencies on biotechnology.

As Mr. Tan shared his story, he traced his lifestyle and leadership back to his humble background. Born in Malaysia to immigrant parents, he received scholarships to study in a private school in the UK and then completed a Ph.D. in biochemistry and was the recipient of a scholarship and four post-doctoral fellowships from the Medical Research Council (UK). He is an elected Fellow of the Royal Society of Medicine.

Today, he is also Co-Founder of the Transformational Business Network, the UK charity with many social transformational businesses in developing countries, including the Kuzuko Game Reserve (South Africa) and the Hagar Social Enterprise Group (Cambodia). He is a partner and advisor to a number of impact investment funds in Africa and Asia and is an advisor of PovertyCure, Sustainia and the John Templeton Foundation.

He describes himself as a 'failed again' leader, as he feels that he has failed academically, professionally, and personally, but has been given many second chances to succeed. Even in his career, he has had many failures but has recovered. Relationally, as a husband and family, he also faces many struggles.

We caught up with him in a café at a Singapore hotel.

 Who or what influenced you most in your leadership development? And why?

 Undoubtedly it would be the servant-leadership of Jesus. He is *the* model for us to follow. His style of leadership is best exemplified by washing his disciples' feet — the work of a slave. Humility undergirded his words and actions. But he showed that you can be gentle without being a push-over, strong without being arrogant. He always looked for potential in others and restored them when they failed. He led with compassion, looking for justice and was willing to confront injustice.

His style of leadership has of course inspired countless others down the centuries, including Martin Luther King, Jr., and Nelson Mandela, two of my heroes.

Whom do you admire as a leader in the corporate world?

One of the many people I admire is Sir John Templeton, the American investor and mutual fund pioneer, whom I had the privilege of meeting and sharing at two conferences he hosted.

I consider him to be the most successful fund manager ever. After his retirement, he sold his fund management company, which later became the Franklin Templeton Fund. He was known for his 'avoiding the herd' and 'buy when there's blood in the streets' philosophy. He literally left the financial herd and retired to the Bahamas.

He was a most thoughtful and humble leader. It was his policy to fly economy and not first class. He was quiet-spoken, dressed modestly, and drove an old Oldsmobile. He gave most of his wealth towards setting up the Templeton Foundation[1].

Sir John is one of the few truly successful entrepreneurs I have met who built his business from scratch. It's one thing to inherit a family business and grow it. It's another to build a new business when you come from a poor family with no capital. Hearing his story was an encouragement. Sir John also articulated and practiced servant leadership. He showed that you don't have to be loud and showy to be a leader. He was an antidote to the cult of celebrity leadership.

 What's your leadership style?

The model of servant-leadership led me to formulate four characteristics I look for in people I choose to work with.

- Intelligence: In our business, the people we work with must demonstrate high intelligence and competence.

- Diligence: He or She must be hardworking and self-motivated. I had a female colleague, a Cambridge Ph.D. holder, who wanted to start a

---

[1] The Templeton Foundation encourages research into 'big questions' by awarding philanthropic aid to institutions and people who pursue the answers to such questions through "explorations into the laws of nature and the universe", to questions on the nature of love, gratitude, forgiveness, and creativity.

family and needed to work two days a week. I had no problem with that because she was smart and hardworking. What she did in two days was worth more than what most people can do in five. When I review CVs, I look to see if they flipped burgers or stacked supermarket shelves or volunteered for charitable activities. Or in my case worked as a cleaner and hospital porter.

- Integrity: A person can be very bright and hard-working, but without integrity, that person will destroy him/herself and your business. The financial meltdown in 2008 on Wall Street was after all brought about by very bright and hard-working bankers.

- Modesty: We have a policy of traveling economy, renting modest cars, entertaining modestly and staying in four-star hotels. You can tell if a person has this sense of modesty by the way they dress, the way they speak and conduct themselves, the cars they drive, and their social interests.

I need to add a caveat to the principle of modesty. I believe God allows every one their indulgences. I have no problem with people who fly business or first class, or drive a BMW or Mercedes Benz. That's their indulgence. Enjoy it!

So, what's your indulgence?

My indulgences are rugby and a safari game park. I invested in a professional rugby club, Saracen Rugby Club in England, even though I recognized that it would be a loss as a financial investment.

Saracen was transitioning from an amateur to a professional club when I was invited to invest and join the board. We flirted with relegation in the early years to become one of the top clubs in England and Europe. Interestingly, the club motto "Work rate, Discipline, Honesty and Humility" is displayed in large letters over our Allianz Park stadium. This club also uses rugby to serve the community and reaches out to about 70,000 school children each year. The players put in time to help students in their schools.

The Kuzuko Lodge is a safari game park in one of the poorest regions of South Africa. We built it from scratch with 40,000 acres of degraded farm land. Kuzuko is now a game park with a five-star lodge and a "Big Five" game experience. The highlight of this project was the re-introduction of elephants, lions, cheetahs and rhinos into this region of South Africa after 150 years of absence. One of my indulgences is to go there to enjoy the wilderness, walk with the cheetahs and drink in the sight of the amazing Milky Way at night. But the other joy is to see how our business is alleviating poverty through economic stimulation of the district and how our staff are developing their God-given potential.

 Share with us one memorable life-changing experience that has impacted and shaped the way you lead?

 Definitely, it is my childhood. We grew up poor in rural Malaysia.

My father was an immigrant from China before the Second World War and worked as a coolie. Like many immigrants, he would send money back to his family in China. When he had some savings, he bought a bicycle to sell vegetables. He would ride from Klang (small town) to Kuala Lumpur (capital of Malaysia) to buy the vegetables to sell them in Klang. Later, he bought a truck to transport latex and finally built a sundry shop in rural West Malaysia.

My recreation was catching spiders and fighting fish in the surrounding padi fields. We often did our homework in candle light because of the regular power cuts. We had a smelly outdoor dry toilet where the bucket was removed by a 'night-soil man' during dawn. Our grandmother had a well in her backyard. Our tap water was always brown and had to be filtered and boiled. All this has taught me the virtue of hard work and modesty and shaped the way I lead.

 Some people start well but end up differently. How do you sustain this value and practice it constantly?

 First, it's remembering my past. Each time, I visit my parents, I am reminded of my past. Of course, Seremban is now more developed. You must never forget your roots.

Second, experiencing the poor. When we encounter the poor, we encounter the divine. God's heart is broken to see poverty in such tragic surroundings. Spending a lot of time building businesses among the poor in Africa and Asia keeps you grounded.

Third, I used to live in a community for eight years. There were 40 of us in 12 houses. We shared all things, except our wives and books! I learned how to simplify my life and lifestyle. This has helped me deal with the addiction of materialism. Only when I am faithful with little, can I be faithful with much.

 What is the most crushing adversity you have ever faced in your leadership? How do you deal with it?

 Not getting into medical school. It was a big dash to my ego. I thought I had done well enough to get in. I ended up doing my undergraduate and Ph.D. in biochemistry at the University of Surrey in Guildford.

I was told by friends that David Pawson was a great Bible teacher and that he was in Guildford, so I chose the University of Surrey to do my undergraduate studies so I could attend his church and be taught by him. Those were formative years and from David Pawson, I learned to be a better Bible teacher. It was at Surrey University that we started practicing the Jubilee principles of economic-sharing and community life. At Surrey University, I got excited about the relatively new field of biotechnology, and that led me into the biotech world and finally into my present work in impact investing.

Had I gone to medical school, I would not have ended up doing all the things I am doing now. I realized that when God closes one door, He opens another one.

 What is your greatest weakness?

 My biggest battle is with materialism and all that comes with it. We live in a very materialistic society. We are lured to have designer-everything. It is so easy to be seduced by the world and its bright lights. It is very easy to justify the need for nice things and enjoy the good life.

It is easy to be seduced by money. In this world, money can buy influence and publicity. That's why I prefer to stay below the radar. I seldom give interviews. This is one of the few.

What is one legacy you have left behind in your organization?

I am trying to write a book entitled *Failed Again Christian*. This will be my epitaph. I am acutely aware of my failures. I am a failed scientist. I wasn't good enough to win a Nobel Prize, that's why I left research. I am a failed CEO. I didn't enjoy hands-on management. I also failed as a father, as I wished I had spent more time with my two boys. I have failed as a husband and a son because I haven't given enough time to my wife and parents. I travel too much.

I have a deep awareness of my failures. But instead of allowing our failures to crush us, we should use them to make us more determined to keep trying. There is forgiveness for failures but not for giving up. And when we lead knowing our own failures, we lead with humility. That's the legacy I wish to leave behind.

What is one piece of advice you would give to emerging leaders?

I think I need to share more than one.

Go find a mentor. I wish I had a mentor when I was younger. In the business realm, I wish I had a business mentor.

Study the Bible until it gets a hold of you. The Bible has shaped the way I think. It is my source of inspiration. It has changed me. You must allow the Bible to change you, the way you think, and the way you behave.

There is a true story about this farmer in China. He had just become a Christian. He lived at the top of the hill. Every day, he had to pump water to his home and farm up on the hill. However, a farmer living at the foot of the hill stole his water by releasing the valve and diverted the water to his own farm. He went to a more mature Christian, who advised him to go the second mile: to pray for him and exercise grace and forgiveness.

The next day, it happened again. He pumped the water but it was stolen again. The farmer went to the mature Christian who now advises him to turn the other cheek. He felt he needed more grace.

The third time, it happened again. This time he was very angry and disturbed. He went again to the mature Christian to ask for counsel. This time, the mature Christian asked the farmer to pray and decide what he should do. While they were praying, the farmer finally had an inspiration. Every morning, he would fill up his neighbor's field first, before pumping up to his own. The stealing stopped and they lived in peace.

The Bible does not give us answers to every situation. There is no verse in the Bible that says "fill up your neighbour's field first before filling up your own". There are no chapter and verse for every conceivable event. But if we allow the Word to infuse our lives, we will be guided to walk in 'The Way'. The Bible may not make us clever but it will make us wise.

Practice stewardship of everything. Your business gift is also a gift from God. God will hold us to account for all our gifts, be it in business, law, teaching, music, art, medicine or whatever. Use it for the good of all. Learn to be thrifty with ourselves and generous towards others.

No sacrifice, no eternal value. If our giving, whether of time or money is not sacrificial and has not cost us, it will be of no eternal value. If it costs you nothing, it is probably not worth giving anyway. It's easier to write a cheque for a charity than to give our time and talent.

Finally, walk humbly with your God and his creation. We are all scumbags saved by God's mercy.

> The next generation must build the relationships themselves, to develop a common aspiration that they want this company to continue. The aspiration must come from them.

LEE OI HIAN

The Succession Planning Leader

r. Lee Oi Hian's love for agriculture began at a young age, when he would follow his father on visits to the plantation estates. Today, he is the Chief Executive of Kuala Lumpur Kepong (KLK), a giant Malaysian company with plantation, resource-based manufacturing and property interests.

The 61-year-old had always enjoyed a close relationship with his father, the late Lee Loy Seng, who bought land from British merchants after Malaya's independence and turned them into plantations.

Mr. Lee recalled: "He taught me the values of integrity, honesty and hard work. He kept speaking about these values and showed it through his lifestyle. He was quite helpful to people and was well-respected, a man of wisdom…I was quite close to him. When I finished school, I went to work for him."

The Ipoh-based tycoon, together with his brother Lee Hau Hian, have been named Malaysia's 40 richest by Forbes, with a combined net worth of US$1.1 billion.

Mr. Lee joined KLK as a marketing executive in 1974 upon graduating from the University of Malaya with a Bachelor of Agricultural Science degree. He then obtained his MBA from Harvard Business School in 1977.

He returned to KLK in 1979 to head the production control division before joining the board in 1985. He became KLK's chairman and chief executive in 1993, following his father's death. As a firm believer of good corporate governance, he stepped down as chairman in 2008.

Mr. Lee has had his fair share of challenges in life, such as steering the family business following his father's death. "I made mistakes — one was the diversion from the main core business," he admitted.

An example was buying over the globally renowned retailer of bath and body products Crabtree & Evelyn in 1996. The retailer's US operations had to file for Chapter 11 bankruptcy protection in 2009 before Mr. Lee's wife Sandra was parachuted in to turn it around. Eventually, Crabtree returned to profitability in a year. In 2012, it was sold for US$155 million to a Hong Kong-based group, resulting in a US$41 million gain.

We meet the down-to-earth tycoon for tea at his apartment in Singapore.

Who or what influenced you most in your leadership development? And why?

 My father — he was the one who nurtured me from very young. He taught me the values of integrity, honesty and hard work. He kept speaking about these values and showed it through his lifestyle. He was quite helpful to people and was well-respected, a man of wisdom.

He was a man of deep conviction. He never liked the gambling business because his father at one point lost quite a lot of money gambling and my grandmother had experiences of gambling debts.

I was quite close to him. When I finished school, I went to work for him.

 What is one memorable life-changing experience that has impacted and shaped the way you lead?

 There wasn't a single major one. There was an incident — the management which I had depended on in a certain section 15 to 20 years ago suddenly decided to leave to join another company.

It taught me not to panic, and also not to be wholly dependent on one team as there'll be other people. It taught me to open my eyes to see the possibilities of younger people. Basically, it also taught me to focus and know my people much better, especially the junior ones.

There were also other instances in KLK where I could have stepped in earlier to resolve conflict, such as infighting among senior management and when they are not speaking to each other.

 How do you resolve conflict among high-level management?

 When the issue comes up, give it a bit of time, don't be impulsive but at the same time, don't let it fester. When certain people really cannot work with each other, you have to move them apart. After talking to them, if it's still not working, maybe you have to make choices.

We can separate them into different areas of responsibility. But it's not ideal. When it comes to working together, you will not have true cooperation. This has an element of building warlords.

Eventually, the organization should be united together.

 How do you choose your leaders?

 You need a cohesive team. It's about choosing the right leader, who's able to motivate the young people to express themselves well, and who's open. All leaders will always think they are open, but they may not reflect this to others. The tendency to have this dictatorial attitude always comes through.

 How does one avoid this dictatorial attitude?

 You have to recognize that your words carry a lot of weight. Sometimes, we must express our opinion carefully, with a lot of deep reflection. You don't have to express your opinion first — you can let others people talk first. As my father used to say: "In the end, the power is yours." If you speak your mind first, they will not be able to speak frankly. After hearing them, though, you still have the power to make the final decision.

 What is the most crushing adversity you have ever faced in your leadership? How did you deal with it?

 We were very lucky, because my father's philosophy was never to be too ambitious. He was a cautious and satisfied man. He came from nothing, and reached the pinnacle of his career when he died, having established an organization which had close to 150,000 hectares of land.

He really built up his business in the plantation industry. My grandfather was in tin mining. At that time, he was the first one to take over British companies. KLK was very big, but because of his caution, he never over-extended the company.

There've been good times and bad times. During bad times, our profit may have dropped significantly but our business has never been threatened for survival. Plantation has also been a lucky industry. Financially, we never went through a crisis.

But we went through certain challenges.

When he passed away in 1993, I was still not very wise. Sometimes it was about siblings, sometimes it was about getting acceptance for the transition, sometimes policy direction. I made mistakes — one was the diversion from the main core business.

I focused quite a bit on downstream, later on Crabtree & Evelyn. I should have focused more on the core plantation business instead of diversification because that is our core business. We should have focused on that which we can build on to become a key player in. In the end, many of the non-core businesses were closed down and we sold some of them. Now we are more stable, more focused.

I think diversification is good, but once you choose an area to diversify into, you must have a strong management team. You allocate your time carefully but not at the expense of your core business.

For example, with Crabtree & Evelyn, we didn't have a very strong management. It's a new business, so we didn't understand it from the macro picture and that we needed to get a good CEO to run the business. We had to change a number of CEOs — many CEOs paint a very good picture but can't deliver.

In 2008–2009, we went into Chapter 11. It was tough — Sandra did most of the restructuring, and turned it around quite quickly. She took over the brand, rebuilt it along the brand values and made sure it didn't deviate from brand values. In a year, we returned back to profitability.

 Let's move on to your family life. How do you maintain a strong family in spite of all the travel and business commitments?

 Sandra spent a lot of time with the children. When they were young, she opened a kindergarten for them in Ipoh. Ipoh was an isolated town away from the big city, and that helped with raising a family. The obligations and temptations are more in a big city.

The children had a lot of core values transmitted to them, from us, from my father. They had a stable environment.

It's about a lifestyle and talking about certain core values. When the children were bigger, we moved on to a Methodist church and that had a big impact on them. It had a good Sunday School and youth fellowship.

They also went to government schools. They studied Chinese until Form 5. Ipoh didn't have many private schools and we didn't believe in sending young children abroad too young — most of my children went to the UK only after Form 5. Some of our friends sent their children to Europe and the UK very young, and most of them regretted doing so.

In Ipoh, there was also a good group of friends surrounding us. Sandra was also involved in a lot of charity work. The children were brought up in an environment surrounded by good examples.

I was traveling quite a lot, but basically our industry is not a very intense one. It's not like investment banking, where you are so hard-pressed for time. Our company was quite laidback — we never really pushed for high growth.

Our culture was that we worked hard but it wasn't the same pace as investment banking, so most of my weekends were free to spend with the family.

 Looking back, what would you have done differently with your family and the business?

 I would have exposed the children a little more, because they were mixing a lot with church people in a safe environment. Maybe I should have exposed them more to the businesses at a younger age.

With the business, perhaps to be less cautious, take more risks and not to be a slave to fear but to trust God more.

 KLK is a prominent family business in Malaysia, so the issue of succession planning in a family business is very relevant. How do you make sure the wealth isn't depleted beyond the third generation?

 It's easier said than done. When you are a first-generation patriarch, you can do a lot more — you build the business up, and most people will obey you and follow your vision. As we move to the second generation, we have to build up the second team, expose them to the business first and put them in a culture of participation and responsibility in the business.

When they were small, the cousins were quite friendly with each other, we go on holidays together. That's very good to build unity. The next generation must build the relationships themselves, to develop in them a common aspiration that they want this company to continue. The aspiration must come from them. They'll have to work with some professional managers and take an interest in the company.

 Q **Do you deliberately expose your kids to the business?**

 A It mainly started when they graduated from university and finished their education. Maybe we could have done more before that.

You have to see where you can fit them into the company according to their skillsets. YTL's Francis Yeoh, one of Malaysia's most successful corporate tycoons and leaders,[1] has done quite well in that aspect.

Some leaders will develop among them, and that leader will have to gain their acceptance and trust. Meanwhile, they have to recognize that they want to carry on.

Second is to ensure that they are reasonably well-off, that they have assets of their own outside of the company. If they don't, you'll have problems.

There are some Chinese families I know where the eldest is the head of family. The siblings will think it's not very fair as they still want to hold on to some power of their own and other people's assets. Sometimes they're very unfair in their allocation.

When you have such unfair structures, families cannot last, companies also cannot last. The fairness must be there, and they themselves must cultivate a sense of fairness and cooperation.

When they are coming into the business, you must encourage them. Let them work with a management group by themselves so they'll learn faster.

Good mentors are also very important. Help them find good mentors — senior people who are very experienced, almost semi-retired and who

---

[1] Read about Francis Yeoh in Chapter 6.

have the time to mentor the children in certain skillsets. We have found one such mentor and we are trying to build up more mentors.

  What's your biggest business challenge currently?

It is how we can make a quantum jump in productivity. Wages keep on escalating and expectations keep on increasing. It has become a problem for regional economies because when there's too much income inequality salaries are too low. It's difficult for governments, so governments are pressing us to have higher salaries.

In Malaysia, they are proposing a minimum wage. Every year in Indonesia there's a mandatory increase in minimum wage. It's for the whole industry. The problem with the Indonesian minimum wage is that there are 33 provinces, and every governor imposes their own minimum pay, and it's always in the double digits. So you can imagine the pressure on us. But because of this pressure, we got to improve our productivity a lot to keep up with this.

  What is one weakness and how do you deal with it?

Not consciously building enough depth in the organization. Sometimes, we leave a lot to the top guys when we ourselves need to go deeper into the organization and see things from another angle, not just what they are telling us. It's about getting deeper and setting the cultural mode of the organization, such as the welfare of workers in the plantation.

For example, their housing. We built many of our houses some time ago. Currently, some of the houses are being rebuilt. But now the workforce has changed.

In the Malaysia plantations, 60% of our workforce are Indonesians. The Indonesians come over alone. Under government law, they are not supposed to bring their families here, so their housing needs are very different from the locals who have families. We've to understand how they live. Some of them have a grouping of 4 or 5 where they cook together. So instead of building houses individually, we built houses for groups of 5 to 7, so they can have a big common kitchen. Things have changed. You can see such issues when you have a multi-disciplinary approach.

At one time, our facilities were mediocre, but they've improved a lot over the last five years. For instance, we know an NGO (non-governmental organization) that specializes in play schools, so we send our teachers to them in Jakarta for training and they come back and teach in the play schools in our estates. The children are taught values from young, the values of honesty, being good to your parents, of cleanliness, responsibility, values which are good for all.

So we're giving them a much better living environment. Some of our estates do very well. In Sabah, they've their own sports days, community celebrations, and competitions where they perform.

 What is one advice you would give to emerging leaders?

 Always understand the macro picture of the businesses you are in, and also be very detailed on the micro. If you are not detailed on the micro level, sometimes you'll lose touch with the business or you are not able to come up with innovations. Innovations only happen when you know how the macro and the micro are tied together.

You have to think outside the box — what makes sense, what doesn't make sense. You have got to keep to a basic understanding of the business — why are you doing this? Knowing the micro means knowing how other people do it and finding out if there is any innovative thing that you can learn from other industries.

There are people who have done it very well in Malaysia, like Hartalega the glove manufacturer. They are very innovative in their machinery, they claim to have a 20–30% advantage over their competitors. That's a big advantage.

 What is one legacy you hope to leave behind?

 We are stewards, we cannot take anything with us, but hopefully we leave behind a responsible second generation who also have values very much driven by honesty, integrity and hard work.

Our industry is very labor intensive, so we are responsible for the well-being of many people. So we have to enable them to have satisfaction in their working life, to make them feel proud of themselves even in their menial work.

We must have different levels of recognition, good compensation and a good environment to live in. We must have a holistic picture of the people who are working in our company, starting first with our own family. Without that, it'll be very hard to leave a legacy.

"

The night is always the darkest just before dawn. Things will get worse before they become better. When you are at your depths, it will pass. When you are at your heights, it will also pass.

"

LIM GUAN ENG
The Prison to Parliament Leader

eeting the Chief Minister (CM) of Penang, Mr. Lim Guan Eng is truly an honor. He became CM after winning the Air Putih State Assembly seat as well as the Member of Parliament for Bagan (a constituency in Penang) in the Malaysian General Election in 2008 and again in 2013.

His story is one of love, courage, faith and endurance. He was imprisoned twice. Together with 106 opposition politicians and activists, he was arrested in 1987 in Operasi Lalang, under the Malaysian Internal Security Act.

On April 1, 1998, he was again imprisoned for championing the rights of an underaged Malay girl who was raped, under the Sedition Act and Printing Presses and Publications Act (PPPA). The Court of Appeal upheld this and they increased the sentence to 18 months imprisonment. He confessed he was seething with anger because he knew he was framed. During that period in prison, he went through a time of soul-searching.

He did not want to come out bitter and warped, as "that would satisfy my tormentors." He thought, "I'd turn out to be like my tormentors in my hate." He understood suffering in a deeper way and found God. Nelson Mandela took 27 years to bring about positive changes. He realized that if he wanted change, he had to give something.

Under his leadership, Penang today ranks among the top in the investment charts in Malaysia, attracting RM40 billion from 2008–2013 as compared to a similar 6-year period of RM21 billion from 2002–2007. Consequently, the public debt has decreased by 95% from RM630 million to RM30 million in 2011. It is one of the fastest economic growth states in Malaysia. He also championed the concept of Competency, Accountability, and Transparency (CAT) to propel the State Government to achieve efficient, responsible and clean governance.

Born in 1960, Guan Eng is currently the Secretary General of the Democratic Action Party in Malaysia. He is married to Betty Chew and has four children. His daughter is 23, and his sons are 21, 20 and 8.

This is Lim Guan Eng's story.

 Who or what influenced you most in your leadership development? And why?

 The person who influences me the most is my father, Lim Kit Siang. My father is a very learned and educated person. Another influence is my own life experience and through reading books.

My father taught me the importance of discipline and humility. He taught me through his own example and hard work. He was a very humane person and finally, he taught me courage. I often wondered where his source of strength came from. It was through reading books of right and wrong, fighting the good fight and holding on to your principles. He impressed upon me that we should open our minds and not be brainwashed to accept something as the absolute truth. He had a very enquiring and questioning mind.

However, I had to take a leap of faith, which was not a forethought but an afterthought. That came when I converted to Christianity very late in my years, when I was searching for answers. I found them in the Bible.

My father, Kit Siang, knew no fear. But we often feared for our safety and future. When I was 8 years old, my world revolved around my parents. When one of them was not around, I felt very alone. When my father was imprisoned for sedition, my mother cried herself to sleep every night. She tried to put on a brave front and not let us know what happened to dad. My dad was the source of strength for the family and also for our political party (Democratic Action Party). He was our inspiration and strength. When he was not around, we were very vulnerable. As a young child, when he was not around, it impacted me a lot as it created worries and doubts.

 Did you at any point think that your dad was crazy to stand for these things, that he might be wrong?

 Of course. Why is he putting the family's happiness and welfare at risk? Why is he doing all this? But during those times, we never questioned our father. We asked these questions in our minds. We had unquestioned faith in our father. When he went to the prison, we thought our father must be a bad person because only bad persons go to prison. It was quite traumatic because your whole image of your father was shattered. It was revealed slowly. My mother told us that it was not that my father was a bad person. Our relatives told us that it was not like that. Slowly, we grew out of it. In the beginning, my grandmother scolded him, telling him in Hokkien, "Don't get involved, he insists on getting involved!" ("*quo yi mai*

cham, yi tio qi cham" in Hokkien). When we were in school, we were mercilessly taunted for having a father in prison.

 What was the turning point in your life, when you understood that your father was standing up for justice and righteousness? How did you turn around?

 There was no turning point. There was no epiphany. No St. Paul type of experience with Jesus on his road to Damascus. It was through repeated instances, his rallies and through reading his writings and speeches. It made sense, as I read, compared, contemplated and reflected.

 What is one memorable life-changing experience that has impacted and shaped the way you lead?

 I read the Bible cover to cover. Three times. I requested for the Bible when I was in prison in 1998. I read the Bible the first time when I was young. It didn't make much sense to me then. And even now, I still cannot comprehend fully. But now it makes more sense to me.

When I was a bachelor, if I die, I die. But during my second imprisonment in Kajang Prison in 1998, being a family man, I had to worry about my wife and children. So it was much more painful. You realized suffering. Then I looked at the suffering that Christ endured. I read in some of the passages about how he was dragged along the streets, how he suffered shame and pain. There is this beautiful film by Mel Gibson, *The Passion of the Christ*. Jesus Christ even had doubts. There was a human-ness in him even though he was divine. He had to bear the sins and the consequences of humankind. The suffering that he endured gave me strength. What was my suffering compared to His?

When reading the Bible, I was also more fascinated with the Book of Revelation. I was more interested in the future and what hell was like. The first time I read the Psalms, I thought to myself, "Luckily I am not a Christian. I have to memorise all these verses." I enjoyed Solomon's writings: Proverbs, Ecclesiastes, and Songs of Solomon. They have wisdom and are filled with hope.

When I was in my 40s in prison, I really appreciated the Bible. But I could never understand the Bible fully. I could understand a fraction of a fraction of its meaning: an infinitesimal fraction!

I even had to battle with demons and spirits when I was in prison. In front of the maximum security cell were the gallows, where they hanged all the condemned people. At night, I could hear 'cranks'. I was in the dungeon, in the middle of the jungle. How can there be cranking sounds in the middle of the night like trap doors being opened? The other inmates told me it was the ghosts of people who were hanged. It was eerie and frightening. Some of the prisoners were possessed by demons. They had to call the *bomoh* (Malay word for witch doctor) to come. You could feel the wind blowing around the cell.

I was in a cell, and could hear the wind whirling. In front of my door, there was a painting of a Chinese god. I had to face it. I said to them, "If you want to come, come. I will take you on. I have nothing to lose. You are dealing with a desperado. Even if I lose, even as a spirit, I will hunt you down!" I had to pray and ask God to give me strength to fight these demons. With His blessing, I can overcome these demons. I never saw anything, only felt the wind blowing.

 What is the most crushing adversity that changed your life and really transformed you?

 My life is not that dramatic. There was no drama. There was no one event or epiphany. It was something that evolved slowly. It unfolded. My love for books is what I acquired from my father. I slowly got immersed in it. Similarly, when it comes to adversity, it comes to you when you are in prison, you have to struggle with daily needs, you have to face humiliation and ridicule.

Even my own daughter questioned me, "Why are you so stupid — helping people who are not helping you? Because you are helping people, you are depriving me of what I deserve." All this made me feel that I had failed my family and my daughter.

When I first came out of prison, I was left with nothing. I could not even practise my chosen profession: accountancy. They took away my professional accreditation. I sold my car and got a smaller car. I cut down everything. I was struggling a bit. I tried not to deprive my daughter. I found other work just to make ends meet. Life was a never-ending struggle. My family felt the deprivation.

I just told my family that as long as we are together, and there is a family of love, that's most important, although I didn't think it registered with my kids. I could take them to places of 'makan' (eating places), we could go on cheap holidays, that was more than enough. They learned how to be part of the ordinary public life.

Of course, after I became Chief Minister, my daughter stopped complaining about her deprivation!

 What kept you going?

 My family's love kept me going. My family's love helped me a lot. They stayed with me and continued to encourage me. Even though my daughter told me I was stupid, she told me to hang on so that I could come back safely so that our family could be together.

I kept telling them to just look at the Bible, look at the characters in the Bible and the other members of the society who had suffered much more. Or those earlier days when we had suffered much more.

My father was more hurt than anyone else. Which father wants to send his son to prison? He felt responsible as if he had sent his son to prison. But he did because of a principle he had to uphold. I think he wished 1,000 times that he could take my place. I would feel the same way if it was my son. I would suffer much more than he would. So did my dad. He suffered tremendously. He never said a word but he did.

It was also my father who kept me going.

Also, it was a renewal of faith. *It was a test to see if I really believed in this enough for me to say that I have to endure and overcome.* Also, a blind faith that I was going to prevail even though I could not see the light at the end of the tunnel. You must have faith. That's why you need to read the Bible.

I always tell myself, "It is always the darkest night that is just before dawn. Things will get worse before they get better." This is how I console and comfort myself. I kept telling myself that the people in the Bible suffered much more. As long you have faith in God, just do your best and let God do the rest even though it may take some time.

Q **There must have been times during that period when you felt like giving up.**

A Of course! I felt like giving up many times. I celebrated my Chinese New Year Eve alone for the first time in my life when I was in maximum security prison. Anywhere you go, you would always see a Chinese celebrating Chinese New Year Eve. But at that time, I could not celebrate with my family or anyone else. I felt really alone. I felt very small. There were many times I felt like giving up.

But I prayed. In the depths of despair, I prayed. I think God answered my prayers by reaching out to the inner parts of my heart. I felt smaller and receded inwards. I believe I heard the voice of God. Just by being silent and by praying, you can go into that state of meditative suspension. It was in that state, in complete solitude that I had to surrender myself. I had to submit myself fully to Him and prostrate before Him without any ego whatsoever. I don't think I can go into that state now.

It's so ironic that you had to be in prison to find yourself and to find God — to see whether you are worthy of His love, and whether you are worthy of your own love. There are some people who cannot face themselves. That person they see in the mirror is a terrible person that they have to live with. So, when they are alone, they are terrified.

Sometimes, you feel ashamed of the things you have done. At the same time, you come to terms with it because you have done more good than bad, and you are capable of doing more good.

Q **In your adversity you find yourself. But sometimes it is in prosperity, at the height of your popularity and fame that you lose yourself. How do you deal with success at the height of power, with being a Chief Minister and a hero?**

A Four words: *"This too shall pass"*. When you are at your heights, it will pass. When you are at your depths, it will also pass. When I was suffering,

I also reminded myself that this too shall pass. Have a sense of balance. Keep your feet on the ground but reach for the stars.

I am the same person now as I was before. Many people tell me that I have not changed: You move around like before as though you are not Chief Minister. I don't have security personnel following me. I know where I come from.

I have, to use a Hokkien term, "*jia kor*" (literally: eat bitterness). I can go back anytime to that state, right? How do we know? Don't forget how you came up to your present position. So much struggle, so much effort. And so many people helped you to be where you are now.

At the same time, I grew up under a banyan tree. It is not easy to grow up under a banyan tree, who is my father. I really have to struggle and strive, to prove that my accomplishments are my own, and not because of my father. So, that will make me value more what I have achieved.

 Kindly elaborate on this fact that it is difficult growing under a banyan tree. Sometimes in trying to prove yourself, you can over-reach and overshadow your dad. How do you maintain the balance?

 I have come to accept a long time ago that I can never be my father. My father is unique. He is a legend. I cannot be smarter or more disciplined than him. I cannot surpass him: he is a once-in-a-generation leader. I have come to terms with that. I want to be myself. I want to excel in things that I think I can do well.

I am in a different era. In his era, it requires people like him to lead the way, to be the warrior, to be the one who paves the way forward. For me, I am just doing his work so that his accomplishments can be maintained and endured. So, it is not easy to grow under a banyan tree.

It gives me some space to cultivate the values I believe in but at the same time, it is through sheer persistence that I am able to achieve these accomplishments.

I am more of a Manager-Leader in the modern contemporary sense. I come from a different background from him. He was fighting right from the moment he was born. He set the dream, the vision and the plan, we are the implementers. I had some exposure to corporate management and to the modern world. It requires a different skill set. He can mobilize people but I am able to mobilize people to work as a team, to maximize and optimize. I get all the inputs and get things done. Right now, I rely on a younger group of people, like Tony and Anthony (both DAP Members of Parliament) to get things done. We sit down to talk and strategize.

Q **Has your dad complimented you on your achievement?**

A My dad is very stingy in his compliments. He is a typical Chinaman. The fact that he doesn't reprimand you, that's his approval and it's good enough!

He doesn't spare himself. He is harsher on himself than others. He always wants to prove that he can do better. Despite the fact that he is in the opposition, he inspires so many people. So many people still look up to him, even the Barisan National leaders and ministers. Ong Tee Kiat said, "Lim Kit Siang is my hero."

He was the one who held the torch during those dark days, asking others not to give up. Despite the fact that he had no power, the force of his ideas and the spirit of his courage really lifted many Malaysians. Even though I am the Chief Minister, my father is an even bigger hero than me. People want him more than me. To the older folks, I am known as Lim Kit Siang's son!

Why? He was every person's hero. To every person in his generation, he was the man. He fought for the ordinary folks. If nobody wanted to fight, they would say, "Find Lim Kit Siang. He will fight for you." The fight is more important than the outcome. Sometimes victory is not the sole purpose. The struggle for what is right is important, even more important than the outcome! Yes, we may lose the battle but the fact that you have fought for something that is right, means you have won the war!

Q **How do you deal with disagreements and differences with your father?**

A Of course, we do have differences. We agree to disagree. We look at it from different perspectives. But that doesn't undermine the love and the bond that is there. He never lost faith in me because I was not an easy child. I am not the brightest in my family. The brightest in my family is my younger brother, a cardiologist. I was a very rebellious and difficult child.

I suffered trauma when I was younger. I was taunted by my classmates. They formed a circle around me and taunted me by saying that my father was a bad person. I was not a popular person among my classmates. I was very introverted and quiet. We moved a lot as a family so I did not form many lasting friendships. I went to many schools and many states. I made a few friends that lasted for a long time, but I was a bit of a misfit. I was not the smartest, not the brightest, not the most popular kid, but one of the quietest in class.

I never expected to be where I am today as I wanted to lead a quiet ordinary life. I never had any ambition. It is a calling and I have to accept it. If you were to ask my teachers, they would be surprised and would never believe it. They look at me now. They see me as a very different person from who I was as a student. They didn't see any leadership quality in me. I was very quiet. I kept to myself, reading books.

 What is one weakness that you have and how do you deal with it?

 Impatience. Sometimes, I am a risk taker. Sometimes, we have to let things go at its pace. You got to pace yourself, just like a plant. Go with the season. There's a time to sow and a time to reap. There's a time to live and to die. There's a time for everything. A time to love and a time to hate. We cannot say that hate is wrong. Hate is part of God. God hates sin. Hate is part of love. Without hate, you can't know love.

 Let's explore this a bit more. You mentioned before that you can forgive but you cannot forget. Would you like to elaborate?

 You have to forgive the person. If you don't forgive the person, you are not forgiving yourself, and you will become what you hate. Why do you become what you hate?

Let the enemy wallow in his own hate, but don't forget the evil he has done so that you can seek justice and make sure that justice is done. Evil is still evil. God can turn that evil into something good.

The other fact is that I am not like Jesus. Jesus can forgive and forget, but I am human. I cannot forget the evil that was done to me, but I will forgive him so there is no hate in my heart. Whenever I see my "enemies", I still shake hands with them. I still give them the respect for their positions.

If Jesus can forgive our sins, we must also forgive. It doesn't mean that when we forgive, we are weak but that we are strong enough to let go. When the Bible tells us to turn the other cheek, it is talking about not taking vengeance. *Forgiveness is not laced with vengeance but is laced with justice, tempered by mercy and compassion.*

 What is one advice you would give to emerging leaders?

 We are leaders but we are also servants. Look at Jesus, he was a leader but he was a servant of God. Why did he wash the feet of his disciples? Because he wanted to inculcate the value of servanthood. You are a servant. A leader is a servant and a servant of the people.

 How do you work this out practically?

 In a democracy, you are serving the people. You serve their interests, not your own interests. You must always fight for and protect the weak, the sick, and the poor. Never lose sight of them. They are the ones who will always be lifted up by God. Blessed are the meek for they shall inherit the earth. We should do good work. We wiped out poverty in my state. Poverty is defined as people living below a certain income level, which is RM770 per month per family here. So, I just top up the difference every month. There are 2,000 of such families. This costs us RM20 million a year.

 How do you keep your focus?

 It's the comrades and friends. Sometimes, it is the people you meet on the street. When they come up to me, I see the hope burning brightly in their eyes. That will always remind me what I am here to do for them. This is the reality check.

Don't lose yourself because they all depend on you. Young kids. Older folks. They place so much hope in you. They listen attentively. They hang on to every word you say. Hope. Not for themselves but for their kids. They see something better for their future. They give the same kind of look as they give to their movie stars! They hang on to your hands. They feel that they have a better tomorrow. This is the feeling that many people in Penang have. Even for those outside Penang.

Actually, we have not done anything special. We just followed international norms. Do what is right. Don't steal people's money. Stick to the rules you have set. I keep on plugging the message again and again. When I travel to Singapore, I travel on economy class. People ask me, "Why don't you take business class? Why fly economy? How much money can you save?" I agree with you I can't save much money. But I want to send a strong message to my civil servants. I want to cut costs. If I can save, you can also save. If I can take economy, you better follow me by cutting costs.

It's not that I want to show off. That's the message I want to send: If we can save, we save. You are the custodian of people's funds. You must uphold the sacred trust.

> Think big, start small, dig deep. Keep what works and chuck what doesn't work. Always be prudent.

LIM HUA MIN
The Responsible Builder Leader

Building a sustainable and successful global financial business for the long haul has been a hallmark of Mr. Lim Hua Min's life in the last few decades.

The Chairman of Singapore financial conglomerate Phillip Capital — a privately held multi-billion dollar firm with a presence in 15 countries — is also no stranger to leading through systemic crisis, having steered his company through the 1985 Pan Electric debacle which had threatened to derail the local stock market.

The former Victoria School student studied chemical engineering in university before obtaining a Master's degree in operations research and management studies from London's Imperial College.

He then worked at energy giant Shell for three years before joining the stock exchange as a research manager.

In 1975, Mr. Lim then embarked on his first key business venture with three partners by taking over a stock-broking firm which had gone into receivership. Gradually, he ended up steering the ship with three family members after his partners had sold their respective stakes.

Leading the company through the 1985 Pan Electric proved to be one of his toughest challenges. "I was hauled up into MAS office at 5 pm on a Friday. All the CEOs of the other firms were there. We were put in that room and I didn't leave the room until 3–4 pm the next day, almost 24 hours," he recalled.

He added: "This incident tells me that even as an institution, you are no longer your own. You have a public responsibility."

Phillip Capital has grown from a Singapore-based entity into one with a visible presence in countries such as the United States, Britain, Japan, India, Australia and most recently Turkey.

But Mr. Lim is not daunted by the task of leading such a diverse global business. Instead he believes in building a strong business eco-system which can deliver in the long term. "The more important thing is building the clock rather than telling the time. In other words, you build the system to tell the time."

The straight-talking, bespectacled man also believes that CEOs should not be paid on contractual terms with commissions and special bonuses. "Whenever you fix the salary of a CEO on a formula, he will become a product of the formula. Running a business is more complex than a formula. The way you pay the piper sets the tune. Too often, in the confusion, we end up paying people to bet the firm."

We chat with the visionary builder at his Raffles City office.

 Who or what influenced you most in your leadership development? And why?

 It's a range of people. But if you really ask me, it's my father. He taught me more by example than by precepts. He taught me enterprise and integrity.

He was a small businessman in tyres, first a tyre shopkeeper then a wholesaler. He had such integrity that business people trusted him greatly. For example, they trusted him even to the extent of asking him to help distribute the inheritance to the descendants after their death, as one of them had three wives.

Enterprise with integrity is a powerful combination. His enterprise and integrity have an imprint on me and underpin my own journey. And in subsequent years, this was reinforced by my own Christian faith — what I learned from the Bible.

 What is one memorable life-changing experience that has impacted and shaped the way you lead?

 There were two major ones. The first was in the late 1970s or 1980, when I was a junior partner of Phillip and I offered to sell it. Under those circumstances, I offered to sell it not because I could not manage it or grow it. However, my other senior partner, who was dying from cancer, offered me his share instead because he couldn't raise the capital to purchase it, given the time frame. So he had to sell to me instead.

That was how I became senior partner of the firm. But I had to really give it up first. When you are the primary party that builds it, you learn that "What you can take up, you can also give up." You learn to look at the transient nature of things. Once you make the decision to give it up, it releases you of that burden and allows you to start anew.

What was your thinking process at that time? How did you come to that decision?

 It was a combination of factors. It was either to sell it or to fight and end up destroying the company. I chose to sell it and move on. Learning to give up, especially with what you have built, is quite an experience. But there is a chance to rebuild. I was a young man then. Today it will be a different consideration.

You look at life as an essence of stewardship — the transference between ownership and stewardship becomes clearer.

 Any other life-changing experiences?

 That was when I went through a heart by-pass 10 years ago. A lot of well-meaning friends advised me to slow down. You realize you only have this one life, so you'd rather have a full life than an empty life. So you might as well take charge and move ahead — it is not so much of having a long life, as the essence of having a fulfilling life, a sense of calling.

A few days before my operation, I realized that I was going through the whole experience. What concerns me most is not the fear of death but the responsibilities and people I leave behind. Now, I work even harder than before. I also watch my diet and exercise — I swim and excercise three times a week.

 What about the stock market crisis in Singapore in 1985?

 That was an incident which changed my thinking — it was the Pan Electric crisis. I was hauled up into MAS office at Treasury Building at 5pm on a Friday. All the broker firms, all the CEOs were there. There were 19 of us plus the bankers. We were put in a small room and we didn't leave the room until 3–4pm the next day, almost 24 hours.

At that time, the decision was to come out with a lifeboat to save the industry. We were all damaged in the market fall-out. Seven out of 19 firms went under. Of course, the unhealthy ones would sign anything; the healthy ones were made to sign a $6 million guarantee. One broking firm said his capital was only $3 million, how would he sign a

$6 million guarantee? We were not the party at fault, but I realized that there was a public responsibility.

This incident taught me that even as an institution, you are no longer your own. You have a public responsibility.

 How did you come out of it? What went through your mind at that time?

 We still made money that year, only about $100,000. I was thinking, "How do we solve the problem?" We offered 50% of our brokerage to contribute to the fund. In the end, we paid 25% of brokerage to the fund and signed the $6 million guarantee. We were told we couldn't leave the room until the matter was settled.

From this incident, I learned that even though it was not fair, we had a public responsibility. When the system fails, individual institutions and individuals are impacted. Therefore, we have this responsibility to preserve the viability of the system.

 How do you lead this large organization today?

 The more important thing is building the clock rather than telling the time. In other words, you keep building the system.

The fundamental problem today is the failure to distinguish between core and contractual staff. You should never pay core staff, which includes your CEO, on contractual terms — commissions and special bonuses, turnover commissions like remisiers. When you confuse the two, you create the rogue trader — he is paid to bet the firm. If they lose, at most they lose their jobs. As a shareholder, you lose the whole firm. You need the core to control the contractual. Too often we have allowed the contractual to run the company.

A lot of people fail to understand that the shift of the industrial economy, in which the means of production rests with plants and machinery, to a knowledge-based economy in which the means of production rests in the individuals e.g. financial services, changes the means of production.

Unfortunately, a lot of internal controls, inspection checks and independent audits don't cover this area. They always cover internal checks. But if both core and contractual staff are paid on contractual terms, sales turnover and trading profits, they can collude. Then, who will check on whom? You have to separate the two, so that one can check on the other. That's the deficiency of the whole financial system. This is the essence. I make sure none of my CEOs are rewarded on that basis.

 How do you keep your senior staff motivated?

 Yes, I lose some staff, I lose talent. But those who stay understand this. At the end of the day, the difference between the guy who builds a house with a strong foundation and the guy who builds a house with a weak foundation will be known.

We emphasize on and inculcate these key values in my organization. The foundational values in my company include Enterprise and Integrity. Enterprise is setting the vision. Integrity is setting the values.

Building the trust with my people over the years is critical. Trust is two-dimensional and on a continuum. The two dimensions are 'Alignment of World Views/Values' and 'Ability to Deliver'.

There must be a constant alignment and the strengthening of the world views/values with the staff. But to build trust, the second component is that staff must be able to deliver. They have to deliver 'over-time' rather than 'a-point-in-time'. Then, bonus will be given to the staff based on the performance of the company 'over-time'.

People before things. Many leaders over-emphasize products, processes, platforms, and results. In the end, it is people who deliver and make things happen. God has valued people more than things. It is not that things are unimportant. The way we approach issues should be people before things. Our DNA and perspective should be governed by this principle. We can afford to lose money on things from time to time. In the end, it is more important that people learn from the losses.

Better before cheaper. It is very easy in business strategy to drop prices and to sell things cheaper. It is much harder to do things better. Of course, we want to be better and cheaper. The focus should be on being better.

'Over-time' before 'a-point-in-time'. I learned this from the late Mr. Lee Kuan Yew. When he passed away, suddenly the whole nation looked upon him 'over-time' rather than 'a point-in-time' as he has served the nation the last 50 years. In that context, we felt he was worthy of our respect. Many of us queued up for eight hours to pay our last respects to him.

Unfortunately, we tend to look at issues in life at 'a-point-in-time' and not 'over-time', whether we look at job or credit. Some staff tell me, "I don't like my colleague, therefore I resign" or "Somebody offers me a few dollars more, I resign". Too often, we are too short-sighted and only look at single issues at 'a-point-in-time' rather than 'over-time'. If we look at issues over long term rather than short-term, I believe we will have a better perspective in life.

I asked my core staff if they want to be commissioned. They said no, because if you are commissioned you will work on an individual basis, and start fighting like cats and dogs and no longer work as a team. Such methods pander to the immediate rather than long-term sustainability.

Once they stay with us for five years, they will stay for a long time because they know the difference.

How do you lead in times of crisis and also when times are good?

You build when times are bad, but you harvest when times are good. So when times are good, you don't expand, but you harvest. When times are bad, you can then use your spare resources to innovate or diversify for the next lap.

When times are good, all your capacity is fully utilized. Therefore, you should be harvesting. You should take the opportunity to maximize your sales and profit.

When times are bad, you should either go for organic or acquisition growth. When times are bad, you will always have spare capacity to build and diversify for the next phase of growth in the company. You can also grow geographically. Another way to grow, when times are bad, is acquisition growth. The price will be right. When times are good, the prices will be exorbitant.

Good companies make money all the time, in good and bad times. In bad times, if you're losing money, you're playing with fire. The role of business is to provide a value proposition to customers. And therefore, at all times, you should be making money. Of course, you probably make less during bad times.

 How do you build businesses for the long haul?

 There are two types of errors: (1) Not doing the right thing and (2) not getting it right. Most of our errors are type 2 errors, which has to do with execution. 95% of our errors in business are type 2.

Execution has to do with the four Ps (Platform, Product, Process and People). These are essentially the business drivers. Then there are the three Cs (Compliance, Capital and Customer), which are hygiene factors or results.

I find that a lot of people cannot distinguish between drivers and results. Budgeting, accounts and financials are results, i.e. telling the time rather than building the clock. Too often in management and board meetings, we concentrate on the results rather than the drivers which lead to the results.

For example, my staff come to me with a problem. They tend to blame it on a type 1 error — they blame it on the sales, something apart from themselves or they claim they chose the wrong people or that the platform is deficient. But I will always ask them if it is a type 1 or type 2 problem. If it is a type 2 problem, it is their problem, not mine. I ask them to go back and solve it. In that way, I don't have to micro-manage them. If it is a type 1 error, it is my responsibility.

If you concentrate on these four Ps, the other three Cs will flow smoothly.

You have a financial conglomerate with people in 15 countries. How do you manage all of them?

 Trust and transparency are important. Don't micro-manage — they submit monthly reports all over the world to me. We interact as and when necessary, sometimes they fly to me, sometimes I fly to them. Twice a year, we have a whole global conference for two days in Singapore or Malaysia: one conference for the retail business and another for the corporate side.

They submit their reports twice-yearly and we brainstorm. It's most transparent. One reason for my not having gone public is that we are more transparent internally than public companies. We have risk management and audit teams that go around the world to ensure good governance standards.

As I have mentioned previously, trust is two-dimensional — it's an alignment of values and character and the ability to perform. Trust is not discreet, it is a continuum. You move from a situation of no trust, where everyone is independent, to a situation of advisory and to trust. You keep shifting that continuum upwards.

To avoid politics and sectarianism in the company, we always try to meet in groups. Rarely do we meet on a one-on-one basis, unless for personal counseling. But for most normal issues, we always meet in groups, especially from the CEO's perspective, so as to provide openness, inclusiveness and transparency.

 How do you steer Phillip through crises well?

 We always feel that crisis is an opportunity. Every situation has its own silver lining. I believe that all good businessmen have to be an optimist fundamentally but operating quite often as a pessimist. It's the whole idea of healthy scepticism, because out of a hundred business offers, you may take only one or two.

We go through crises in different parts of the world all the time, but we've had less and less life and death crises. However, as you grow, decay sets in, wrong habits, bureaucracy — you're fighting more on diseases rather than calamities, and these can be cancerous. So there's nothing like reflection and reading to help you see another paradigm and then shift the paradigm.

If you are a single product and single platform, it's very simple. But as you move to multiple products and multiple channels, it gets more complex and all this complexity creates even more complexity. So how do you keep things simple? For example, having thicker and thicker reports doesn't make you a better manager. Also, having too many choices creates complexity.

Then there's the principle of postponement. If you're doing mass production, the concept is to move the choice right to the final client interface, i.e. move the choice up the value chain. This way, I keep it simple. For example, in Subway's choice of sandwiches, they offer many sandwiches but they don't make them all and wait for the customer to choose. Instead, they just manage their inventory of ingredients and wait for the customer to choose before making. This way, I just concentrate on maintaining my 10 ingredients instead of having to manage a 10 factorial (10!) inventory.

 What is one advice you would give to emerging leaders?

 Think big, start small, dig deep. Keep what works and chuck what doesn't work. Always be prudent.

Shift from interest to responsibility — maturity is to move towards this direction. If you emphasize too much on rights based on your interests, you are still operating as a student. I'm not saying that having personal interests is wrong, but responsibility and interests come hand in hand. What is a company? It is a group of people coming together to be responsible for one another.

What do you think about at your death bed? What are you interested in? You are concerned about the responsibility that you have left behind.

 What is one legacy that you would like to leave behind?

 Creating and building a healthy eco-system — shifting from individual to corporate to communal to networks to eco-systems.

The challenge for me all the time is to build a network of eco-systems. Whether you are talking about business or even community in terms of microfinance, it's the same. How do you build a network of eco-systems to ensure sustainability?

The guiding post is sustainability, and this is about ensuring a decent return underpinned by the common good.

Think future, think people, think excellence.

LIM SIONG GUAN
The Future-Oriented Leader

r. Lim Siong Guan has had an outstanding civil service career. He has served as the Permanent Secretary of the Ministry of Defense, the Ministry of Education, the Ministry of Finance and the Prime Minister's Office. He was also the Head of the Civil Service from 1999 to 2005.

During his time as a civil servant, he was a very well-respected leader, mentor and teacher. He has documented many practical leadership lessons in his book, *The Leader, The Teacher and You … Leadership Through the Third Generation*, which has become an instant best-seller in the region.

Presently, he is the Group President of the GIC, the fund manager for Singapore's foreign reserves. The Prime Minister of Singapore, Mr. Lee Hsien Loong, writes in a tribute to his accomplishments, "Throughout your career, you have established an unbroken record of understanding Singapore's challenges and developing a vision of how the Public Service should respond to these challenges. You have turned this vision into strategic ideas and programs."

There is no doubt that Mr. Lim is more than a civil servant who simply follows the Minister's vision for each ministry. He is an innovator and future-oriented leader. Under his leadership in the Prime Minister's office and then as Head of Civil Service, he launched and championed PS21 (Public Service for the 21st century), a strategic initiative that made the Singapore Public Service become more forward looking, responsive to change, performance-driven and more customer-focused.

This initiative galvanized officers at all levels in each ministry to anticipate change, welcome change and execute change. He is truly a future-oriented leader. We speak with Mr. Lim over tea to hear his leadership perspectives and insights.

 Who or what influenced you most in your leadership development? And why?

 I served the founding Prime Minister of Singapore, Mr. Lee Kuan Yew, for three years as his Principal Private Secretary from 1978–1981. He was a wonderful mentor. I had the opportunity to sit in all the meetings with government leaders, foreign dignitaries and other world leaders. I traveled with him on many overseas trips. He often shared his concerns for Singapore. He was a big picture person, excellent in strategizing and planning for the future. He always focused on the fundamentals and had very strong convictions. For example, he strongly believed that what is needed for a small country is meritocracy and racial and religious harmony.

He was also concerned about essential details and what many could even consider as non-essential details. Thus he had the vision for the greening of Singapore with a passion, and looked into an enormous amount of details as to what and how trees and plants could grow well in Singapore. He didn't want Singapore to be a concrete jungle and came out with the road map for the 'Garden City'.

Also, in the merger of the National University of Singapore and Nanyang University, he attended to a lot of details while focusing on the critical issues.

The other person who influenced me most was the late Dr. Goh Keng Swee, who was Deputy Prime Minister of Singapore and variously the Minister of Defense, Minister of Finance and Minister of Education. He was a tremendous implementer. He was also a great experimenter and lived well the principle of learning by doing: "If it works, nice. If it doesn't work, move on."

He introduced many national initiatives, like the transformation of Jurong from a mangrove'swamp wasteland into an industrial estate. He created the Economic Development Board to attract foreign investments into Singapore. He was the driving spirit in the creation of the Monetary Authority of Singapore and the GIC, known then as the Government of Singapore Investment Corporation.

He also had the 'softer touch' when he formed the Singapore Symphony Orchestra and wooed Singaporean Choo Huey back to Singapore to be its first resident conductor and music director. And no doubt his greatest achievement of all was the creation of the Singapore Armed Forces to be a well-respected defense force to maintain the peace for Singapore.

I will always remember Dr. Goh's famous quote, "The only way to avoid mistakes is not to do anything." He had the insatiable energy to keep imagining and doing. He has been the encouragement to me to think deep, think long term and move. He had a lively mind, always curious and willing to try things. It was this that gave me the impetus to first start the

MINDEF Productivity Movement in MINDEF, and then PS21 (Public Service for the 21st century) as a big drive to encourage the whole civil service to pursue excellence and to be the best that we can be.

The goal of PS21 is about desiring people to operate to their maximum capacity. We need to anticipate change, welcome change, and execute change. It rests on three key ideas: (1) Using scenario planning as a means of imagining the future, the idea being to be in time for the future. (2) Next is recognizing change as an unending process. To welcome change is to be open to change. We formed work improvement teams (WITs) so that everyone can be a part of the change initiation and change process. (3) Finally we need to execute change well i.e., how to make things happen and derive maximum effectiveness. The general principle here is: "evolution in execution, revolution in result".

 What is one memorable life-changing experience that has impacted and shaped the way you lead?

 The most transforming experience for me is becoming a Christian, striving to live by the precepts of the Bible. For example, the importance of loving my neighbor and forgiving people. I also learned that the role of a leader is to serve people and help people to be the best that they can be.

 What is one legacy you have left behind in your organization?

 Every organization I have been at, I would like to leave behind a place where people want to be the best as an organization and be their best as individuals. Especially for Singapore, we need to have people who are top class and future-oriented. We cannot be complacent about the future. We need people who are thinking and making themselves better all the time. We need to be really good on a sustained basis.

It is a frame of mind of wanting to be No. 1. The mentality of being No. 1 is learning as much as we can and having the ability to create our own thing. The mentality of No. 1 is different from the mentality of No. 2, which is simply to be faster, and better by (often blindly) copying.

The mind of being No. 1 is to explore the possibility of what can be and understanding why others are doing what they are doing. It is learning to think independently and learning from all relevant sources. At every place I go, I start off by sending an email to everyone in the organization, asking what three things they think we should stop doing and what three things we should start doing. This gives me a very quick sense of what people consider to be important in their work.

I believe that people want to do a good job and they want to succeed. We need to find out what the impediments are for that to happen. We must remove the impediments. We must allow people to share their dreams. I don't believe in the charismatic visionary leader because then there is only one acceptable vision. I would rather have people sharing their visions and dreams, and then creating a composite vision.

 What are some practices that you maintain in your personal routine?

 First, reading. I read anything that may be interesting. I like to then create my own perspectives and theories based on the reading, as this would allow me to create useful ideas.

Second, I like talking to people, asking them what they want to do and what they know. I am open to learning from others.

Third, listening is a skill that I have cultivated, to listen carefully to what people are saying at all levels, both verbally as well as non-verbally.

In all these, I recognize myself as a steward as told in the parable of the talents where three different individuals are given 10, five and one talent. The ones with the 10 and five talents multiplied their talents while the one with the one talent hid it in the ground.

That is why I keep desiring to be as good as I can be and lead the organizations to be as good as they can be.

 What is one most crushing adversity you have ever faced in your leadership? How do you deal with it?

 I don't have any crushing adversity as such. It's because I have this frame of mind. If I fall, I learn from the opportunity. I keep short memory. Even when people have fallen, I try to help them recover. Of course, there are people who see negatives in everything. I try to counsel them.

If they are cynics and try to undermine their own future and, even worse, the future of the organization, I have to try to prevent them from doing so. Some people don't know the effects and impact they have on others.

I work with those who are willing and to those who are not, I tell them that they are not going to do well in the organization. Unless they modify their behavior and are aware of their impact on others, they will end up removing themselves. I would not want to undermine their future, and would always give them an opportunity to change. But there are times when I have to make the hard decision to remove them for the sake of others.

Generally, people will be prepared to listen to you if they believe that you care about them and want them to succeed. I have to help them believe that I am not here out of personal ambition. If they believe in you and you have their trust, they will be open to bad news, even news like their having to leave the organization.

Some leaders are not prepared to confront those who are not competent. They are not able to give people feedback. We must give people opportunity to improve. At the same time, we cannot allow incompetent people to carry on. Sometimes, job fit is the problem. For example, some people cannot live with ambiguity and, they want clear rules on what they have to do, whereas others want to be told just the final goal and be given the freedom to figure out how to get there.

We need to focus on people's strengths and help people to get the right fit.

 One of the main themes of the book is dealing with uncertainty. What advice do you have for business and investment leaders dealing with turbulent times?

 Uncertainty is a given in life. But we need always to seek to be "in time for the future." All organizations have to anticipate the future as best we can. We look at the competitors and the geo-political situation in the world, and have to develop the capability to respond and react to unexpected situations.

The capacity to respond lies in emotional resilience and perseverance. We need cool-headed people in a crisis to apply first aid, stop the bleeding as quickly as possible, and figure out what needs to be done to solve the problem and be better for next time.

We must be prepared for unanticipated situations. We need to run crisis management exercises and never assume the system will not break down.

  What is one advice you would give to emerging leaders?

The advice that I would like to give to emerging leaders is: Think future, think people, think excellence.

Success today is not good enough. We have to think future.

Help people become what they can be. Think people. They have the potential and they must see the potential for themselves.

And never be satisfied with being anything less than what you can be. Think excellence.

  What is one weakness that you have?

I don't believe in weakness *per se*. I believe that the flip side of every strength is a weakness. In other words, my strength can also be my weakness. For example, in wanting to help people learn from their failures and succeed in the best way possible, I could be much too patient with them and not recognize enough that those around them are having to carry the consequences of their lack of competence.

Love your life, Love your
dream, Love your job, Love
your problems, Love your
time, Love things with value,
Love your clients, Love 360
degrees, Love the country.

MONTREE
SORNPAISARN
The Rich in Love Leader

he first thing that strikes you about Mr. Montree Sornpaisarn is his infectious and hearty laughter, which frequently punctuates a conversation with him.

Mr. Montree has been the Chief Executive of Thailand's largest stockbroking firm Maybank Kim Eng Securities (Thailand) since October 2001, and is responsible for its overall brokerage business and investment banking business.

The Bangkok-based Mr. Montree is known for his unassuming and candid demeanor, despite his illustrious career which includes becoming a CEO at just 37 years of age.

Mr. Montree has also served as a Member of the Board of Governors at The Stock Exchange of Thailand from May 2008 to May 2010, and as a Governor of the Stock Exchange of Thailand from October 2001 to May 2002.

He has over 25 years of experience in the securities, investment banking and fund management businesses, and has seen first-hand how his country's companies were crippled by excessive borrowing during the Asian Financial Crisis in the late 1990s but emerged stronger during the recent Global Financial Crisis.

He recalled: "Back in 1997, the whole country was over-spending, over-speculating and over-borrowing, not following our King's philosophy of being a sufficiency economy. But when it came to the Global Financial Crisis in 2007–2008, no firm went bankrupt although there were high losses. So, we can see that Thailand passed through the crisis strongly.

The 50-year-old has also written books in Thai, with a recent one entitled *Being Rich In Love*. He has also produced DVDs featuring famous Hollywood movies such as *Toy Story* and *Finding Nemo* to introduce great movies which illustrate the importance of family values and being rich in love.

He said: "I wrote in my book that
'Being Rich doesn't mean Happy.
Being Happy doesn't mean Rich.
You can be Happy, when you are Rich in Love.'

We catch up with Mr. Montree over tea at his Bangkok office.

 Who or what influenced you most in your leadership development? And why?

 God. I came to know God when I was 11 years old. I was the only Christian in my family and among one or two Christians out of 40 to 50 students in my class. The rest were Buddhists. God grows me spiritually through the Bible. He has helped me to love people more and more.

There is also my mother — she was a role model for me. She was kind and nice and loved my father so much. I grew up with five brothers. After my father passed away, she had to work so much harder. The biggest challenge was when our grocery shop in Chinatown burned three years after my father passed away.

Then there are also my elder brother and wife, who are always supporting me.

 What is one memorable life-changing experience that has impacted and shaped the way you lead?

 The real change came when I knew God at 11 years old. I joined a Christian camp and saw that the people in camp were really happy and loved each other. I thought that "this is the life that I would like to live" and "this is the society I would like to be in", so I accepted Christ.

 What is one legacy you have left behind in your organization?

 It is the lesson of being rich in love. I wrote in my book that

"Being Rich doesn't mean Happy.
Being Happy doesn't mean Rich.
You can be Happy, when you are Rich in Love."

Love your life,
Love your dream,
Love your job,

Love your problems,
Love your time,
Love things with value,
Love your clients,
Love 360 degrees,
Love the country.
My value as a CEO is to make sure that we can be rich in love.

 How do you inculcate these values in a dog-eat-dog industry?

 I was appointed CEO at 37 years old, so I have a lot of subordinates who are older than me. We were formerly two firms — Kim Eng and Yuanta. Previously, we were competitors, now the two firms are one family. I had to lay off 10–20% of the staff to reduce cost.

This was a source of conflict. After the merger, a lot of staff saw new colleagues sitting in the seats formerly belonging to their friends who were laid-off. One might think "Is it because of you that my friends have to leave? If you go, my friends may be able to stay."

I encouraged them to accept one another as new friends when the two firms merged. I challenged them to trust in the good parts of their new colleagues. Even between the front and back rooms, I cheered them to fulfil each other's roles, forgive each other, trust each other, and to be kind to each other.

I need to model these values to my staff. For the front-line staff, I cheer them on to stay together. Together, we become No. 1. We have to connect the train carriages to each other, and to move in the same direction side-by-side to gain momentum. We prevent fighting internally but allow competition externally. Therefore, we do not allow marketing staff to take clients from one another.

At annual seminars, most are bored because we only talk about problems, and thus, everyone felt such seminars were a waste of time. Instead, I now ask them to send the problems to one another in advance. During meetings, I let those who learned from their problems share the problems and then their proposed solutions. That's a solution-based approach, instead of just a forum for complaining or blaming others.

Right now, our market share is about 12–13%, double that of our nearest competitor.

 Give us a glimpse of your daily routine. And why do you keep these practices?

 I like to identify long-term problems early and prepare for them. I encourage people who have done well or have succeeded. People can also learn lessons when they fail but these lessons can be painful. So I prefer to do it the more constructive way. People who have done something right and well, I always try to encourage them. To correct people who have done something wrong, I express what they have done right first before saying where there is room to improve with encouragement.

People already know what's right, they just need encouragement. I see problems instead of blaming the person. I communicate inspirational messages with my staff by email daily. If I am inspired by events, then I will send out an email. For example, when Maybank acquired us, I highlighted the positive — that Maybank is the No. 1 bank in Malaysia.

Some lessons from movies, some good strategic ideas from any industry or some problems which happened to our competitors can be valuable to share with staff at the appropriate timing. We also need to keep "thinking ahead" in order to be among the leading groups in the industry.

 What is one advice you would give to emerging leaders?

 Love your life, find your mission and gift, discover your dream and realize it. Feel proud when you can make your life valuable for others. That's the way to have unconditional happiness and success.

 Why and how did you change a purely money-making culture into one that is driven primarily by love? How do you balance that with the need to deliver healthy profits?

 You need to choose the right time to deliver a good message. The most important weapon of a hunter is time. We may have a series of messages, which if we send out when it's business as usual, no one will listen. For example, when a speculative stock crashes, I use that time to talk about lessons. I use real-life lessons to teach people. I have about 1,100 full-time staff. Of them, around 800 are remisiers. I send 20 to 30 emails a year, about two or three emails a month.

You have to care for self, care for family and care for clients. The client is the source of all our benefits. This is the way of sustainable growth. We must work hard to give good and suitable advice to clients. Although no one can give the right advice all the time, we need to do our best. We don't push them to trade actively in the market when the outlook is negative. We emphasize the message of love and sincerity to clients. Our motto: "Clients' benefits are our goals". Our clients come first.

 How do you keep a healthy family life, nurture your children and have a happy marriage in your busy work life?

 I make limited time high-value time. When we are tired with work and have little time for family, I don't think our family will be pleased with us. Instead, we must please our spouse. Our spouse might be lonely when we are busy. You have to understand your spouse, be humble towards her, see her positively, and forgive each other.

 How do you make limited time high-value time?

 I learn to say sweet words and make them happy. These will have strong impact on them. The secret of saying sweet words is to start with your heart and use your eyes to connect with them positively. To the younger generation, I try to think what will make them happy. It may be different from what makes me happy. Keep the relationship positive and waste little time to fix the relationship when it's not working well.

 You must have seen many financial crises in your leadership journey. What are the ways to lead through a crisis effectively?

 In 1997 during the Asian Financial Crisis, I was still only in middle management, so it's hard to say how I managed the organization through the crisis. I was working with Jardine Flemming at that time. We worked professionally, ethically, prudently and with discipline.

Basically, before that, a big bubble in the securities business was building up: full of greed, high margins, and speculation. When the problem came, some stocks dropped very sharply.

During those times, most securities firms would negotiate with their clients to relax on their force selling as clients were not happy with their losses, if they were forced to sell. Other brokers might also encourage them to increase collaterals, instead of cutting losses. My company chose to trigger the forced sale method. As a result, we made minimal losses and our clients had fewer losses than their friends, who held accounts with other brokers. For those who held on, the stock prices dropped much more and their losses were so much greater.

The keys to leading through crises are prudence, ethics and professionalism. Don't just follow the book but follow with good understanding — follow the 'spirit' of the book over the 'law'.

Back in 1997, the whole country was over-spending, over-speculating and over-borrowing, not following our King's philosophy of being a sufficiency economy. But when it came to the Global Financial Crisis in 2007–2008, no firm went bankrupt although there were high losses. So, we can see that Thailand passed through the crisis well.

For example, in 1997, debt-to-equity ratio was 2:1. After the Bank of Thailand floated the baht, a lot of companies borrowed in US dollars, so the value of debt became much higher and equity became lower. Debt-to-equity then was 5:1. At the end of 1997, during the pre-Lehman crisis, our debt-equity became only 1:1, much lower than 1997. We were so much more prudent. At the banking level at that time, US banks and Lehman had debt-to-equity ratios of up to 30 times. So through the crisis, Asian financial institutions with debt-to-equity ratio around 10–12 times, became much stronger than Western ones.

As my ex-boss Khun Korn Chatikavanij used to say: "We may make profit for seven to 10 years, but a loss in one year may wipe out the company."

In 2001, when I became the CEO of Kim Eng Securities, I learned one more lesson from my client. He said, "The securities business has a lot of manipulators who maneuver certain stocks for artificially high prices.

Most of the time, the end game is to put those stocks in the hand of brokers." This was a very good warning for us. We always allow people to invest in the market but we will not support manipulators — for example, to create false market signals: fake turnover and/or fake performance.

How do we prevent such manipulation? We are more conscious of company owners' account, when they buy a lot of their stock to keep their share price higher. Basically, they borrow money to buy their own shares to make the price go high artificially.

We have a prevention policy — a credit line cannot hold any stock over half of the credit line. Usually, the manipulators will borrow money just to buy one stock, so when we have this kind of tough prevention policy on the credit line, these manipulators will open accounts with other brokers instead.

During 2008–2009, the SET (Stock Exchange of Thailand) Index was as low as 380 from around 900–1,000 points. There was a case of a listed company in Thailand, a stock whose market capitalisation of 20 billion baht dropped to 200 million baht in eight days. So some securities companies made big losses. Our company was still okay, but those who supported manipulation suffered.

 What personal lessons did you learn from the crisis?

 I learned many lessons.

1. Learn to see all events positively.

Even if 30% were positive and 70% were negative, we can still count our blessing if we believe that everything is under God's control.

2. Bad things may not be bad.

In 1994, I was headhunted by a Hong Kong bank — they flew me business class and drove me around in a Mercedes. But I did not get the 'exciting' job in spite of me spending a lot of effort on it. I finally gave up. I believed that if God did not give me the job, he had something better for me. Two years later, the firm closed its operations in Thailand. Only then did I realize why God did not give me the job in the first place!

3. Learn to trust God.

In October 1997, I went to find a new job but couldn't find one that suited me. So I prayed for a new opportunity. I met a Singaporean, Low Poh Weng, CEO of Vickers Ballas in Thailand. He recruited me. Initially, I thought the position would not suit me. During the interview, we discovered that we were both Christians, and I sensed that this was a gift from God for me. So I resigned from SG and joined Vickers Ballas.

Little did I realize that God's plan for me was only two years later. DBS Bank, a top Singapore bank, acquired Vickers Ballas and my boss had to leave. I suggested that he goes to Kim Eng Securities in Thailand. After the interview, he told me that they were looking for a Thai. That was how I came to join Kim Eng Securities!

4. Don't blame God for our greed.

In 1997 I suffered some personal losses. I speculated in shares, gained 8–9 million baht but during the crisis I lost 10 million baht. I asked God, "Why did this happen to me?" He told me, "This is a lesson on risk." I asked him, "Why don't you teach me in a nicer way? Why do you need to make it 10 million?" God replied, "I tried to teach you many times but you didn't listen when you were losing 1 or 2 million baht."

5. Don't ask why, but ask what blessing I can get out of this.

Lately, I don't ask God why anymore when something bad happens to me. Instead, I will ask, "What blessing can I get out of this situation?"

During the financial crisis, 56 securities firms were shut down and 100 senior executives lost their jobs. This gave me the opportunity to join the senior executive level. Otherwise, I would still be languishing at the junior level. It was in 1998, after the financial crisis in 1997, that I wrote my first book about the lessons I learned.

I learned to:

1. View the world positively.
2. View my work passionately.

3. View and love others heavenly (i.e. in God's way).
4. View my challenges constructively, creatively and purposefully.

 What's one weakness which you have?

 Sometimes, I'm too relaxed. I also should learn to be stricter with the goals of the organization and people, and at the same time keeping to my values of 'love' and 'kindness'.

> We have acquired gourmet taste but have no clue how to fry an egg … If you have plateaued, you should vacate the job. Your highest decision is to know when to quit.[1]

NGIAM TONG DOW
The Moral Courage Leader

---

[1] Ngiam Tong Dow. Let's get our young talent job ready. Speech to the EDB Society. Mar 27, 2013. The Straits Times.

giam Tong Dow was a former Permanent Secretary (Administrative Vice-Minister) of the Ministry of Finance, Ministry of Trade and Industry, Ministry of National Development, Ministry of Communications and the Prime Minister's Office of the Government of Singapore.

He also served as the Chairman of the Singapore Economic Development Board and the Development Bank of Singapore (DBS Bank). Presently, he is an independent non-executive director of Yeo Hiap Seng.

He started life from a humble beginning. His late mother was illiterate but had an indomitable spirit. She toiled as a washer woman and maid servant to send her children to school. She used to say in Hainanese: "If you have one talent which you excel in, you will never starve." The best thing she did was to earn enough to educate her children; of the four boys, all of them went to university on bursaries or scholarships. Tong Dow was a beneficiary of this as he became one of Singapore's brightest scholars.

Tong Dow acknowledges, "I would like to say that my civil service career flourished because I was fortunate to have (the late former finance minister) Mr. Hon Sui Sen and (the late former deputy prime minister) Dr. Goh Keng Swee as mentors in my formative years. They were truly selfless men."

Tong Dow is one person who will speak his mind. He openly suggested to the late Prime Minister, Mr. Lee Kuan Yew, that his ruling People Action Party (PAP) should allow for serious political challenges to emerge from the alternative elite out there, or else the incumbent elite will cruise along.

With regard to the PAP's long-held belief that there is a shortage of talent for "A" Team, he argued, "You have to allow some of your best and brightest to remain outside your reach and let them mature spontaneously. How do you know their leadership will not be as good as yours? But if you monopolize all the talent, there will never be an alternative leadership. And alternatives are good for Singapore … I think our leaders should accept that Singapore is larger than the PAP."[1]

---

[2] Ngiam Tong Dow. **"I suspect we have started to believe our own propaganda."** **Interview with Ngiam Tong Dow.** May 20, 2010.

He is not afraid to question and challenge conventional thinking and government policies.

He also wondered about the necessity of raising Goods and Service Tax. "Why tax the lower income, then return them in aid package? It demeans human dignity and creates a supplicant class who habitually hold out their palms. Despite the fact that we say we are not a welfare state, we act like one of the most 'welfarish' states in the world!"

With such audacity and radical insights, it is no wonder that he is a much sought-after thought leader and speaker. Although his candid forthrightness has earned the chagrin from some leaders in Singapore, Tong Dow remains a leader who has earned the utmost respect of both his friends and not-so-friendly foes. Why? Because he speaks with moral courage.

We caught up with Tong Dow over tea in Singapore.

 Who or what influenced you most in your leadership development? And why?

 Dr. Goh Keng Swee, the former Deputy Prime Minister of Singapore, was my mentor and hero. When I became Permanent Secretary (Perm Sec), he called me and said, "Your job as permanent secretary is to raise the competence of your team to a higher plateau. However, if you have plateaued, you should vacate the job. Your hardest decision is to know when to quit." I will never forget that.

Therefore, my job in any organization is to raise the bar of the whole organization and ministry to a higher level. When I cannot lead my organization to a higher level, I will quit.

Many leaders overstay their usefulness. They think they are gods. They think they are the best just because they were the founders and had built up the private business or the organization. You have to be honest with yourself and ask, "Can I bring the company to a new horizon?"

Nelson Mandela is a great example of such a great leader. He knew when to quit. He became the President of South Africa, after he got out of jail. On 14th June, 1999, he handed the presidency to Thabo Mbeki. He was a truly great statesman. It was Lord Nelson, the admiral who defeated the French at Waterloo, who said, "When I leave command of my fleet, I do not look over my shoulder neither do I spit on the deck."

Deputy Prime Minister Goh Keng Swee knew when to quit. When I asked him, "Minister, you are in politics. Don't you want to be the prime minister?" He said, "I don't have the prime minister's charisma. I cannot be the prime minister." To him, loyalty to the party is greater than his ambition.

Dr. Goh Keng Swee taught me when to quit. He had the courage to do so.

 What is one memorable life-changing experience that has impacted and shaped the way you lead?

 I believe in the native wisdom of the common person. As Perm Sec, I was faced with a great crisis. My job was to close down the then Singapore Traction Company (STC). It was bankrupt. I didn't know what to do. There were 2,000 or 3,000 conductors and drivers who were losing their jobs. God was kind to us. There was a Mr. Lee, a trade unionist of STC, who came up to me and said, "Can I help you? Let me give you a suggestion. We will tell them that the routes have been taken over by Chinese companies, Tay Koh Yat, Green Bus and Hock Lee Bus Company."

So, on that day, we drove to Kallang and locked the buses from STC and invited all the drivers and conductors to register for jobs at the other bus companies. In a twinkle of the eye, the whole crisis was resolved.

That experience taught me humility. With all the education I had, I learned to find wisdom from the common people. It was a very humbling experience; I had to listen to the people on the street, instead of just the Harvard Business School graduates. That took away my arrogance.

If you listen carefully to the common folks, there are pearls of wisdom. Unfortunately, those who are educated become arrogant and prideful.

 Tong Dow, how do you remain humble? It must be tough especially when clever people surround you.

 We need to keep being sensitive to people. We must continue to have compassion for people by understanding the poor. I consciously and constantly remind myself about my past and where I came from.

What is your greatest weakness?

 My handicap is always to look at the bright side of a person. I look for what talents a person possesses as opposed to a person's weaknesses. I normally give people the benefit of the doubt. The problem with my judgment is that I am always too generous. When they fail, it is too late. I sometimes fear to do what is right. I always make way for the other guy. I am not assertive enough.

 What is one legacy you have left behind in your organization?

 I would like my children and successors to judge my legacy. What I want my Singaporean friends to remember me for, is that I made good, rational and God-fearing decisions. To be rational is not to take the easy road to success.

To me, the casino decision was an easy road. We sacrificed our values just to create jobs and increase revenues. We need to earn our keep the honest and hard way. I have challenged the Ministry of Finance to do the cost-profit analysis. I am not certain that the taxes collected from our casinos outweigh the increased cost of policing, social welfare, and breakup of families.

Singapore was on a good trajectory 30 years ago. We were doing all the right things based on the right values. But the casino decision was very corrosive. When the Singapore Government invited Mr. Li Ka Shing to join up Suntec with the casino, he said, "My policy is not to profit from human misery." That is the right moral decision.

 What is one advice you would give to emerging leaders?

 I would like them to look at problems rationally and not take the short cut. You have to earn your keep through the sweat of your brow. Work hard and be honest.

> **I find that building bridges always works better than building walls…**

PAUL CHAN
The Corporate Bridge-Builder Leader

Twenty-seven years in the same company is no mean feat these days. Mr. Paul Chan not only survived but also thrived while serving in Compaq and Hewlett-Packard (HP), even when both organizations went through tumultuous times, including mergers and acquisitions and the stochastic ups and downs of sale cycles.

A former Hewlett-Packard Asia Pacific Managing Director, Paul Chan was a blue-blooded corporate leader for many years. In 2006, he stepped down as Senior Vice President of HP's Technology Solutions Group (TSG) and Managing Director of Asia Pacific/Japan after 27 years with the company.

Paul was the Managing Director of Compaq Computer Asia Pacific (1995–2002) before the company's merger with HP, and was involved with Compaq's acquisitions of Tandem Computers in 1997 and Digital Equipment in 1998.

He has served on the board of directors for Singapore Telecommunications Limited, Singapore Power Limited, and SIA Engineering Company Limited. Currently, he is on the board of National Healthcare Group, SP Services and Integrated Health Information Systems. Paul holds a B.S. degree in physics from the University of Singapore and a marketing diploma from the Chartered Institute of Marketing, UK, and is a Fellow of the Singapore Institute of Directors.

Throughout his leadership journey, he has always served as a bridge builder in order to navigate the complexities and challenges of corporate life.

He had resigned to spend time with his family and to embark on church work. His work ethic has remained the same — building bridges wherever he is placed. He is soft-spoken, unassuming, never brash or boastful, a true gentleman and a people person.

If you see him, you will not know that he had brushed shoulders with the who's who of the IT industry.

Over tea, Paul opened his heart and shared his experiences as a corporate leader.

Who or what influenced you most in your leadership development? And why?

 When I first joined HP, the then General Manager of HP Singapore, Malcolm Kerr, left a very strong impression on me. He exemplified a man who always puts the company's interest first. He taught me to assume ownership when doing a job, not to give excuses, but to come up with solutions, not problems, no matter how difficult the job is.

He said this to motivate me because he saw positives in me. I was a rookie then. He could see the potential and he allowed me to make mistakes, learn through the process, always giving me sufficient push through the years, even when I no longer reported to him when he was transferred to the US. He was very much a person who walks his talk, a leader who was very committed to the company.

It was much later on that I found out that he had cancer and had gone through several rounds of chemotherapy, and that he was in remission when he was my boss. Subsequently, he succumbed to the disease. While he was in remission when in Singapore, he was still very much focused on the company. He focused on what needed to be done.

In one of my early projects, I had to go back to him with my problems. He said, "You have to solve the problem. If you are unable to find the solution, please let me know, there are 10 others waiting for the job." I was not threatened by this. I felt encouraged by it partly because of his character and his tone. He was telling me the reality. If I was unable and unwilling to do it, there are others more willing and capable to get the job done. He was a man of integrity, espousing the company's values.

This lesson was something I kept in mind and put into practice throughout my career. If I had a job that needed to be done, it was up to me to bring to bear the necessary resources to get the job done.

If not for him, I would not be in the company. When I was interviewed for the job in HP back in 1978, the other interviewer didn't think too highly of me, but Malcolm thought otherwise. He gave me some books to read and I sat for a test. For some reason, he could see the potential despite the lack of experience.

What is one memorable life-changing experience that has impacted and shaped the way you lead?

 The most difficult and toughest time was when I was in Compaq in 2002, and we were acquired by HP. It was not really great being acquired by another company. It represented a lot of disruption to people's lives. We had to reduce the work force. Product lines overlapped and we had to make decisions to shut down certain product lines.

I remember the date very clearly. It was September 3, 2001 when they announced the takeover. On September 11, my Compaq bosses were doing the road show and the 9/11 disaster happened. Compaq lost five people in the tragedy. Four of them were in the building making a presentation to a customer and one of them was on the flight which was heading towards the Pentagon.

 What was particularly challenging in this takeover?

 As head of Compaq, I knew HP and I also knew that HP had changed. I was more concerned for the people in Compaq. I did a few things to try to mitigate the pain and smooth the transition for my people. Because of my prior knowledge of HP, having been there before, I gave them an understanding of how HP would operate differently from Compaq.

For example, in Compaq we had more direct management. We had more autonomy for what we did. But in HP, it was more complex as they had matrix management. There were lines of businesses for products and services and geographical lines. It was common to have multiple bosses.

In a matrix organization, there is greater ambiguity, and the bosses may not necessarily agree with each other. The products and services lines would hold the resources and budget while the geography lines have the task of developing the appropriate go to market model which may be a mix of direct, indirect and on-line models with its accompanying cost structures. This interplay of products, services and geography adds conflicts as well as interdependencies.

Tell us, Paul, how did you manage the matrix organisation effectively?

With matrix management, we need to recognize the added complexity. If we don't do it properly, we can make good and effective managers become ineffective. The matrix can potentially slow down the organization. We don't get things moving because we can end up fighting internally, trying to allocate resources and arguing over go to market models.

Clarity is No. 1. This is most important. We need to be clear about who is accountable for the different outcomes or KPIs. Hard measures require soft skills because the soft drives the hard. By this I mean that people skills, recognizing interdependencies and teamwork bring about the hard results. Even in the evaluation process, we must agree who does the evaluation and who provides the input.

Another important aspect is learning to build trust. This is the other most important and the most difficult part. You have to build trust to operate in a matrix organization. You have to strengthen personal relationships. When you do that, people are more amenable to help you, if you are willing to make certain trade-offs. One way of building trust is to choose which battle to fight. You must be prepared to give up some rights.

Third, we have to make the tough decision about choosing the right person to do the right job. The best person is not necessarily the right person. Apart from capability and potential, the fit for the job is important. You have to see if this particular person is the best fit for this assignment. The team is only strong when you can put together different members to play as a team. We don't need everyone to be a forward in soccer.

I had chosen somebody, a very capable person to do a particular job in the team. He later became the CEO of a listed company. I took him out of a CFO role to a front line market role.

As a result, another capable person was left out of the position he wanted. This person was very disappointed that he did not get the job but was placed in another position. Subsequently, I chose him for another role. He did very well in that job but it took time to build the trust. I must give credit to him as he did not let old wounds fester. He became one of the most trusted members in my team. He is now a CEO in another firm and remains a friend till today.

In building trust, we must try to be as direct as possible. There must be no hidden agenda. I explained to him the reason for my selection and also my sincere hope for him affirming his strengths and potential. He did not like it and for a time, we operated in different groups. Subsequently, he came back to the group. We put the past behind us. He did not hold on to the past but looked forward to the future.

 What is the most crushing adversity you have ever faced in your leadership? How did you deal with it?

 There isn't any crushing adversity because at the end of the day, it's not the end. In 2002, I was appointed leader for Asia Pacific and Japan. There were three geographic leaders around the world: Europe which includes Middle East and Africa, Americas and Asia Pacific and Japan Heads. We were all reporting to the Global Head, who was an English gentleman in America. This gentleman reported to Carly Fiorina.

We had very challenging times in HP. We had to meet investors' expectations. There were a couple of quarters in which we slipped in our earnings. There is a particular third quarter in 2004 that I remember. On August 12, I was in Australia when I received a call. The company had missed the quarter. The call was to inform me that my boss and my two colleagues will be leaving the company. Overnight, I was the only one left on the frontline. I wasn't sure if I would keep my job.

When I told my wife about this, she sent me a passage from the Bible — Psalm 84:5–7.

> *Blessed are those whose strength is in you, whose hearts are set on pilgrimage. As they pass through the Valley of Baca, they make it a place of springs; the autumn rains also cover it with pools. They go from strength to strength, till each appears before God in Zion.*

It gave me deep assurance that my security was in the hand of the Lord. If God wanted me to go, I would go. If not, I will stay.

I felt secure. The next week, I was told by Carly that she had confidence in our team. I was reassured. I was not fired. The HP years were tough years. My best corporate life was when I was in Compaq My colleagues who left the company were capable leaders and did well subsequently. One of them is now the CEO of a European company.

 Q **Would you like to elaborate on that when you said the best years of your corporate life was in Compaq? Why is this so?**

 A This was because I made my faith clearly known to my colleagues and direct reports in Compaq. I was able to practice my Christian faith openly and actively. Many of my colleagues in Compaq were Christians and we encouraged each other in the faith. Even though we have gone our separate ways and are no longer in the same company, we are still very good friends and still keep in touch with one another.

When I first visited India, I told the country managing director and president about my faith. In India, sometimes as part of the custom, they would have religious blessings, like putting a red dot on the forehead. I explained politely to him that I appreciate the blessings and thoughts but would rather not have the red dot placed on my forehead. The leaders there respected that. I had a wonderful time in India over my many visits throughout the years.

When I was in China, as you know, the Chinese have a strong drinking culture when they are entertaining their guests. I had to explain that I could not drink too much. My president was kind enough to take care of it. He only gave me one glass and stopped at one. They nicknamed me *Chen Yi Pei* — The Chan of One Glass. They knew about my faith.

When I left Compaq, the Chinese colleagues were nice to give me a book with photos and other articles. They penned blessings and Bible verses in their compilation. So I felt happy that I had wonderful colleagues.

In spite of all these wonderful things and people, I am sure there must also have been some colleagues who might not like you or the way you handle things. How did you deal with these people?

 I had a very experienced Australian head. He was older than me, a very capable person, much more experienced than I was. He was a tough and seasoned leader who originally came from Scotland. When I was appointed Head of the division in Compaq, he could not understand why I was made Head of the division and not him. In fact, to be honest, I was also surprised that I was appointed to the position. I thought he deserved it more than me. I felt that the job was too big for me. At that time, he lobbied the boss of Compaq about this and for the position. Whatever the reason, the position was thrust upon me.

During my first visit to Australia with my team, I chaired the meeting to review their business in Australia. In the boardroom, the start of the meeting was rather confrontational. He challenged our credentials to review them, since Australia was much larger and they were more experienced than us.

So, I prayed. I did not respond in a hurtful or angry tone. I basically explained to them that we were not there to tell them what to do, but to work together and to sharpen each other to improve our market capabilities for the benefit of our people. Thank God, immediately after that, the whole atmosphere changed and there was a marked change in attitude. He was much more open to talking with us. Over time, we became good friends and had shared a common goal of doing well for our division. When he got married to a lovely lady of Indian descent, I was invited to his wedding.

 What is your greatest weakness?

 There are two things I struggle with. One is to build bridges and not walls. Through my experiences at work, I found that building bridges always works better than tearing down walls. Always build and don't tear down as much as possible. If you have to tear down walls, it is best to know what the walls were built for in the first place. That has helped because with building bridges, we recognize our interdependencies and work towards a shared future. We can't do everything ourselves. We need helpers, people to work with you.

One practical way to build bridges is a willingness to give up your right sometimes. Give in. Not on principles but to commit your resources to help another person or help another organization grow. Be willing to let other people take the credit.

The other thing I believe is that in this industry and environment, things change very quickly. Whatever we know will become obsolete quickly. You need people who are learners. We need to give people the opportunity to learn, to try and to fail. When you pick a leader, the best indicator that leaders can succeed in the future is their ability to learn.

The leader also needs to have integrity. They must be able to bring people along. If you are a leader, you move ahead and look back to find that there is nobody following you, it's useless. You have to bring people along to overcome hurdles and difficulties. The leader will inadvertently fail sometimes. They have to learn. There is no set formula to achieve the goal. You need to adapt and learn what will work in that situation.

Many of the leaders, whom we have groomed and have taken on bigger roles and positions, are great learners. We gave them exposure and opportunities to learn and grow across divisions.

These are the two things I believe in.

For myself, it is not easy to build bridges. It is a real struggle too. I am naturally not the most encouraging person. I tend to criticize and see the negative side, not the positive in others. I really had to struggle: to not tear down but to build up.

We need to give people the chance, to be less judgmental and to be more forgiving. I struggle with this. It took me years to get there. Even at home, with my children. Am I an encourager to them? I have been criticized for not being an encourager.

I remember that I was quite hard on my daughter for something. In a different situation, she showed me how compassionate and kind she was towards someone who failed. By her acceptance, she taught me to realize what an encourager is and how they can affect another person. She taught me humility.

How do you practice being nice and build bridges when you are Head of Sales? There is a perception that to be good in sales, you have to be aggressive and drive numbers.

When you put together the right people, the right resources, the right structure, they will get the results. Building trust is very important. I do have to meet with the big customers. Both being a junior and seller, the element of trust was very important. When we were selling to the Singapore Exchange, I remember having to meet Mr. Hsieh Fu Hua, the CEO at that time. At the end of the day, they bought our products and services based on trust. They chose us because of our commitment. As a representative of HP, my job was to communicate that HP was worthy of their trust.

How do you sustain these values of building bridges, humility, or being more generous in your life? Are there certain routines that you keep to nurture these values?

I read the Bible almost daily. There is no magic to it. Spending regular time with God and the Bible always gives me fresh insights and makes me realize my position. Everything I have belongs to God. We are stewards, we don't bring anything along with us. I try to practice that as well. I learn to give back.

There are many bright people around you. When you honor people, they will inevitably give their best. I am not hungry for power. I did not seek for the promotions that came. Although when we experience and taste it, the privileges and perks that come with it are quite good. But don't get used to it or be a slave to it.

I recall that S. Rajaratnam, the former Foreign Minister of Singapore said, "Never get used to the trappings of the position. When you leave your position, you will not have it." I have to force myself not to get used to it. If we do, we become a slave to it. When I was with Compaq, sometimes,

I used to travel on our corporate jet. They are not yours. Don't get used to the trappings of your position.

 What is one legacy you have left behind in your organization?

 That's a difficult question to answer. Because when I look at the companies now, they have totally changed. Almost all the people I know have moved on. The organization has a life of its own. One thing I know, I am still friends with a lot of people I worked with. In my corporate life, I have made a few precious friends. In our journey, we have been fortunate to make some impact on each other's life. This I know and this I value.

One thing I know. Even now, when I sit on different boards, which I have been given the privilege to do so, I pay attention to the individuals. For those whom I can bring to a new level in their life journey, I would do it as a board member and fellow human being. It's about people at the end of the day!

 What is one advice you would give to emerging leaders?

 Always build bridges, not walls. Always learn and never stop learning. The young have a great capacity to learn, but even people who are old have some capacity to learn. When we can no longer learn, it is sad because we have reached the end of the present road. As long as you are living, you must keep on learning.

> We moved from criticism to
> constructive engagement. When
> we criticize, we must also give
> solutions.

PAUL LOW
The Constructive
Engaging Leader

hen Transparency International-Malaysia (TI-M) President Datuk Paul Low Seng Kuan, 67, was appointed as Minister in the Prime Minister's Department, it came as a shock and surprise to many in Malaysia. He never coveted or dreamed about the job. In his own words, "It came suddenly".

The National Front coalition (the Barisan Nasional or BN) which forms the government and ruled Malaysia for the past five decades — lost its two-third majority in Parliament and the majority in four states in the 12th general election in 2008. In the 13th general election it was unable to regain its parliamentary two-thirds majority in 2013. One of the major issues of concern in these two elections was the perception, particularly by the urban voters, of the high level of corruption under the BN rule.

Immediately after the 13th general election in 2013, he was invited by the Prime Minister to join his cabinet as a federal minister to institute changes in the government to improve governance and integrity.

His sentiments were echoed by Corruption Prevention and Consultative Panel member Datuk Seri Azman Ujang, who opined that Low could help the cabinet in ensuring that its decisions were always above board where projects and procurements are concerned.

"Low himself has been championing the cause of good governance, integrity and transparency in government. And now that he's in the cabinet itself, he has a ringside view of the government and he now can ensure the government walks the talk in tackling graft," he said[1].

Paul Low started his career as an accountant with Imperial Chemical Industries in 1969 until 1973 in Melbourne. On his return to Malaysia he joined Malaysian Sheet Glass Sdn Bhd as an accountant, rising to be its Financial Controller, before he became their Executive Director. He holds a Diploma from the Royal Melbourne Institute of Technology, Australia and is a Chartered Accountant by profession.

---

[1] *Paul's appointment helps combat corruption in Government: Chandra.* Sin Chew Daily, May 16, 2013.

Paul Low was the Federation of Malaysian Manufacturers president for three years since 1996, and was an Enforcement Agency Integrity Commissioner for three years since 2011.

He was involved in the National Economic Action Council in 1998, was a member of the National Economic Consultative Council II in 1999 and a panel member of the Malaysian Economic Research Institute think tank.

He is married to Law Hung Lai and has a son and two grandchildren.

We met up with Paul Low over lunch in Kuala Lumpur as he shares his story of a leader who fought for good governance and transparency but who had to learn first to be a non-fighter.

 Who or what influenced you most in your leadership development? And why?

 There was hardly any individual who influenced the way I lead. But it was experiences in my life that transformed me. I started my career like anybody else — materialistic, performance-driven and self-focused. This is how I was shaped by my worldly thinking as to what constitutes the way to success in the business world. My ambition was to be powerful and to be rich. This was how I was trained.

In the 1970s, I started as an accounts clerk with Imperial Chemical Industries, Melbourne before returning to Malaysia to join Malaysia Sheet Glass, one of the largest companies in Malaysia that was established shortly right after the May 13, 1969 riots. That was the only job I kept for many years, as I was not a 'rolling stone' in my job. Once I was in, I stuck it out in the job. I have a deep sense of loyalty. I developed patience and endurance, and learned not to quit easily. I guess that character development prepared me for my future work.

I rose from the rank and file, from accountant to becoming the chairman of the company in 1994. The company was a joint-venture with the Japanese and my uncle, who was the major minority shareholder. In fact, I was by-passed as CEO several times but by God's grace, I became the chairman in my 40s.

Although I knew God in the early 80s, I was a nominal Christian. The Christian faith did not impact the way I led my life. I was like anybody else, materialistic and ambitious.

I reached the pinnacle when I became the chairman of the company. However, there were some relatives who wanted my chairman post and insisted that I step down. I was asked to vacate that position and I felt unfairly treated.

I began to ask God, "What's happening?" I sought counsel from my pastor and family, and they advised me to step down and not to contest. Remember, I wasn't a quitter and it was very difficult for me. For the first time, I was confronted with a most challenging situation. Either I had to be obedient to God or I had to fight it out. It was during those times that I began to question, "How much importance do I place my faith in God?"

Even my family and my mom advised me to vacate the post for the sake of family peace. Reluctantly, I did but on the condition that I continued to be paid the salary of a Managing Director but without holding any position. Financial security was very important to me. Surprisingly, the board agreed.

Because of that, I had lots of time on my hands. But the first thing that came to my mind was, "If I hold no position, what would people think?" Because my standing in the corporate world was quite high, and if I went from being the chairman to someone without a position, people would think, "Paul must have done something wrong to be removed." That bothered me quite a bit.

I was still serving as a vice-president of a premier and very powerful business association, the Federation of Malaysian Manufacturers (FMM). You see, I had the ambition to be the president of FMM. All my dreams were almost shattered when I was removed as chairman, everything came to zero. At that time, I didn't understand what God was doing.

But it was only on hindsight that I knew it was a process of God humbling me. The top has to go down to the bottom before God pulls you up. That was true of me. It was more easily said than done. I could only say this on hindsight but during that period, it was very difficult.

He had to clean up the ambition in me: the power-crazy, materialistic and self-driven parts. I had reached the pinnacle and now I became a nobody.

The irony was that, despite the fact that I held no position in any company, I still held the post of vice-president of FMM. It was then that I paid attention to God's values and got into studying the Bible.

I began to value dependence on God, humility and servant-hood and not being materialistic. All these began to form my leadership perspective. It was during that time that my values were completely reversed. That was the turning point of my life. I told God, "If this is your plan for me, I am going to leave everything to you now, including my career path." My faith and trust in God began to take root.

The strange thing was that even though I held no position in any company, many business leaders wanted me to be president of FMM. They said, "Even with your position as advisor of your company, we would still want to vote you to be our president." If I were to come in, I would be the first non-Malay to hold this high position, which broke with tradition.

The people wanted to vote for me in 1993/4. Just before the election, one of the four vice-presidents came and asked me, "Can you not stand but please give me the chance to stand." He knew that most of the votes of the Council were coming to me.

My natural reaction was to refuse and keep the position. My initial thought was to go to him and say, "Do you know what I went through in my company when I was asked to vacate the chairmanship, now you want me to stand down again? That would be impossible."

But I didn't go down that route because I had gotten closer to God and learned to trust God for everything. "Why is this man asking me for this?" But God didn't answer me. But I sensed the comfort and peace, telling myself, "If God wanted me to be the president of FMM, He can make it happen." Was it a test? I knew it was to see how much I trusted God.

So, I went to the person and told him I would give up running for presidency and he became the president in 1994 without any contest.

After he became the president, the FMM Council resolved to pass a new provision in its constitution limiting the term of the presidency of FMM to 3 years. The previous presidents served their terms for 18 years and 15 years.

When that president's term expired, the same group came to me and said, "You gave up once but now we want to support you again for the president." In 1996, I was voted in as the president, even though I was not holding an executive position in the company. Not long after, the Asian Financial Crisis hit us.

Within a month, I got a letter from the then Prime Minister of Malaysia, Dr. Mahathir Mohamad, inviting me to do "national service" and be a member of the National Economic Action Council with the main purpose to help Malaysia get out of the financial crisis.

Just think about it carefully. If I had not given up the presidency in the first incident, somebody else would have had the opportunity to serve the nation and not me as my term would have expired then. That was when I became close to many of the Malaysian leaders and many senior civil servants. When I became the president of Transparency International-Malaysia, they knew exactly who I was.

What were the lessons for you?

Don't be ambitious, but go according to God's plan. I could never have seen the financial crisis coming. The company, Malaysian Sheet Glass, that I was relieved from, had to manage the crisis. I was not there to manage the crisis, but was called to do national service and serve with the government. Imagine if I had to deal with the company, I would have been stressed on dealing with the serious problems in the company brought about by the crisis.

As part of the crisis team, my advice to the government was crucial. There was a fierce debate on whether or not to raise the interest rates, and to tighten the availability of credit, because that was what Thailand and Indonesia did in line with proposals by the International Monetary Fund.

I told the Prime Minister then, "This is a financial crisis and not a manufacturing crisis. Manufacturing is not affected, apart from the fact that the currency had gone up. If we looked at all the loans, people who were borrowing foreign loans were the banks. But the local companies and those companies residing in Malaysia were borrowing in local currency.

"When you have a tight credit squeeze, you are actually squeezing the local companies, which are still making money. They are the ones that will save Malaysia as they will export the way out of the crisis. Please reverse the policy of high interest rates and loosen the credit squeeze. The high interest rates may attract short-term capital inflow to come in but would not help the local manufacturers." So we reversed the tight monetary policy and did not raise interest rates or reduce credit facilities to the manufacturers.

Of course, in his wisdom, Dr. Mahathir pegged the Malaysian ringgit to the US dollar. When the government did that, all the Indonesian and Thai orders which could not be fulfilled came to Malaysia. All the expatriates and multinational companies in Thailand, Indonesia, Taiwan and Korea came to us.

We became the main manufacturing hub during and many years after the financial crisis. We were the only ones who had the credit to buy raw material and with the pegged ringgit that provided currency stability, we could buy the material and we could determine the prices. There was stability and order in Malaysia's economy. We exported manufactured goods from Malaysia to many countries. Literally, we exported ourselves out of the crisis!

Without sounding boastful, that was the single most important advice I gave to the government because our decision was based on a survey with statistics to back up our analysis. We found out that the local manufacturers were hardly borrowing in foreign currency especially in US dollars.

Today, the government leaders know me as one of their economic advisors. After that, I was quite comfortable to serve as Economic Advisor to the Government in many government bodies and as president of FMM.

These experiences shaped my values and the way I lead today. From then, I became more confident in God and my belief was strengthened.

What a story of leadership! So, what was the next step for you in leadership?

 I then began to serve God in church. The first job my pastor gave me for two years was to be an usher, shifting and arranging chairs in the church. Mind you, I was somebody in the community. That was a really humbling experience.

At that time, I had already obtained my Datuk-ship awarded by the King for my service during the financial crisis: Imagine a Datuk arranging chairs. But I had no problem. Other people who saw me doing this, felt uncomfortable and had a problem because they could not believe the Datuk was arranging the chairs, wondering if this guy was genuine or just showing off.

I told them that even if you had wanted me to go down on my knees and clean the toilet, I had no problem as well. But I believe it was a test to see if my humility was genuine. Some people say, "I am humble," but if they were asked to wash somebody's feet, would they do it sincerely and whole-heartedly?

Somehow, God gave me the passion for the sick. I asked many questions and attended many conferences and seminars to learn about the sick. It was just a strong passion to help the sick. I could feel a great deal of empathy for people who are sick and God put in my heart a desire to minister to them. I began to learn about diseases, especially psychosomatic diseases and mental illness and tried to uncover the spiritual root causes of these illnesses. Today, I still have all the 260 pages or about 25 chapters of notes on the subject!

God showed me. Now I understand why a person like me doing business had to understand about healing. It was from one end of the spectrum to the other end: from the natural to the spiritual. I began to understand in depth about spiritual truths and how they influence earthly matters. It strengthened my faith and trust in God and anchored my life on His purpose for me.

At one time, I was dealing with 50 to 60 cases a year and helped about 250 people, even people with mental illness. I understand mental illness so well today. Some of the cases I handled were very tough ones.

One of these cases was a 17 year-old boy, who locked himself up in his room for four years. His parents did not see him and whenever he wanted food, the parents would bring food to him from the dining table. He was a schizophrenic. But today, he is back, running his father's business and serving in his church.

I spent the next six years doing healing ministry. I gained deep insights into illnesses, the spiritual world and the healing power of God. I understood diseases quite well and their roots. I could see the spiritual impact of illnesses. I thought my gift was healing and that would be the end of my involvement in the market place. I should leave my job and begin my work in healing.

The financial crisis was over. I had no more companies to run. I thought my work was to be an elder, running the church and doing spiritual work. I was preparing myself to do spiritual battle. I did that for six years and was travelling around the country.

On hindsight, God put me in this work to prepare me for another bigger assignment. I was weak in the spiritual side: the offensive side. People were wondering why I was in business and yet was doing spiritual stuff. I began to realize that there is no dichotomy between the spiritual and natural and began to see things from God's perspective.

 How did you get involved with Transparency International?

 Having said that, that was where corruption came in. We were talking and praying about corruption and corrupt leaders. But nobody wanted to stand up and speak against corruption. They only wanted to pray but did not do anything. Many also felt a sense of hopelessness that nothing could be done to make things better.

That was where Transparency International came in. In 2007, there was a strong disagreement among the office bearers and this caused divisions and infighting, to the extent that there were exchanges of emails being made public. To resolve the impasse, members requested for an EGM (extraordinary general meeting) and the members passed a resolution to remove the executive council (Exco) and to hold a fresh election.

A group of prominent members was looking for someone to take the lead to fight corruption. They wanted me to do it. Frankly, I wasn't keen to fight corruption as it was an impossible job and a dead-end assignment. But people were encouraging me to take up the challenge. I told them, "It is easy for you to say but the moment I take this position, I will be targeted."

I decided to take on the role of Secretary-General at Transparency International for two years, to set up the secretariat which was in disarray. I was an outsider standing against the incumbents but was elected and got a significant majority of the vote. I put my priority in building the institutional capability of TI-M. It was supposed to be two years. Very soon, there was a vacancy for the president's position. I did not want to become the president as he had to be the spokesperson for the organization. Although I wrote most of the press statements, I hardly spoke at all. If I become the president, I would have to be the spokesperson.

The same group came and tried to persuade me to take up the position, telling me that they needed me as I was the only one who could build up the organization. The reputation of TI-M was not good. I told them this was a very big decision and I had to pray hard. I told God, if I can choose, I do not want it. I told Him I had enough already. I really didn't want it. But at the same time, I will not disobey His will.

I read the passage about the story in the Bible about Abraham's servant who was sent to look for a wife for his son, Isaac. The sign was that the first woman in the well who offered him a drink will be the wife for Isaac.

That was the first time I made a covenant with God. I told God if so and so who intended to stand for presidency rang me up to say he was not standing for president and he would support me as president, then I would know precisely that it was His will for me to stand as president. In my heart I thought that this was very unlikely to be fulfilled as that person was very keen to stand for president.

However, two weeks later, that person rang me and said that he would be withdrawing his candidacy and gave me the assurance he would support me. As I knew that this was a serious matter when one made a vow to

God, one had to keep that vow when God had done His part. I chose to obey and stood for election. I served as President for four to five years and during which my priority was to strengthen the organization.

 Tell us more about your work in TI-M.

 In terms of effectiveness, our chapter, TI Malaysia, moved from being the lowest to be one of the top chapters among the 100 chapters in the TI community.

First, I changed the modus operandi. It consisted of NGOs (non-governmental organisations) activists and lawyers. The first thing I did was to stop criticizing the government just for publicity sake. We have to be constructive. We moved from criticism to constructive engagement. I changed from activism to engagement. People thought I had become too cozy with the government. I told them that when we criticize, we must also always give the proposed solution.

 What is constructive engagement?

 The first case we had to deal with was the Port Klang Free Zone case, (PKFZ)[2], a 1,000-acre regional industrial park in Malaysia. It was a RM4.5 billion dollar scandal. Mr. Lee Wah Beng was the chairman and he asked me to help him. I told him, "I just became president for less that one year and you want me to deal with this RM4.5 billion scandal?" Anyway, I got involved in it.

I took the constructive engagement route. They asked me to take on the Chairperson role at PKZ to instill governance inside the organization. I took on the position and brought the whole team inside. There was a group in TI-M that came against me because in their opinion I had compromised the reputation TI.

The then Minister of Transport, Ong Tee Keat told me, "You criticized us, well and good but can you come and help to change things?""

---

[2] PKFZ is a regional industrial park in Malaysia. It offers extensive distribution and manufacturing facilities. It is located along the Straits of Malacca, on Port Klang, Klang, Malaysia.

To such a request, what would one say?

"No, no. My NGO culture would not allow us. We don't engage. We only sit outside and we only criticize and monitor your progress. Everything is up to you and we do not get involved?" That's an activist's point of view.

I looked at it and told myself that we needed 'constructive engagement.' Most activists do not favor such an approach. An activist's approach is to be seen and heard, and to put pressure on the government to act. This may include street advocacy. What I did was not in line with the culture of TI Malaysia at that time. In constructive engagement you criticize but also offer solutions and, if requested, work to implement the solutions in a practical manner on what is doable at a particular time.

To the activists' mindset I was compromising by getting my hands dirty, and if change was not as successful as we had expected, then we would have to deal with the reputational risk.

So, how did you win the Exco over?

I won the Exco over by showing them the kind of work we do. I am very transparent. I had to change the whole organization.

In the past, we depended on volunteers, who were activists. I found that there were some volunteers who were self-serving. When the going got tough, they did not show up. They were armchair critics and would not get involved because it was too much work. That was the other mind-set change we did.

I employed professionals to run the organisation. One of whom was Mark Lovatt. I built up professionalism and brought this cultural change to TI. With greater professionalism, the activist's role grew smaller because the professionals knew more than them. They only knew how to shout but did not know how to implement. I had to shelter them. Professionals would be more impartial in their assessment. Also, funds began to flow in because of our professionalism. People began to see that not only do we talk, but we also deliver.

TI International saw what I did was working and included us as part of the advisory team for equipping other TI Chapters such as Bhutan and Myanmar. It was a recognition of TI Malaysia's capability to contribute to the global movement.

 What keeps you going in TI, despite these many challenges?

 First, it was a call from God. I had to deal with corruption. I had to answer God's call. I am very passionate about fighting corruption as we have to be a voice for civil society.

 What is one most crushing adversity you have ever faced in your leadership? How do you deal with it?

 The most crushing one was after my first year as President in TI, when the PKFZ scandal came in. I thought I was doing the right thing. I came in to participate as Chairman of Governance. A group of highly respected members came against me and accused me of compromise. One of the council members (Mr. X) together with the founder past President held press conferences to criticize me. He said I had brought a bad name to TI and ran it like it was my own company.

Mr. X went on to create great publicity to get himself popular. He was vicious in his attacks and it was relentless. The media loved the excitement of someone trying to bring the President of TI-M down. I came to God and told him that I wanted to throw in the towel as He was not protecting me. I wanted to quit.

I refused to listen to God and blamed Him for allowing such humiliation to be brought upon me. I was so disappointed, but not in an angry way. I just could not understand what was happening. God put me there and I had this guy coming after me. Why was I having all these troubles?

Also I was required to launch the Global Corruption Report published by the TI Secretariat in Berlin. In this report was a section written about the PKFZ fiasco and certain names of the parties involved were mentioned. I was sued for libel after I refused to back down to withdraw the report and to make a public apology to the offending party. A threat was also made to extend the suit to every member of the Exco and this created great uneasiness in the Exco.

Some Exco members blamed me for bringing all these troubles on TI. Mr. X and his group went against me, accused me of getting them into trouble. He went on a relentless public campaign against me. Finally, as I was greatly concerned with the negative publicity that had been created, I made a gentlemen's agreement with him, in the knowledge of other Exco members, that I would take sole responsibility for the article so that the suit would be on me alone. However, Mr. X then told me that I had to resign because I had made a mess of TI, and that he would call off the press conference. I agreed to resign in the presence of the Exco.

I resigned because I was so fed up with the whole thing. It was a thankless job, and my family, especially my wife, was unhappy that all these things had happened to me. I resigned but he did not keep his end of the bargain and did not call off the conference. In that press conference, he kept on slandering me.

Somehow, that council member also sent in his resignation. Two weeks later, a few members and the Exco wrote to me and asked me to stand again. They wanted me to continue to lead the organization, and they would all resign en bloc so as to dissolve the Exco so that an election could be convened. I was really confused. I had just resigned and now I was wanted to stand again.

I went to God again. This time I felt more peace and comfort when I understood that in this way He was getting rid of all the "rubbish" and bringing in a fresh group of people to give me a fresh mandate. So, the extraordinary members' meeting was held and I got re-elected as president, unopposed. And I got a better team. Finally, I understood what it meant by having God to do the battle on my behalf. This was a faith-wrenching experience.

On the defamation suit, I believe God brought Philip Koh, a prominent Christian lawyer, to defend me on a pro bono basis. The suit was struck off at the appeal court.

What lessons did you learn from this crushing incident?

 I learned to trust God more even in the most difficult situations, even in circumstances that are not pleasing to our eyes. He has delivered me every time. When you hit a disappointment, always think of how God has delivered you in the past. God has a way of allowing circumstances to turn to suit His purpose, and often, we can only appreciate His way on hindsight especially when He is bringing us to a higher level of His calling on us.

Secondly, I learned about the heart of people. I tend to trust people too easily without wisdom on the motives of people. This is my weakest point.

 Let's talk about your weakness, Paul. What is one weakness that you have and how do you deal with it?

 I trust people too easily. The ideals of love and compassion can take priority over wisdom. I have to balance them with wisdom. Not everyone appears to be what they are. This is important. I am still learning. People can be very nice to you but they may have evil intentions. I need to know the heart of human beings.

This is my weakness even today. My wife sees too much of the soft part of me and people take advantage of me. I am too forgiving. I forgive but I do not deal with people with wisdom. If you want to be a leader, you want to be inclusive but on the other hand, you have to be firm. That authority is also necessary. People will respect you for that. It is very clear God has the grace but also the truth. He is both love and righteousness. We often easily forget the righteousness and the truth part. We only do the love and grace. Some people get more grace than they deserve.

 What is one legacy you have left behind in your organisation?

 When I was at TI Malaysia I laid the foundation for the establishment of a good team of professionals who are well-trained and competent in fighting corruption. They should reach a level of competency where they are able to help other TI chapters and also be able to generate their own funds to sustain themselves.

Likewise, as the transformation of the government is a journey and may take more than my term in office as a minister, I hope to leave a team of experts in governance in every ministry and agency who will be able to continue with what I started. Hopefully, the portfolio of governance and integrity will be institutionalized in the Prime Minister's office as a permanent function, to continue to enhance the credibility of enforcement institutions and improve processes to provide a higher level of accountability and transparency.

 What is one piece of advice you would give to emerging leaders?

 My advice is that the biggest part of their character should be humility. It goes down to so many things. When you are humble, people will connect with you. People are prepared to work with you in partnership.

Be righteous and have integrity. Relationships are formed by people who trust you. You must also be someone who means what you say. Even when you have to carry out tough decisions, you need to walk the talk. You must be trustworthy. Having no political agenda or ambition does give me an advantage in the nature of job that I am in.

Always bear in mind that you have to serve other people. When you have trust and serve them, people will form a natural affiliation with you.

As a member of the Cabinet of the government, what official power do I have? I am not in an operating ministry with a well-defined official authority. But I have acquired the power to influence. How do you define power? Does that mean direct authority or influence?

In my view, power is influence. You may not be in the line of authority. It is the ability to move people according to what you believe in. It is to convince other people about what you believe. That influence is stronger because it does not come from official authority but from people respecting you and knowing that you are looking after their welfare as much as you are taking care of your welfare.

You are reliable. They know that you are not taking them for a ride. You are sincere and genuine. You help them and you sacrifice for them sometimes at a cost to yourself. That's the power of leadership. You create win-win outcomes without compromising on the principles of integrity. More importantly, they know that I am helping the government to create a better future.

 How do you cultivate humility?

 Just know that God hates pride. When you are proud, you are on the opposite side of God. I believe that very strongly. When you are proud, God will not hesitate to teach you. Of course, He will give you several warnings before the big correction comes. I believe God will put down pride for a good purpose. If you are proud about yourself, you cannot be trusted with greater authority and power. God cannot advance you further as you are likely to abuse your position. If you are a leader, pride is one thing that God has to get rid of.

Please bear in mind that even today for myself, I realize how pride can creep in. That's why I keep saying to you, "I am not boasting." Consciously, when I say I did this and did that, I do not want to be misunderstood. It is always with the help of God.

I am fully aware that pride can easily set in. As much as I am the Minister here, pride can easily set in. This is very subtle. By your behavior, people can see it.

Let me share with you an instance. Last week, my pastor had trouble using the LCD screen as the connection was disconnected. I was the nearest to him. Before I helped him, I said in jest to the congregation, "Here's the Federal Minister fixing the computer for the pastor." What do you think of that statement as someone in the pew? After that, my wife confronted me, "Why didn't you just fix the connection? Why did you need to say, 'Here's the Federal Minister fixing the computer.'" She said, "When I heard you, my eyes rolled. Other members' eyes also rolled."

This was a very simple, innocent act. Because of what I said, it showed that I was somebody higher up fixing a computer. To be frank, it put me out. I thought it was a joke but people thought I was boasting. Last time, when I was the CEO arranging the chairs, I didn't say anything.

Now I must tell people that I am a Minister doing this. Pride is very subtle. It took my wife to confront me.

I am not aware and I need someone like my wife to correct me. When I give press conferences, it is very easy for me to run people down. For leadership, when pride goes in, the other things become unimportant. This is the single most dangerous thing for people in position. It is like a fly falling into perfume. It makes all the good things you have done smell bad!

> **If you punch one hole, and another punches a second hole, we will sink together. Let's behave like a family.**

ROLAND WONG
The Collaborative Leader

ato' Roland Wong is a retired Malaysian businessman and former Managing Director of Wong Heng Engineering Sdn. Bhd. and Warga Hikmat Kejurutaan, which was involved in providing engineering support to the oil, gas and petrochemical industry. Started by his father, Wong Heng had the reputation of being one of the most reliable and reputable contractors in Malaysia at that time. Their clients included Petronas National Oil Company, Shell and Esso.

In 1976, Dato' Roland Wong founded and was the first President of the Negri Sembilan Foundry and Engineering Industries Association (NSFEIA), a position he held until 1993. From 1985 to 1993, he was the President of the Federation of Malaysia Foundry and Engineering Industries Association (FOMFEIA).

He was also a prominent and influential figure in the sporting arena of Malaysia, where badminton is the No.1 sport. From 1985 to 2009 he was the President of the Negri Sembilan Badminton Association (NSBA). He was also the Deputy President of the Badminton Association of Malaysia (BAM) from 1993–2009. He was the co-chairman of the organizing committee for the Thomas Cup final in 1992, when Malaysia won the cup after 25 years. Perhaps one of his most memorable experiences was being the manager for the Malaysian badminton team at the 1996 Olympics in Atlanta, where Malaysia won its first-ever Olympics silver medal by finishing second in the men's doubles.

He is one leader who was able to work with leaders of diverse cultures, backgrounds and races and yet harnessing them to focus on delivering results together.

He always believes in team work either in business or in other social organizations. We met Dato' Wong in a restaurant in Kuala Lumpur, and he chatted openly about his story.

 Who or what influenced you most in your leadership development? And why?

 One of the people who has influenced me is Mr. Lim Bian San of Shell. He was then Engineering Manager in Shell (Pulau Bukom, singapore) in the 1980s. In the 70s, he was the chief engineering and operations manager of the Shell refinery in Port Dickson, Malaysia. He was a strict person, diligent, straight and efficient. He was an example of commitment to work and attention to detail. He was a man of great integrity.

I drew inspiration from his qualities, most of which have become the values of my company: Integrity, Commitment, Diligence and Focus.

Bian San was the one who got me involved in badminton. He had a strong passion and love for playing badminton. Being the Engineering Manager of Shell in Port Dickson, a town in the state of Negri Sembilan, Malaysia, at that time, he was very involved in the Negri Sembilan Badminton Association (NSBA) as Shell Badminton Club was a member of the association.

Knowing that there was a lot of infighting within the NSBA, he persuaded me to run for one of the six vice president positions. Reluctantly, I agreed and became the Vice President of the Association.

I am a quiet worker. I do not like glamor. Whatever I did, I did it for the greater good of the Association. I worked hard at building relationships with my council members and was able to galvanize the leaders to work together as team. I led the way to enable the change of the constitution, to have only one deputy president instead of the usual six vice presidents. I was then nominated to that post and became the first Deputy President and subsequently became President from 1985 to 2009.

 Knowing that badminton is the most prestigious sport in Malaysia, how did you win the trust of the State Presidents'[1] of the Badminton Association of Malaysia to become their Vice President for 16 years?

 I believe in collective leadership. I am a team player. Even when I was the President of my state's badminton association, I personally was never drawn to an autocratic type of leadership; I had no desire to control everything. Instead, I preferred a team model. I consciously made the effort to distribute the work fairly among the council members.

---

[1] To become the Deputy President of BAM, one would require majority votes from all the State BAM Presidents. Dato' Roland had a unanimous vote.

It was the same in BAM. When I was the Deputy President and Chairman of the organizing committee of the Open Championships, I got different people involved. My committee included one person from each of the different government departments, such as the police force, the home affairs department, the tourism board and the immigration department.

Their appointments helped a lot. Whenever we had problems, the relevant department would help us to solve them promptly and swiftly (issues ranging from visa, traffic and crowd control). The organization of the Open Championships was a testament to the great teamwork, as it was one of the most well-organized and successful events to be held.

I allow people to go against my proposals. I don't insist on their following my way. I am prepared to follow the majority. But they must convince the rest that their ideas are better. Although at times I may feel hurt, I still go along and support their decision.

During the Olympics in Atlanta in 1996, the BAM faced challenges with the Sidek brothers. I sat them down together and spoke with them. I pleaded with them, "Please help me to help you. If you punch one hole in the boat, another punches a second hole, we will sink together. So, let's behave like a family."

As you know, managing the pride of these superstars can be very challenging and difficult. It brought me a great sense of satisfaction to overcome these challenges and get the Sidek brothers to work together for the sake of themselves and for our nation. I helped them see the bigger picture. If they bring glory to the country, they bring glory to themselves. They have to put their country first, not themselves.

They were convinced and we became the best of friends. When we stayed in the Olympics Village, I would organize the team and take them out for Malaysian meals which contributed greatly to building team spirit.

Another of my hallmark values is integrity. I am very strict and would not stand for corruption. It is my nature. I consistently remind my people, "We are in the same boat. If we have holes, we will sink." It's probably this aspect that enables leaders to trust me.

What is one memorable, life-changing experience that has impacted and shaped the way you lead?

 I was a rascal. I was proud, status-conscious and bad tempered. I also loved the pleasures of the world and night life, even at the expense of my family. I was a businessman who kept mistresses. During the 1970s, there was the oil crisis. I managed to get through unscathed. During the mid-80s, there was the recession. Again, I managed to get through it. I had a crisis with my brothers and got through it. I thought I was god.

But in 1997, during the Asian financial tsunami, when the US exchange rate fell from RM2.5 to RM4.8 to US$1, it was a disaster. I was the main sub-contractor for Petronas, the largest oil company in Malaysia. I had employed sub-contractors from China and paid them in Malaysian dollars as per our contract. However, due to the crisis, they insisted I had to pay them in US dollars. They even stopped work.

It was the same with my big contract with Shell. I had a few hundred Chinese working for me as a sub-contractor. I owed many individuals as well as HSBC Bank a lot of money, which amounted to millions of dollars. I could not pay suppliers. It reached a point where I was threatened and intimidated. I am thankful the bank never pulled out. I ensured I was honest and open with them.

I could not sleep. My company was on the verge of collapsing. This was an extremely emotionally draining experience. I felt trapped and had no way out. There was no light at the end of the tunnel. And if there was a light, the light was like an oncoming train. It got worse every day.

On the 15th day, being a non-religious person, I began to pray to Buddha. But it didn't work. My wife Amy asked me to give the Christian God a try. One of my auditor friends told Amy to bring me to church. But I was stubborn as I was quite anti-Christian then.

On January 11, 1998, a friend of mine arranged for Amy and I to meet with Dato' Yap and his wife, who shared his testimony. We had never met before. At the end, he asked, "Why don't you give my God a try? You have nothing to lose." They prayed for me.

The following Sunday, I felt the urge to go to church. Dato' Yap and his wife waited for me at the entrance and welcomed me. When they started singing, "God will make a way, where there seems to be no way." I suddenly started crying. You must know, as a proud 'Chinaman', we never cry. We have a Chinese proverb, "We can shed blood but never our tears" (流血不流泪).

I was weeping like a baby. I could not stop crying. Suddenly, I felt a deep peace inside me, which I could not explain. Although the problems were still there, this peace brought me a deep sense of comfort. The same year, I accepted Jesus Christ into my life.

That was the most memorable experience in my life.

 How did you come out of this devastating crisis?

 The problems I had never went away. Allow me to elaborate.

Before the crisis in 1997, my company, Wong Heng and Warga Hikmat was doing so well that we were planning to go for public listing. However, as well as things were going, changes that occurred in the political and economic sphere brought things to a screeching halt. The IPO did not go through. I was stuck with the whole deal. My company was solid. I was looking for a buyer but I couldn't sell. Prices on the second board had dropped drastically. If my firm got listed, I would have been a bankrupt.

What kept me going? God. After the conversion, I had peace. My mind was clearer. Before that, every morning, I refused to go to work because my debtors were hounding me.

But now, I was willing to meet up with them. I explained to each one of them my financial difficulty and challenges. I promised them that I did not want them to take a 'hair cut' (cut my losses and pay them what is left) and short-change them. I paid them slowly. I started to depend on God. At every meeting, I would spend two to three minutes praying. The suppliers trusted me and allowed me time to repay them. I eventually settled all my debts completely.

I am deeply grateful to my wife, Amy, who stood by me throughout this crisis. She went through it with me, through thick and thin. I would not have survived without her. My wife and daughter saw me through this crisis. Amy and I prayed together often which constantly kept me at peace and brought clarity to my thinking.

Finally, a white knight came to our rescue and bought over the majority share of the company while appointing me to stay on as the Managing Director.

Truly, God has seen me through this crisis. We experienced His grace and provision every step of the way.

What is one legacy you have left behind in your organization?

I always tell my people:

Safety

Quality

Efficiency

Schedule.

These are cornerstones of the project and construction industry. Many of my ex-employees continue to follow these simple but important principles in their work.

What is the biggest lesson you have learned from this crisis?

We should live a decent and contented life. I used to be envious of others. I was status-conscious. I liked to compare myself with other rich tycoons and wanted to be like them.

Now I learn to be contented with whatever I have. Don't be envious of others. I don't feel discouraged and jealous. Finally, when we learn to be contented, we will have peace. Or else, we are striving all the time, as we are never satisfied.

What is one advice you would give to emerging leaders?

I would say, four Ds: Desire, Determination, Dedication and Discipline. If you want to be a champion in anything you do, you must have these four Ds. This is how I saw champions being nurtured in badminton. Today, young people are always of thinking of money. When they have it, they would spend it. Or sometimes, they spend it before they have it.

Desire: You must have the passion and interest in whatever you do.

Determination: You must have a sharp and piercing focus in whatever you do, coupled with the urge and gumption to achieve it.

Dedication: You must work hard to fulfill your dream.

Discipline: Nothing is accomplished without discipline. Discipline also means you must have integrity. Be disciplined enough not to succumb to temptation. Simply put, there is no short cut to success.

Roland, you are now retired. I understand that you are helping to run a shelter for Myanmar women and children with HIV. Tell us about it.

I came to know of the organization HIVHOPE (a Christian organization committed to reaching out to those living with HIV/AIDS). It is a home which was initially run by Pastor Andrew Kulasingham. Due to his migration to New Zealand, it was almost shut down.

Rev. Bruce Sonnenberg, of He Intends Victory, USA, met with me numerous times when he was in Malaysia, and persuaded me to continue with the running of the home.

"Why don't you get it started?" Bruce shared. At that time, I was very fearful of the mere mention of the word, HIV. I wasn't sure of restarting the home.

However, I finally decided to get into it. I formed a working committee with a group of Christian brothers. We put up money ourselves to help restart it. When we restarted the home in 2008 with the help of an American couple from He Intends Victory, USA, we kept it to just women and children infected and affected by HIV/AIDS. We named the home Life Shelter.

In the beginning, there was no residence. We rented three homes side by side in Bukit Beruntung. We started to admit the homeless women and children infected and affected by HIV/AIDS. Majority of them were refugees from Myanmar.

God then provided the finance for the three homes. Allow me to share this story. There were three children, who finally immigrated to USA. Before they left, we gave them some ang pows (red packets of money). One of the children, Ruth, asked, "Uncle Roland, can I say something? I want to thank you very much. Thanks to the home and you, I can speak English. Now I am going to America."

My reply was, "Don't thank me. I couldn't have done it myself. It was the collective effort of the committee. But most importantly, thank God." What keeps me going in this work is the love of God. God has been so merciful to me. I could have been a bankrupt. I am always grateful to God.

> As a banker, there is only
> one most important value:
> INTEGRITY. Especially when
> we work in the financial sector
> where TRUST is the biggest
> asset and reputation.

ROOSNIATI SALIHIN
The Trusted and Truth-Telling Leader

Ms. Roosniati Salihin, or Ibu Ros as she is most affectionately known, is one of the most outstanding women bankers in Indonesia, who has not only survived but has also thrived while working in a family-owned business for the last 42 years. The Bank she works for has since become one of the major publicly listed banks in Indonesia.

She is one of the most well-respected corporate leaders in Indonesia, known for her uncompromising integrity, strong values, and industry competence.

She started her career as a banker in Panin Bank (Pan Indonesia Bank), a merger of three private banks (Bank Kemakmuran, Bank Dagang Indonesia, and Bank Industri Jaya Indonesia) in 1971. The Bank was majority owned by the Gunawan family and Mr. Mochtar Riady, who first employed her as his personal assistant. Even though at that time she was approached by a couple of other established foreign banks, she has stayed on with the Bank. Presently, the Bank has assets of more than US$16 billion and is one of the top 10 Indonesian banks.

After completing her studies at UCLA (USA) and Sophia University (Japan), she returned to Indonesia and planned to start her career with a foreign bank.

She was approached by Mr. Mochtar Riady, who was then the CEO of Panin Bank, and she believed she was initially hired because of her ability to speak Mandarin and English.

Even though she was offered positions in two other American corporations, her then immediate boss encouraged her to stay and work for a national bank and help build up the capacity of the local banking industry. Her immediate boss, Mr. Prijatma Atmadja, assured her that the Bank will grow and become one of the biggest banks in Indonesia. He promised her that she will be sent for training in global finance so that she could learn more about international banking practices. She has had many opportunities to learn and be trained at multi-national banks ever since.

With that assurance, she decided to stay with the Bank, and went through four major crises and currency devaluations in Indonesia while working her way up in the Bank. From then on, Panin managed to deliver good financial results and continued to grow from strength to strength. She has been their Deputy CEO since 1980.

As a competent professional, her value is not only appreciated by the founders of the Bank but also by the community of bankers in Indonesia. She is well-connected with people of all walks of life, particularly in the banking industry.

In her responsibility as Deputy CEO, she sometimes has to challenge or confront her bosses or colleagues, if she feels that a decision made was not for the best interest of the Bank. She is always ready to contribute her thoughts to find workable solutions to solve problems. She is also passionately loyal without compromising on her integrity.

She has developed a good rapport with her bosses and has earned their respect. In turn, she also encourages her subordinates to challenge her if they question her decisions. She learned from her mentor-boss Mr. Mumin, who told her that, "If all you want is a yes-man, get an OB (office boy) who never questions your order."

So, how does she flourish as a woman corporate leader in a male-dominated business? We caught up with Ibu Ros over lunch in Singapore.

 Who or what influenced you most in your leadership development? And why?

 Other than my parents, there have been many people who have influenced me at different stages in my life. Different people have influenced me in different aspects of my life. I also look up to some successful leaders as my role models.

My first mentor was Pak Mochtar Riady, who hired me and taught me how to interact with his network and clients. I learned how to make call reports, write business letters and to differentiate between Indonesian and Western strategies when making business proposals.

I was fortunate to be hired and to learn banking from Pak Mochtar Riady. He is a master strategist. He is known as the Father of private national banks in Indonesia. He was involved in founding and developing at least four major banks in Indonesia: Bank Buana, Bank Panin, Bank Central Asia and Bank Lippo. I learned from the best, and he was generous in sharing his vision and his banking knowledge. I owe him my banking career.

My second direct boss was the late Pak Prijatma Atmadja, who was then the International Director of Panin Bank. As soon as the Bank obtained the Foreign Exchange License in 1972, I worked for him in the International Division of the Bank. I learned a lot from him and I started from the bottom. We set up a treasury desk, remittance, import and export departments etc. I learned first-hand to be a foreign exchange dealer and all the international banking products on the job.

He taught me how to do marketing, to write and respond to business letters and proposals systematically, and to deal with domestic and international bankers and clients.

Even though I am an English literature major, making business proposals requires using appropriate banking terms, aside from understanding the products and the clients' needs.

At some points of my career with Panin Bank, I reported directly to the Bank's founders, Pak Mumin and his brother, Pak Gunadi Gunawan. They have also taught me business acumen, to appreciate and understand the clients' needs, and how to differentiate businesses as our clients come from all kind of industries.

The Gunawan family is innovative and forward-looking in their strategy and business dealings. I have been dealing with them as a professional but having worked for the Bank more than four decades, I am now considered as one of their trusted executives.

They have empowered me to represent the Bank in marketing, and in attending various business functions and seminars. I also have the privilege of meeting and learning from the Bank's important network as well as its foreign business partners. I was entrusted to represent the Bank in various joint ventures' supervisory boards.

To have a successful career, one must be willing to invest time, effort and passion to keep on learning. I have been spending a lot of time attending countless business forums and seminars. I am always an eager learner, as there is so much knowledge we have yet to discover.

The Bank has had various joint ventures with international banks. I have had opportunities to learn and be involved in the managements of the affiliated companies. The Bank's joint ventures include ventures with Credit Lyonnais, the Dai-Ichi Kangyo Bank (Mizuho), Westpac Bank and ANZ Bank. Those assignments are also part of the reasons I am still motivated to keep my banking career.

The recent assignment that I cherish is heading the Bank's new venture in developing its Islamic banking. Panin Bank Syariah was established in 2009, and it was successfully listed on the Indonesia Stock Exchange in January 2014. It now has a strategic partner, the Dubai Islamic Bank from the Middle East. Islamic banking in Indonesia has indeed a great potential to grow significantly, as Indonesia has a population of 250 million — the majority of whom are Muslims. Currently, the Islamic banking assets are less than 5% of the total conventional banking assets.

 Share with us your leadership perspective in banking and working with a family business?

 I think working for a family business usually creates a myth in the marketplace that the owners or the bosses are always right. Most professionals do not want to challenge the boss if he happens to be the owner of the business.

However, from my own experience working for a bank in which the founding shareholders are family, I believe that many bosses appreciate and see value in advice and input from their professional management. They do expect the management team to perform above and beyond their abilities as professionals. The shareholders should set the vision, direction and strategy, then engage management to achieve the goals. The interaction between the shareholders, who are imparting their vision and wisdom, and the management, who is implementing the business plans objectively, will deliver a positive synergy and good performance.

In my position as a senior executive, I mentor my colleagues and subordinates to uphold our professional principles. We have to prove that we are competent professionally. A good banker must be able to understand and help our clients to succeed in their business models. It is our duty to invest time and effort, to network with clients as well as other related parties so we can deepen our knowledge and master new skills to render our utmost services.

Bankers are also financial advisors to their clients and communities. We need to understand current market dynamics to keep up with important domestic and international market issues. To succeed professionally, we have to be more prepared and arm ourselves with information, data base, skills and self-taught knowledge which can readily be shared. All these will accelerate our standing with our stakeholders. Positive market feedback and our strong track record will eventually support our professional career in the marketplace.

I believe in leading by example. I ensure that my subordinates are keeping up with me as an A Team. No matter who you work for, everyone in my team has to establish their own professional identity in the marketplace. The idea of employment security in a family-owned business based on loyalty alone is an old legacy.

Technology has been transforming and reshaping our work place. We have to always be responsive to career developments and mastery of new skills to excel in our jobs. Consider this as managing our professional reputation. We should choose to work for companies that will continue to create and innovate, making our lives more meaningful to us and to the communities around us.

 What are some key values in your work as a banker?

 Over the years, I have developed a set of values. As a banker, there is only one most important value: INTEGRITY. Especially when we work in the financial sector where TRUST is the biggest asset and reputation.

I always remind my staff that there is no substitute when it comes to integrity. As a banker, that's the only requirement that will allow your career to succeed professionally. Banking knowledge, like any other business knowledge, can be taught and learned but integrity can only be earned with time and effort.

It is indeed devastating to witness some senior bankers who have been tempted and failed to honor their integrity. I remember my late boss Pak

Prijatna used to remind me that "Every morning when you wake up, you should be able to look into the mirror and feel good about yourself that you have kept your integrity intact". Once we fail, our banking career is finished.

There have been some occasions when clients have sent gifts to our staff, whom as I expected, reported to me promptly. My advice and action was to return the gift with an official letter, thanking the client for the appreciation and informing them that we have a strict policy of not receiving any form of gifts. Any good services rendered are indeed part of our professional duties.

Such letters would be formally signed by me and the staff who received the gift. This is to acknowledge the appreciation without offending the client. At the same time, I coach our staff on how to manage the client's expectation appropriately.

I am blessed that despite the four decades of a challenging career as a banker, I have been able to keep my conscience clear. Obviously, there are temptations and challenges, but with a lot of faith and prayer, I have managed and will continue to maintain the trust that the shareholders have awarded to me.

In a position of power, sometimes it is tempting to make use of or abuse our authority. Four decades is a long journey in my life, and I pray that I will not disappoint the shareholders and my subordinates. I will not waver in pursuing my belief and keeping my core values.

I have had several of my subordinates who were high achievers, and they have become very successful that some of them now have their own businesses. Their success stories mean so much to me. It gives me great satisfaction if they are able to be much more successful than me.

My passion is to help my colleagues and subordinates to prosper. One of the highest achievements in my career is my former staff, who became one of the younger generation of tycoons in Indonesia. He always shows his appreciation and tells people that "If it were not for Ibu Ros who gave me the opportunity to start establishing my own business, I would not have succeed and I would not be who I am today."

Being human, regardless of my values, at the end of the day, I need to look up to the Lord and ask Him to show me His guidance, wisdom and grace as I do not know any other way.

 Can you share any experiences where you had a major disagreement with your boss? And how did you deal with that?

 In the earlier time of my career with the Bank, the founders were still involved mostly in the strategic direction of the Bank. They set up the vision and mission of the Bank and appointed the management for the day-to-day operations. The Gunawan family has been engaging shareholders who are always ready to give business guidance to the management. In my experience, a family business will thrive if the shareholders understand clearly the business model they are engaged in. In the case of our boss Pak Mumin, he is an engaging boss who is innovative and has a strong entrepreneurial background.

Fortunately, he always encourages the management team to speak up and to give our input before he makes any important decisions. His interaction with management allows him to evaluate issues objectively. I think this is his strength, and also the reason Panin Bank has been steadily growing for the past decades and even survived the worst of Indonesia's economy in 1999. Panin Bank was the only one among the top-10 banks which did not require the government assistance in recapitalization programs, thanks to its strong capital adequacy and liquidity ratios.

There had been many discussions, arguments and disagreements with the shareholders along the line of my responsibilities as one of the Board members. If there is a disagreement, I will be prepared to give an explanation. I would be ready with all the data for discussion — market information, risk evaluations etc. I will also give alternative options if there are any. The key is that you need to be well prepared if you disagree with the boss. The boss will always argue but if we prepare all the points professionally, so far the conclusion has been that eventually, the decision made is for the best interests of the Bank.

Because of the commitment that the Gunawan family has to the Bank as its founders up to now the family has managed to be the only original founders who are still major shareholders of the Bank, whereas the other top nine banks prior to the 1998 financial crisis have all changed ownership.

Having differences with others is also a learning process for me. At the Bank, we currently have more than 30,000 employees. The learning process is on-going and we complement each other in managing our differences. We have an Indonesian saying, "Teeth sometimes bite the tongue even though they are supposed to function together."

 As a woman leader in a pre-dominantly male-dominated industry and Muslim nation, how do you deal with this issue of woman leadership?

 I think I am fortunate to start my career in a private sector enterprise, as we understand that in Indonesia, the government enterprises are mostly male-dominated, while in general, the private sector has always been more performance-oriented. Up until recently, the gender issue was more due to a cultural reason, as males have always been seen as the breadwinner of the family while females are homemakers.

It has been a norm that in most companies, male employees are generally preferred to female employees, as men being breadwinners are considered to be more committed in their jobs. In my case, I studied overseas in the USA and Japan, therefore, I am more outspoken, confident and independent. I also was brought up by my parents who believe in giving the same opportunity of education to their sons as well as daughters.

If not for the overseas education, I might have fallen into the same cultural trap. Moreover, I was fortunate to have very supportive bosses all along. When I started working, I did not see it as an issue, therefore, I have never felt threatened in a male-dominated work place. For the past two decades, I have been the only female member of the Board for the Bank and its subsidiaries.

In Indonesia, it has not been easy to break the glass ceiling. Aside from cultural and education issues, there is resistance from the female workers to climb up the corporate ladder beyond a certain managerial level. The reasons given are, among others, some want to get married after reaching a certain age, some who are married do not want to have higher positions than their husbands, others have to look after their children, etc., which undeniably still revolve around female dependency in our society.

As Indonesia's economy is growing and we are better educated compared to four decades ago, I am pleased to see that women, who comprise 50% of the workforce, have succeeded in playing important roles in the government and in the society. We are having more impressive women leaders who become our good role models.

In the financial sector, we are seeing more women in the workforce from junior to senior management roles. At Panin Group, we promote female staff and managers based on their own merit. I hope that I have made some impact on many of my fellow women staff and colleagues, as I believe regardless of the gender, women can be as successful. The survey of women leaders by McKinsey stipulated that top corporations in the world which have two or more women on their Boards have better corporate governance and deliver excellent financial results. Women by nature are more loyal, focused and able to multi-task in the managing of their responsibilities. I may be biased but it's a fact.

 Maybe they are threatened by you?

 I have been working with male colleagues for decades. My subordinates are mostly men and I think they should not feel threatened. I like to think that I have always been fair and have given the same opportunities to both genders. In Indonesia, the workforce consists of both men and women. If women do not play active roles in the economy, we will be wasting half of the nation's income.

In my corporate role, I try to get to know every member of my team. We work and interact like a big family. I make it a point to get to know everyone's spouse, so as to better understand them. I am fortunate to have mostly long serving executives in my team, despite the very competitive market to get good banking professionals. I guess trust and loyalty go hand in hand, but most importantly, I believe that our success is contributed by great team work.

 Share with us, Ibu Ros, after being in the bank for so many years, what's your next phase? What's the future?

 Life is a journey, during which we meet various people. Some have more impact than others but we keep learning every day from people and circumstances. After four decades of my career, five years ago, I realized that

I have been working for success and power. I thought those are all I need to achieve. I am glad I have been able to use the gifts and skills to help many others to prosper. I thought that was enough.

Going forward, I want to do what I love not because I have to. I want to contribute to the communities and do work which will energize me and give my life meaning. I have decided to chair a foundation promoting education for underprivileged children in Yogyakarta.

For the past five years, I have been the Chairperson of the Titian Foundation, which has a holistic approach in helping underprivileged children. For many years prior to that, I have already been involved in several social activities, donating and helping friends with their causes. I used to think that a philanthropist is someone who donates money, but now I understand that being a philanthropist is not only about donating money to the needy but also about getting involved with the people we are helping, understanding their needs, working and helping them to have a better future.

Titian, which means "a small bridge", provides education to more than 600 underprivileged children. We have a wholesome approach in educating the children, improving the teachers' quality, providing life skills to the community and extending microfinancing to the parents of the children to help them improve their living condition.

We motivate them to produce arts and crafts, which they are very good at. We mentor them to produce better products, which can be marketed in the city, as well as by setting up a gallery to display their products.

I look forward to building more small bridges for the less fortunate people in remote villages. We believe in the power of education, as it is the only option to empower these children to get out of their poverty cycle and have a better future. As we all know, it is indeed more blessed to give than to receive. Success means we are in a position to share what we have. That includes knowledge as well as other material possessions.

What is the most crushing adversity you have ever faced in your leadership? How did you deal with it?

 Throughout my banking career, Indonesia has gone through four major devaluations in the four decades. The worst crisis was the 1998/99 one, a multi-dimensional crisis from the social, economic and political aspects. The whole country was at a standstill, surrounded with much uncertainty. That was when one would wonder what the meaning of life is.

I was frightened, as suddenly my Chinese race was a liability. Many Chinese Indonesians left the country. I took refuge in Singapore and came back still uncertain of my future at that time. That was the time when I learned to depend more on God's provision. My faith has deepened since then.

During the crisis which lasted about two years, the Bank's Board of Directors and commissioners held meetings with every level of the management teams and branch managers across the country on a daily basis to update them on the situation. We made sure that everyone was well-informed. We had open communications with the authorities and we maintained our close relationship with the clients. My main responsibility at that time was to supervise the assets and liabilities management of the Bank.

I thank God that almost all directors of the Bank had many years of banking experiences, and we managed to steer the Bank out of the crisis. Panin Bank was one of the only few banks which did not require the government's recapitalization program. The rest was history.

The two most important lessons I learned during the crisis were:

Firstly, banks must have a strong capital base, both in paid-up capital and in its Capital Adequacy Ratio. Secondly, banks must manage their liquidity ratios. Therefore, implementation of good corporate governance and risk management are mandatory requirements by all central banks, and it is regulated based on international standards, particularly in Indonesia, where capital and money markets are still in the developing stages.

What is one advice you would give to emerging leaders?

Never stop learning. Success is earned over the years and is never instant. We can learn from every situation by evaluating it and drawing a conclusion which will add value to our future decision-making. I have read the best selling book *What They Don't Teach You at Harvard Business School*, which is really interesting.

Education is like a white canvas, our experience will be the painting on it. What I learned during my education in America and Japan is valuable and has given me a strong educational background. But in building a career, I need to slowly gain practical knowledge from my daily activities to excel. One advice on how to be a good banker is to uphold one's integrity, and to have the humility to learn all the time.

What is one weakness that you have and how do you deal with it?

My weakness is perhaps that I am too emotional. When my mind is set on learning about something, I am focused and I am passionate to do the best I can. On the positive side, I am a hardworking person, but I also expect others, including my subordinates, to share the same values, which may also be my weakness. I am trying to be wiser and to not expect too much from others, as they have the right to have their own opinions.

As I grow older, I have learned to be more patient, and I realize that life is indeed a short journey. Every day is God's precious gift, and I want to stop and smell the roses from time to time to make every day more meaningful.

We need to laugh and pray more, but most importantly at the end of the day, we ought to always count God's abundant blessings.

> If children are important to you, be prepared to put them first and sacrifice career advancement for them.... In order to lead, I must have a very clear vision and mission. I must also share them to get ownership from the key leaders.

SANDRA LEE
The Ipoh Housewife
to Global CEO Leader

n 2009, Ipoh housewife Sandra Lee was catapulted into the global spotlight when her favourite body and home products brand Crabtree & Evelyn filed for bankruptcy protection in the United States.

She was appointed as Crabtree & Evelyn's Global Chief Executive, with the aim of rescuing the famous brand and turning around the business — 27 years after she had left the corporate world.

After obtaining her degree in business administration majoring in marketing from The American University in Washington DC, Singapore-born Sandra worked as a brand manager for several fashion labels and cosmetics companies before moving to Ipoh and becoming a full-time housewife.

Her husband is none other than Lee Oi Hian, CEO of Malaysian palm oil giant Kuala Lumpur Kepong Berhad, the company that had bought over Crabtree & Evelyn.

Despite her long hiatus from the corporate world, Sandra had lost none of her business mettle. Within a year, the company became profitable again. Three years later, it was sold to Hong Kong-based Khuan Choo International for a handsome profit of US$41 million.

The secret of Sandra's success: her experience in managing Daybreak, a vocational training centre she founded in 1992 for the physically disabled in Ipoh.

We get her insights on leadership, motherhood and faith in an interview with the outspoken mother of four at her home in Singapore.

 Who or what influenced you most in your leadership development? And why?

 It was more an experience rather than a particular person. 17 years of running a vocational training centre for the disabled and managing a group of volunteers instilled in me leadership skills that would come in handy later at Crabtree.

It was the most challenging time for me, as I had to start the NGO from scratch. I started it with the church to do social work. We had no model to follow. I had to lead a team of strong-minded people, and had to lead with vision, clear goals and integrity.

I faced a barrage of objections from concerned critics who thought their efforts were a waste of time, church money, and manpower. Some of my critics pointed out that this had never been done before. Was I for real? Was I there just to kill time as a housewife?

It was no easy feat, balancing between pleasing all the stakeholders, and making the right judgment call. Though I believe in consultative leadership, I knew that as the leader, I had to share my vision with my members and hope that they buy into it. Through day-to-day interactions with my team members, my leadership skills were honed. It was a steep learning curve, full of tears and sweat.

What were the challenges involved in starting Daybreak?

First, it took a lot of money and resources. It was very challenging, not like buying and selling clothes.

Second, I had to hire the right person for the role. Instead of saying "I'm not the right person for the job", people have a tendency to say "This organization is bad". A lot of it was about getting the right staff, learning how to identify strength and talent. I later applied that to Crabtree & Evelyn. If the person is not the right person, don't hang on to him or her; learn to cut your losses.

Third, I had to set up the operational system and train people. A meeting in 1996 with Mr. Robert Styling of The Phoenix Society, a pioneering social enterprise in Australia, delivered the breakthrough I needed to bring Daybreak to the next level. After undergoing intensive training with Mr. Styling in Australia, we applied our newfound skills to Daybreak and developed five types of vocational training modules from scratch. We finally had a professional team and operational systems.

How did you use your experiences with Daybreak to set your priorities in Crabtree & Evelyn?

In order to lead, I must have a very clear vision and mission. I must also share these to get ownership from the key leaders. Then, you set your three-year goals. I had to identify key leaders, know their strength and competence and whether they were loyal to me. Then you empower them and give them enough leeway to run with the ball, and entrust them with the job.

 What is one memorable life-changing experience that has impacted and shaped the way you lead?

 It was a series of obstacles which I had to overcome. I was born in Singapore, then I went away to the United States for five years to study and work. I was in brand management, and led a very glamorous life. Then I got married and moved to Ipoh in 1981. I believe that family comes first, so I quit my job to be a full-time wife and mother.

Nobody prepared me to live a very laid-back, country life. I had to learn a new way of life, new roles, and new rules. Moving to Ipoh challenged my value system, lifestyle, and interests because it is a very conservative town.

As a devoted wife, I have only one choice: to change. I had to dig deep into my inner resources to totally change and adapt to the environment, to find God, find myself and a new meaning to my new role as a wife, mother, and daughter-in-law.

So to go from a glamorous, single working-woman life, to being married and having four children in six years (every other year I had a kid), was certainly a dramatic turn and life-changing responsibility. I had to completely give myself to be a wife and mother.

In the mid-80s, my family started going to church because of a family crisis. Seeking God was the only way we could find peace. It turned out to be one of the best decisions we ever made because it brought us closer — we found that we share similar values.

 What are your most difficult challenges as a mother of four?

 The imparting of values. Each child is so different — you can't use one formula. The first child was the most challenging; you make every single mistake with the first. Our anxieties were passed onto the first child as they also tend to be the most high-achieving. The youngest, however, tends to be the happiest and most easy-going. We had to make sure we practiced no favoritism.

Up to 12 years old, we were very strict about routines, going to church, keeping to homework schedule — it was the only opportunity to instill self-discipline. During the teenage years, we started to let them go. After O-levels they went to the UK at 17. We were confident then that they could make their own choices. To us, education is second to family life. It's about building a strong foundation.

 You and Oi Hian have been able to maintain a healthy marriage. How do you do it?

 If I could go back 20 years, I would have asked to be mentored. I wish I had one. I learned it the hard way and it took a lot of effort and a long time! Modern women want to fulfill their own goals — they are very strong and seek career advancement. We forget our priorities.

Once you are married, submission to your husband is very important. It doesn't mean being a doormat or a second-class citizen, but submitting and respecting your husband. A woman's job is not to fight with her husband all the time. I want to support and encourage him in what he does.

I've found that a very important factor is to have a good support system of family, friends and the church.

Next is to be clear and to set my priorities: If children come first, then set boundaries at work, especially when my children are young. In this way, I made sure that I had time for my kids.

Third, stay focused on our core values. Both of us share common values of God and family. This keeps our marriage together.

 What's your advice to young women in leadership on how to balance family, career and business?

 To younger women, it is important to balance family, career and finance. We can be a great help-mate to our husbands. If children are important to you, be prepared to put them first and sacrifice career advancement for them. You must learn how to plan and manage both personal and family finances.

My biggest lesson is to wait on God. I do it more and more as time goes by. Don't carry problems with your own strength. Personally, I find that I have been able to overcome even the most difficult challenges if I pray and depend on God.

 What is the most crushing adversity you have ever faced in your leadership? How did you deal with it?

 That was when we faced Chapter 11 bankruptcy protection when I was running Crabtree & Evelyn.

From 2009–2011, we had to restructure management in the most difficult market — the UK. The UK had very tough labor laws. We had to be well advised by lawyers every step of the way in the UK.

I overcame these problems by persevering and consulting the right people at every step without rushing forward. I learned a tough lesson: people you think you can trust a 100% can let you down!

 How did you turn Crabtree & Evelyn around and what were the challenges involved?

 We had a financial crisis when I stepped in in 2009 but we made a profit within a year, by 2010. The turnaround was very quick, because I pulled together a global team.

We had an American CEO in 2008. He came from a competitor who was very American and mass-market oriented, and wanted to rebrand Crabtree in a way that went against the core value and DNA of the brand, which was more of an English lifestyle. He wanted to throw away practically everything English, and make it modern.

When we found out what he was trying to do without telling us, I was parachuted in in January 2009. From an Ipoh housewife, suddenly I was a global leader, after having left the corporate world for 27 years!

I had been tracking the brand from the outside, but had never been involved in the management. My challenge was to understand the female consumer and the essence of the Crabtree brand. We evolved the brand from something dated into a modern British lifestyle brand. Many wondered how an Ipoh housewife could handle the role of global chieftain overnight!

I would say that it came from the combination of being a mother of four, a penchant for shopping, and the experience of running Daybreak. Voluntary work teaches you about perseverance, commitment and dedication to a task. Managing a group of volunteers forces you to step up and in the process you gain skills you never knew you had. In the corporate world, you can hire and you can fire. But volunteers — if they don't like what you do, if they don't believe in your vision, or they don't think you're authentic — they can walk out anytime. If you can lead volunteers and retain them, you can lead a company.

The skill set was already embedded in me; I just had to draw it out. As I was already a loyal fan of the brand, the job was made a little easier. I did not see it as just a job, because when it becomes just a job, it becomes too overwhelming. The brand was my passion. My vocation was my vacation.

Within a year, we turned profitable again. The experience taught me that no matter what we are given, do it with all your passion and do it well. Leading with a clear vision and mission was also important. I sat down with my key leaders and said I want to make the brand profitable within three years. I wanted to either hold an IPO or sell it within three years. It was a risky move, but I got a buy-in. All my people were excited by this mission and we sold it in three years.

 What's next after Crabtree & Evelyn?

 I often get asked whether I will return to the corporate world. You'll never know. I'll try to stay out of the radar screen before I do something else. Right now, I want to learn more about social enterprises. I have been very fascinated by the model of making charities sustainable. Instead of the usual hand-outs, I want to learn how to build sustainable social enterprises. Every NGO struggles with the challenge of finding the right work that is income-making, sustainable, yet meaningful. My dream is to use my experiences to help other NGOs to be self-sustainable.

 Give us a glimpse of your daily routine and you keep these practices.

 Discipline is key. So is quiet time for myself. I spend a few moments by myself every morning to set the tone for the rest of the day. I also exercise three to four times a week — cycling, swimming, and doing weights to keep myself fit.

I make it a point to take time out for friends and socialize and have fun too. I enjoy good friends, good conversation, good food and wine. I also love to spend time with my family. We are now reaping the rewards of the last 25 years of child-rearing. They are grown up now and all are involved in the family business. My role as a mother and mentor continues.

I'm grateful that my husband has been my pillar of support and that my children see the value of what I do too. I believe that my work in Daybreak encourages and inspires them to take on responsibilities in life.

 What is one weakness and how do you deal/cope with it?

 I am a typical type-A personality, impatient and quick-tempered. In hindsight, I wish I had learned to use more diplomatic words earlier — how to say no or to reprimand someone constructively, without tearing that person apart.

 What is one legacy you have left behind in your organization?

 It has been my greatest joy to say that I have run the race, I have not wasted any of my God-given talent or resource. I have given my full effort in any role that I have played. My greatest hope is to leave behind a legacy of contribution and a tradition of excellence for them to carry on for future generations.

What is one advice you would give to emerging leaders?

After 30 years of experience, I would say, bring problems to God first. He has it all planned out. Why struggle? Ask Him to lead and be patient.

Also, be brave. Hold on to your faith, keep moving forward, and don't be fearful. If you have set your mind to do something, just do it.

> During a crisis, I prefer to eat a lot and exercise. You have to put yourself in a good condition and not let your mind be clouded, because a lot of bad decisions are made under stress.

STEPHEN RIADY
The Crisis-Calming Leader

r. Stephen Riady has been a corporate titan both in Singapore and Hong Kong for many years. The younger son of Indonesian tycoon Mochtar Riady, Mr. Riady is the President of Lippo Group, a US$20 billion conglomerate spanning property, health care, financial services, media and retail. He is also Executive Chairman of Singapore-listed property firm OUE Limited.

Mr. Riady made his first million at the age of 22 from investing in stocks while still studying for a finance degree at the University of Southern California. Before that, he had already honed his entrepreneurial skills by helping out in the family business during school vacations.

"From my school days, I never had a holiday. Every time I had a school break, my father would ask me to come back to spend time with him and to just follow him. He would rotate me among the different departments," he recalls.

His family's 'worst crisis' came during the Asian Financial Crisis in 1997, when the Indonesian rupiah fell sharply against the US dollar in a short time. He was based in Hong Kong at the time. Mr. Riady says the ability to stay calm and his faith in God helped him through that turbulent period. "You must believe that there's always an element of luck, or if you are a believer — God's grace," said the devout Christian.

He also learned from his father how to remain calm amid adversity. Said Mr. Riady, "When crisis comes, my father is always calm, and he doesn't give up easily or get disappointed. He's always positive… he will just relax and read newspapers when he's in the office. He doesn't usually play golf. But during a crisis, he will also play golf to show people — even if there is a big problem, he can still play golf."

Mr. Riady made a splash in Hong Kong's business scene in the 1990s before he decided to shift his focus from Hong Kong to Singapore in 2003. In 2006, he teamed up to buy a 55% stake in OUE from United Overseas Bank, before gaining a controlling stake in 2010.

A year later, he was named strategic investment entrepreneur of the year in Ernst & Young's entrepreneur awards for Singapore.

Mr. Riady is not just an entrepreneur but also a firm believer in giving back to society. In fact, he derives more satisfaction in being a philanthropist, and he and his family have donated large sums of money to prominent universities and hospitals.

We catch up with the amiable and astute businessman at his Sentosa home.

 Who or what influenced you most in your leadership development? And why?

 Obviously it's my father, Mochtar Riady. From my school days, I never had a holiday. Every time I had a school break, he would ask me to come back to spend time with him and just follow him. He would rotate me across the different departments. He would talk to me and ask me what I had learned today. What had I seen? How good was the manager seated next to me? One time I made my father really happy. By the time I was 18, I had gone through many departments. Then his friend asked me, "What's next?" It so happened that my last department was just next to my father's office. So I replied "Next, I will take over my father." That was at the age of 18.

 What did you learn specifically from your father?

 He's really humble. He likes to listen and talk to people, whether they are high ranking or low ranking — everybody has access to him. He treats everybody the same whether they are important or unimportant. He would still invite them for lunch or dinner.

He never changed his lifestyle. When I was six, seven years old, we lived in a two-storey house. We lived on the second storey. The first storey was a warehouse. It was dirty, and had trucks, goods and so on. Then of course, I saw him prospering and prospering. But he didn't change his lifestyle — he kept his old car and never looked down on other people.

He also kept reminding me — don't change your lifestyle just because you've made more money. He respects people who have made lots of money but are still simple and are still the same.

So I learned from him. I learned to be humble even when you are getting successful. Don't show off.

Another lesson is how to handle a crisis. When there is a crisis, he's always calm, and he doesn't give up easily or get disappointed. He's always positive.

He learned that if you have a crisis, you should not pretend that you don't have a crisis. Rather, you should face the reality. You should face the creditors and tell them you will find different ways to solve it. If you do that and you are sincere, people will trust you and give you a second chance. The worst thing to do is to try to run away.

The first people he must calm during a crisis are the employees. So when there is a crisis, he will just relax and read newspapers when he's in the office. He doesn't usually play golf. But during a crisis, he will play golf to show people — even if there is a big problem, he can still play golf.

 What are the keys to leading well during a crisis?

 Our worst crisis occurred in 1997 during the Asian Financial Crisis. Indonesia was the worst-hit during that crisis, when the rupiah collapsed from 2,000 to 16,000 to the US dollar. That meant that if you borrowed US$1 million, it became US$7–8 million. It even became life-threatening — do you stay or leave? Do you just protect your life and run away? All the biggest banks collapsed one by one or were taken over by the government.

When Indonesia went through this situation, I was also affected in Hong Kong. I owned a bank in Hong Kong with 40 branches. Every day, I couldn't sleep, because I was so worried that the rumours would spread to Hong Kong and affect my banks there. At the same time, some banks were lending but others were cutting bank credit lines to my property business. So you tried — pump in resources from the property and retail into the bank business. I remitted all my money from Hong Kong to Jakarta. Every day we were worried, whether the bank would collapse the next day.

Every day, you would wait for 6 pm to see if the Central Bank has cleared you. Upon seeing your deposit balance, you would find out if you are black or red. Somehow when you showed red, someone would leak the information out that the next bank to collapse is yours. We were one of the last few to show red.

Here's a lesson, if you're one of the last few to collapse, that's all right because the government just cannot allow any more collapses, so they had a new regulation of a government guarantee for deposits. We would have been dead if we went on for another three months without the guarantee.

You must believe that there's always an element of luck, or if you are a believer — God's grace. The crisis lasted almost two years in total — it was really serious.

What kept you and your family going at that time?

First of all, my father was the leader. He was very calm and slept very well. He was able to think and then go to sleep, and wake up the next day fresh to think again.

My mother was worried too, but she made sure we stayed healthy, ate good food and had enough rest. If we were talking late into the night, she would remind us that it was 10:30 pm and gave us another half hour before we slept. She also said that we must do some exercise. More importantly, she prayed a lot and shared messages with us.

During a crisis, I prefer to eat a lot and exercise. You have to put yourself in a good condition and not let your mind be clouded, because a lot of bad decisions are made under stress.

That's the time I also grew a lot spiritually. Under such challenging circumstances, you're easily close to God. During those times, when I opened my eyes, I felt God's presence. You're just grateful for a new day, when you can wake up and walk and feel healthy, something which you used to take for granted. You realize that life without God is terrible. During a crisis, the experience of God is deeper. During the smooth and good times, you don't know what hidden manna is. During a crisis, outwardly, you may be suffering, but inwardly, you still have joy because you have the supply of hidden manna from God — you're not so thirsty, you still feel contented.

After that experience, I became more serious in pursuing God.

From a leadership standpoint, how do you manage a crisis in terms of your employees, customers and debtors?

 My father's teaching is to learn to do things preventively, not only when you get into deep problems. There are always cycles in business. You want to buy low and sell high. You need to borrow money in business but you can get carried away. You can buy for ego, for money and get emotionally attached.

'Preventive' means when you buy low, you can be emotional (i.e. positive or brave), but when it goes high, you must be rational and not get emotional (be brave to say "no"). If you are not brave to say "no", you may make a mistake and regret. Therefore, always act preventively. For example, in Hong Kong, I bought low in 1987 and 1988. But in 1993–1994, when the price had gone up 3 or 4 times, I started selling. But people said "Why so silly?" If you listen to too many people, you may get too emotional and too greedy, so do not worry about what people say, even if it is still up the following year. You must think "what if it goes down", not "what if it goes up".

What does over-gearing mean? Is 60%, 70% over-gearing? The gearing ratio is not the only criteria. You must also consider how much you pay for it and the interest rate. Don't be too greedy. Don't believe a lot of bankers and analysts — people want to make money. Trust your own feelings.

 Anything else?

 You must have an international perspective and vision. Look at the world and also at the market you are in. For example, in 2000, I had no business in Singapore. When Hong Kong recovered in 2002–2003, I monitored the market for two to three years and asked myself how come Hong Kong was doing well then while Singapore was still relatively quiet.

In 2004 and 2005, the Singapore government started debating whether to have an integrated resort — this was an important issue. I talked to people to understand more. The government's vision was to make Singapore the best city to play or work. By 2015, it was to remake the city. I saw that the government wanted to achieve by 2015 — a River Safari, two casinos, integrated resorts, water sports, etc. When you see that, you ask yourself if you believe that. I think I was one of the few businessmen then to believe that vision so I came to Singapore. People were still saying "Why do you come to Singapore? Hong Kong is better." My response was that the Singapore government had a good track record.

So we moved from zero in 2003 to S$10 billion today. Leadership for a company which you start from small (e.g. One Newton) needs soft management. But for a company you buy over, you need tough management (e.g. Mandarin Hotel). For example, you hire someone to cut costs — food and electricity waste management.

 You run business as business. How do you correlate your business practices with your personal values?

 First you must know that there were a lot of problems in the company so I hired somebody to look into the details. I don't bother with the details. For example, in the hotel business, there was pilfering and loop holes. For instance, the door man and concierge knew the preferences of repeat guests and arranged cars for them. However they did not use the hotel car, but their own company or friend's company's car.

Once, I got a complaint from a Member of Parliament (MP) because a staff who had worked for 30 years was asked to retire. The MP asked us to reconsider. We offered him a different job because his age did not allow him to carry luggage but he rejected it because his tip was more than his salary. I said we could not offer him the same job because my service quality would be affected. So we told him he had to go.

I need to hire someone who is tough to handle such details. It is not my nature to be very tough. I am more 'big picture' so I need someone different from me.

We have the best buffet with nine different types of cuisines. But every time we have almost 100% occupancy, there will be a very long line. So what do I do? I reduce the food so that people don't spend too much time there. Other people say open another ballroom, hire more people. But why do business in such a way as to create more cost? Another way is to have younger people as they tend to work faster (i.e. productivity) and are less set in their ways.

Be creative. Don't implement things in the easiest way and increase business cost.

  What is one advice you would give to emerging leaders?

Work hard and save money — don't spend beyond your means. These are the basics and they are also the basics of management too.

How do you increase profit? One is to reduce cost, the other is to increase revenue, but reducing cost is the fastest way. For example, do you offer a set menu or a la carte? A la carte is usually more costly because you have to buy many things.

You must learn how to cut cost — cut electricity usage, reduce full-time staff and as your requirements increase, increase the number of staff. You need them to work longer hours on busy days, but on weekdays they can go home early. Good managers manage costs well. Every division must have its own profit and loss statement. Bonus is awarded to those who make money.

At Chatterbox, I asked my staff to increase revenue by 40%. I challenged them to think beyond the restaurant space e.g. venture into home catering, banquets, functions like Formula One, etc.

I also check on my senior management to ensure compliance and minimize the possibility of fraud. I check whether they use pirated software and check the systems from time to time. This is the style that must be used — if you are the head, your subordinates must have access to you. They can write and complain to me.

 What are two most intense tensions between faith and business that you have faced? How do you manage them?

 Business is business — just because someone is Christian doesn't mean that you should give him special treatment. In the past, I made a mistake. I trusted a person because he was a Christian but in the end, he didn't do his job. Do what you must do — get the facts, but also care about his feelings.

If you need to correct someone, speak to the person personally — do not embarrass him in front of others. Treat the person with dignity. Be sensitive about it, and be nicer to older people.

In Mandarin Hotel and OUE Management, there was duplication and we needed to cut people. That is the correct business decision, but we can do it differently. I asked HR to help them look for jobs and relocate some jobs. For those that cannot be re-employed, be nicer, talk to them nicely.

We had a cleaning lady who was sick so we had to ask her to leave to take care of her health. Emotionally, it was tough. What I did was to ask her to clear her leave and then personally, I gave her an extra six months of salary. I also told her that if she still couldn't find another job after one year, to talk to me. I do these by exception but I do not expect my manager to do that. If he is supposed to be tough and I ask him to make such exceptions, it would confuse him.

 What's your personal weakness?

 It is not in my nature to be tough. And so people sometimes take advantage. For example, one staff said that we never offered him another job. In fact, we had but he didn't want to accept that job.

Some people say their pay is not enough, so they write letters to me. But the positive side of giving all my staff access to me is that people become more vigilant and are less likely to commit fraud.

Sometimes, I just walk around to make my presence felt. I don't need to say anything. Rather, it is to remind people not to do dishonest things. Sometimes, I go to a crowded area just to watch the staff work. I don't need to give them any instructions. I just watch and observe.

> ## People must come first, with no hidden agenda.

TAN CHENG BOCK
The People-First Leader

r. Tan Cheng Bock made the headlines in Singapore in August 2011, when he participated in the island-state's hotly contested presidential election — the first in 18 years.

The former Member of Parliament's (MP's) campaign tagline of "Think Singaporeans First" won the hearts and minds of many of his fellow citizens. He lost to former Deputy Prime Minister Tony Tan by the slimmest of margins (0.34%).

In a statement delivered just after the election results had been announced, Prime Minister Lee Hsien Loong described Dr. Tan as a "highly respected backbench MP", adding that he called Dr. Tan to "thank him and his supporters for having fought an effective and dignified campaign".

The man who contested for one of the highest positions in the land had lost his father to tuberculosis at the tender age of 16. Despite the challenges, Dr. Tan did well academically at Raffles Institution and eventually made it to medical school.

His medical career began in 1971, at a spartan wood-and-zinc shop-house in the rural farming community of Ama Keng Village in secluded Lim Chu Kang. "My friends were shocked by my choice. But it became the best 10 years of my life," he recalled.

The father of two entered politics in 1979, before becoming MP for Ayer Rajah in 1980. That was a post he held until 2006, including a 88% win at the 2001 polls — the People's Action Party's best result for any constituency in 31 years. During his time in Parliament, he gained a reputation for speaking vocally against government policies which he disagreed with, such as the Nominated MP scheme and the foreign talent push. He also served as the first head of the government's Feedback Unit, and sat on the boards of the Land Transport Authority and SMRT.

On the corporate front, Dr. Tan has served as non-executive chairman of investment holding firm Chuan Hup Holdings since 1991, and sat on the board of ING Asia Private Bank from 2008–2009, playing a major role in its sale to OCBC Bank in 2009.

We caught up with the people-centred doctor-politician, who enjoys playing the ukulele, gardening, keeping koi and golf, at his home for a morning chat.

Who or what influenced you most in your leadership development? And why?

 It was not a person but a particular experience.

My dad died of tuberculosis when I was 16 years old. Mum said that my father was entitled to some gratuity from the Singapore Harbour Board (SHB), where he had worked. So I went, but to my horror, I was turned away by the union guys. I went again and was told that my dad was in arrears of union subscription so I was not entitled to the gratuity, which amounted to $28,000, a handsome sum then.

When I looked into dad's box of personal belongings, there was a union receipt dated a month before he passed away. I went back to the union but they still didn't give me the money, maintaining that my father was in arrears. Moreover, they told me that after a change in the constitution the sum involved was only $14,000 and not $28,000. I said, "Never mind, $14,000 I also take." I didn't know whether it was correct or not.

I kept pestering the union, because I was advised by an uncle that my dad probably was up to date with his subscriptions as he had that receipt. I decided to fight the union. My mother was pressuring me to get the money, as there were seven kids in the house to feed. So I gave tuition, studied and chased the union for money at the same time but to no avail.

I was in Raffles Institution (RI) and my classmate Peter Chua, whose father was Justice Chua, advised me to seek help from the Legal Aid Bureau. I went and talked to an officer and he drafted all the letters for me. They said not to worry and they will take over the case. But I didn't hear from them. I kept pestering but they told me, "Young man, you don't understand. There are a lot of things involved, a lot of politics." SHB was run by Jamit Singh then, and he was very close to Lee Kuan Yew.

When l went around my estate to ask for help, everybody told me that it was political. I did not quite understand but l persisted. This lasted for one year. I did everything I could to help my mum financially, including writing a PSLE workbook which I sold. My studies suffered and l wanted to leave school, but the RI principal Mr. Ambiavagar got me a bursary.

My routine then was: give tuition, sit outside the Legal Aid Bureau for information and face the unions. It was very frustrating but my determination paid off. One day, I read in the newspaper and heard on radio that there was a split in the PAP. A new party Barisan Socialist was formed. Jamit Singh sided with the Barisan Socialist and a change of leadership happened at SHB union. I told my mum that I think we can get our money back. I went to the Legal Aid Bureau and waited. Soon, I got my cheque of $14,000! After paying the family debts, we bought our first family fridge.

 Seems like your first brush with politics. What did you learn from all that?

 This experience taught me that you must have the resilience, the stamina, and the will power. I believed my father had the right to his money. I will stand up for what I believe is my right. I was not intimidated.

I found that after this incident, I grew, I changed. I managed to scrape through school, got a bursary and went to university to study medicine. I didn't do too well in medical school because I was too busy with the student union. I never took a lead role but I had the knack to get people to support those who I believed were good people. I have a rallying power — I don't know how but when I talk to people somehow they believe and they trust me.

 You lost your father at the young age of 16, how did that affect you?

 When my father died, I remembered I was really lost because we always had a very close relationship. I remembered that when I studied, he would sit next to me. He was not a very educated person but could read and write, and worked as a clerk in Singapore Harbour Board. He could not impart all the things he wanted to, so he would bring me old newspapers and made me read the editorials. He told me that would keep me abreast of what is happening, but it was beyond me.

He told me ancient Chinese histories of people with honor, valor and patriotism. He was an ardent admirer of Lee Kuan Yew. He smoked heavily and was always ill. His death was a loss not only to me but also the children of our estate who loved him for his kind and caring ways. They called him 'enche', or 'uncle' in Malay.

Your national service experience was also a difficult time. What happened?

 After medical school, I was among a group of 12 in my class of 50-odd Singaporeans called up to do National Service (NS). To me, this was not NS, as NS should involve all eligible Singaporeans and not only the 12 of us. Something was not quite right. Sadly, there was no separate NS program for doctors then. We were all for NS, and we knew that the army needed doctors, but this was not the way.

We crafted a paper on how to deploy doctors in the army and health ministry. It must have embarrassed them. The paper was rejected. We went through tough basic military training and we did well. Then they dropped a bombshell telling us the rank of a doctor would no longer be captain but a lieutenant. We protested as we knew rank was very important in the army, especially when we were field doctors and we had to command officers. We argued with them. They threatened to charge us with insubordination.

After an exchange of letters, we were given the option to leave NS — but this was not correct as the constitution did not allow for such an option. However, there was a catch that came with the option. The officer told us that if we sign the letter, we would not be able to get employment in the public sector.

I was so angry. Was that a threat? If after having studied in medical school for so long, I cannot fend for myself, then all that I have studied in medical school would be useless. So I signed the option, and the rest followed me and signed too. True enough, I was rejected by the Ministry of Health (MOH) when I applied to join them even though I had to serve a seven-year bond. It was a very vindictive move.

When word went around that the 'dirty dozen' was 'out', nobody dared to employ us. I went to work for Dr. Sheng Nan Chin as a locum for a few months. He happened to be in the opposition camp. When Dr. Sheng wanted to quit his practice, he asked me to take over his clinic, but I had decided not to be an 'ordinary GP' treating just coughs and colds. I wanted to put my training as a doctor to better use. As a result, I was unemployed for a while. Later, I worked as a locum until I found my ideal practice at Ama Keng.

How did you end up as a village doctor in Ama Keng? Tell us about your experiences there.

 Medicine is my first love, politics is my calling. When my classmates were studying medicine via the books, I was in the hospital wards learning about diseases first hand from doctors and patients. This way, you learn about clinical acumen, empathy and care. One day, a cigarette seller friend told me about this village needing a doctor. So I went and knew that was what I wanted. It was a rundown shop-house — half zinc, half attap roof, with mud flooring. My friends were shocked by my choice. But I began to enjoy the best years of my life practicing rural medicine there!

My patients were farmers with simple needs. When they see you, they are really ill. They trusted me and I looked after their social and family needs as well. I never worry about payment and some paid me in kind with their farm produce, including eggs, chickens and durians. I remember one particular case.

One day, a very sick boy was brought to see me. He had severe asthma and was very ill. His father had no money and offered his wedding ring as payment, but I didn't accept his ring. I attended to his boy and told him he need not worry about payment. He could bring his children to see me any time there was a need. I think they were very grateful. Many years later, when I became an MP, the boy came to see me at my resettled clinic saying, "I am Cheong. My mother said, before I go away for further studies, I must come and see you to thank you for looking after me. You must take the hamper." For the first time in my life as an MP, I accepted the hamper.

You must have faith in people. Don't worry, they won't run away. So many people who didn't pay me, subsequently they came back and paid me. But sometimes I tell them, "Never mind, now that you have made it, give the money to charity".

 How different are doctors these days?

 Today's doctors face many problems. Many are driven by different motives, perhaps because their needs and expectations have changed. The environment has also changed with the internet influencing and raising expectation of care from patients. Medicine is now an industry, hospitals and even private practices get listed on the stock exchange. This raises expectations of growing profits and higher healthcare costs. So the question asked is this: which will prevail? Patient interest or shareholders interests? Advertisement has changed doctors' behaviour too. Is it good or bad? Monetary consideration over patient care has altered priorities.

My generation of doctors was better off. Clinic rentals were cheaper and more affordable. Houses and cars were also cheaper. Nowadays, high rentals coupled with financially lucrative procedures have driven many young doctors to practice aesthetics medicine. It is a choice and I do understand. However, my wish is for disease management at ground level to be encouraged and supported more by the Ministry of Health (MOH), as the population ages and chronic diseases are on the increase. As more and more doctors opt for aesthetics medicine, what would happen if we are hit by an epidemic like SARS (severe acute respiratory syndrome) and there are not enough primary care practitioners to manage it?

As a doctor and a politician, you must have very strong views about Singapore's healthcare policies. What are they?

Politicians want to win elections. Therefore, most of their policies are tailored towards gaining votes. But in the field of healthcare, I feel that we shouldn't do that. Instead, changes must be geared towards the general outlook of what the health of the population is going to be. The current emphasis is too institution-based, i.e. towards hospital care. Everyone now looks to hospitals for treatment. This has increased health cost — but the real problem to tackle is at the ground — the prevention aspect. The current state of health financing is 70% towards institution-based care. I would prefer to redistribute this expenditure more towards the preventive and primary care areas.

Having created a high-cost healthcare system, we are now building systems to sustain the high cost! One factor causing this is the use of Medisave and insurance schemes based on the Central Provident Fund (CPF) to pay for hospital care. This easy source of financing treatment has made hospital administrators think less of the cost benefits of procedures. They are 'chasing health cost' not 'containing health cost'. They are always working out 'how to pay for it' and not 'how to manage the cost'. Thus the many insurance schemes being evolved and the irony of it all is this: people are using their own money, through their CPF, to pay their medical bills and the huge administrative costs involved. I am sure a big chunk of our healthcare cost goes to administration.

Instead of spending billions to build new huge hospitals, why not build smaller ones and spend more on primary healthcare — outpatient departments, old folks' homes, nursing homes etc? An army needs a good infantry. You do not fight from the headquarters. The real battle is fought on the ground. You must think long-term — preventive care, downstream health matters and activities for the aged. It is the ordinary doctors and allied health and medical personnel, not the specialists, who are the real gate-keepers of health in this country.

 How can leadership in Singapore be improved?

 Our leadership suffers from intellectual arrogance. Our leaders come from very good schools, and are very good students. They've always been praised, never been caned. They think they can do no wrong. They consider the discontentment swelling from the ground as noise.

But if you think you are so clever and think you cannot do wrong, then this is a problem. Such leaders must come down from their high chair. One simple observation I make of telling whether that MP has a way with people is the handshake. You will know the type of person you are going to deal with after a handshake. Some don't even look you in the eye when shaking your hands.

 How can one hone moral courage and integrity as a leader?

 We will have integrity only if we have the moral courage to do what is right by our beliefs. When I was the Feedback Unit Chief, l gave space for people to speak up. This was not well-received by some of our leaders but l kept up my style. Our talk-down style would not be accepted by the younger Singaporeans. I took the trouble to find out in detail the problem, because it is incomplete to simply listen and pass on the information to the ministers. If you do that, one important element — the emotional expression of the feedback — is missing. Therefore, l recommend more constituency walkabouts. You got to go to the ground and listen to the people — you can't expect the ground to come to you. Some ministers do not like what l do and l was accused of personalizing the Unit. Some pass strong comments when they read bad reports. On one occasion, I cut off my feedback to a minister who was not happy with what I gave him — he asked me whether I had anymore worthwhile feedback. Another time, l received a strong rebuttal in parliament from ministers and later a public scolding by the late Mr. Lee Kuan Yew for challenging the foreign talent recruitment policy, but l stuck to my conviction of "Think Singaporeans First". I was very hurt but that was not going to stop me from saying what l believe is right.

When I voted against the Nominated Members of Parliament (NMP) bill, I told the House that my conscience would not be clear if I supported the bill, as I believed the NMP scheme was not in the interest of the country. Parliament is for elected members who have a moral duty to those who voted them in.

I worry that NMPs only represent sectors of our community which nominated them. It is divisive as other sectors that are not represented will be unhappy. To allow such interest groups, who do not have a proper mandate by the people, into parliament to push their cause is inviting trouble for the country. This is wrong. MPs should push legislation which is good for all Singaporeans, not only special interest groups. I voted against the NMP bill even when the whip was not lifted.

Also on a point of principle, I resigned from the board of Jurong General Hospital when the government approved naming the hospital after a private individual, whose family paid only one tenth of the cost of the hospital. To me, that is not philanthropy but buying a name. This is wrong, as such public institutions should only be named after prominent Singaporeans who have a history of contribution to our country and have impacted our lives. Money should not buy one's name to public institutions.

 What are the three biggest challenges facing Singapore, and how would you tackle them?

 Healthcare — it's a hot political potato. We must restructure our thinking — move from high-end healthcare delivery system to a lower, less-expensive and wider-base system. We must refocus on primary community-based care.

Otherwise, there will be increased demand for expensive hospital-based institutional care.

Next, managing the new media. This is very important. Young people are watching and using new media platforms to know, learn and question. And they are the future voters. Many have stopped reading the main-stream media like *The Straits Times*.

Thirdly, our leaders must stop labeling Singaporeans as xenophobic. We need to bring back the pride of being a Singaporean. We have lost a lot of our pride due to over-championing of the foreign talent policy. Our lead-ers are too quick to label Singaporeans' behavior if they react strongly against foreigners. It is only natural to express our displeasure if our pub-lic space is being taken over.

We must "think Singaporeans first". I'm not against foreigners. We should welcome the real talent, not those who cause our wages to be suppressed or those who displace our PMETs (Professionals, Managers, Executives and Technicians). We must adopt certain changes to our policies — Singaporean companies must stay Singaporean, the supporting cast can include some foreigners.

The head can be a foreigner only if there is proof that no Singaporean can be found for the job, but if everything is equal then the choice must be a Singaporean. We must guard against foreigners hiring their own people at the expense of locals, all under the pretext of talent.

Companies like the power, gas and telecoms firms are our national treas-ures; we cannot lose them to foreigners. Some people say I am old-fashioned but sometimes I think old-fashioned ideas, like having control of our daily essential services, should always be with us. Don't let others make you believe this is wrong.

 What leadership lessons did you learn from the 2011 Presidential Election (PE)?

 If I were to do it again, I would still do it the same way. I don't think I should change because that was my style — hold a dignified campaign and if we lose, lose it gentlemanly. We must fight honorably. I hope my PE campaign helped Singaporeans to better understand the difference between PE and GE (General Election). However, there was one issue which some older Singaporeans advised me not to bring up. That is: if I become President, the government must leave the Istana and only the President's office will be there. I believe the arrangement of the offices of the Prime Minister and the office of the President should be separate and not be sharing the same building. The current arrangement does not reflect the political changes resulting from the conversion in the office of the President from an appointed to an elected one. The role of the President is no longer just ceremonial but also custodial, i.e. his approval is needed for use of the country's reserves and appointment of key personnel in the civil service.

I believe the physical separation of the offices of the President and Prime Minister must reflect this political change. This is to avoid any suspicion of collusion and compromise. I was merely addressing the need to right a wrong arrangement.

Singaporeans have learned to exercise their own judgment and voted as they wished. Don't underestimate Singaporeans' independent thinking. My campaign showed the will and determination of young Singaporeans campaigning for me through the use of the new media.

  What is one advice you would give to emerging leaders?

You must be honest. Be yourself. If you really feel you are coming in to do a job, you must do it well. People must come first, with no hidden agenda, then you won't go wrong. You must also be prepared to listen to advice, because sometimes you may be wrong.

It's important to mix with people, all strata of people. When I was MP of Ayer Rajah, I made it a point that the one who picked me up weekly for the Meet-the-People session was always a different person. This way I got to listen to different views. So one week it could be a hawker, another week a taxi driver, and the following week a managing director who picked me up. I listened and checked all feedback, and if I found that a certain view I held might need modifying, then I would do so — there is no shame to change. I am prepared to concede if they are right.

“

Live with no regrets. Do things honestly. You don't have to be rich to live comfortably.

”

TANRI ABENG
The Value-Focused Leader

anri Abeng was one of Indonesia's most astute corporate executives, serving as a cabinet minister during the Suharto and Habibie administrations. He is Founder President of Tanri Abeng University. The 73-year-old was born in a rural village on the island of Selayar in South Sulawesi, Indonesia. His parents were poor farmers who were very resilient and adaptable.

He had to sell bananas to fellow students to make enough money to buy books and materials needed for school. By the age of 10, his parents had died and he was sent to live with relatives in Makassar.

To finish his education, he sold stenciled copies of school notes to his fellow students. Recognizing that he needed to do well in school, he worked hard and earned money by tutoring students whose grades were not as good as his. He was awarded a scholarship to spend a year as an exchange student by the American Field Service (AFS) to study in the United States.

This was a defining moment in his life, as he learned to speak English and was exposed to the openness, creativity, and achievement-oriented nature of the American culture.

He continued to learn and grow, taking many management development courses and attending the Advanced Management Program at Claremont Graduate School of Management (where Peter Drucker was the professor) in California. He worked hard. Finally, he earned his Master of Business Administration (MBA) from the State University of New York at Buffalo, supported by the Gibsons — an American couple.

He joined chemical company Union Carbide as a management trainee in 1968, and three years later, he was appointed to be the finance director and corporate secretary of the Indonesia office. After five years, he was transferred to Singapore to direct the consumer goods marketing operations for the Middle East, Asia and Africa, and he posted record profits every year.

In 1979, Heineken was looking for someone to turn around its Indonesian operation and appointed Tanri as CEO. He did this by restructuring the organization and simplified the over 100 distributors (many had bad debts) to just 12 major distributors. They also diversified to sell non-alcoholic products, like Green Sands Shandy, and bottled and sold Coca Cola instead of depending on a single product — beer. Within three years, the company was taken public.

In 1991, he was appointed to the top job at Bakrie and Brothers, Indonesia's leading indigenously owned conglomerate. He said, "I wanted to direct my skills and knowledge to the development of an Indonesian company as I had been working for foreign companies." Again, he restructured the large corporation into three main industries — telecommunications, infrastructure support and plantations, as well as made strategic investments and alliances in mining, petrochemicals and construction.

The rest is history. The transformation made Bakrie and Brothers one of the most profitable companies, and its sales shot up from US$50 million in 1991 to US$700 million in 1995.

During the Asian Financial Crisis in 1997, the Rupiah exchange rate plummeted from Rp2,000 to Rp13,000 for US$1. Many state enterprises were either bankrupt or close to bankruptcy. In March 1998, Tanri was personally appointed to be the first Minister for State-Owned Enterprises by President Suharto to avert the bankruptcy of these state-owned enterprises. One crucial and pivotal rescue that Tanri oversaw was the turning around of Garuda Airlines, the Indonesian national carrier. He was appointed to the National Economic Resilience Council to advise on economic policy.

To turn these enterprises around, Tanri launched a reform program that took his same guiding principles to enhance the overall value of these state-owned enterprises. He planned and introduced a range of regulatory reforms, privatized five leading state-owned enterprises, and formulated a detailed and coherent plan for future state-owned enterprise reform.

After his stint with the government, he was appointed Chairman of Telkom, the largest telecommunication conglomerate in Indonesia. Blessed with a good education, Tanri is now committed to developing leaders and managers with good values and strong competence. Hence, he founded the Tanri Abeng University (TAU), with the aim of nurturing the next generation of leaders and managers for the public and private sectors in Indonesia and the region.

We caught up with Tanri over tea and he shared his story of transformation.

Who or what influenced you most in your leadership development? And why?

 There is no one person whom I learned from. Over the years in leadership, I learned many lessons from a variety of experiences and from different companies and organizations including the government, which I am privileged to be associated with.

When I was with Union Carbide for 10 years, leading the marketing operations in 62 countries, I learned the fundamental principles of leadership: focus on the fundamentals to create value for the company. I learned too about being adaptable to different cultures and different people.

For example, when I worked with Indonesians, Singaporeans, Middle-Easterners and the Dutch (while in Heineken), I learned that people are very different. You have to be very adaptable to work with them. Yet, at the same time, focusing on the fundamental principles of vision, values and people.

I developed my leadership skills from the different experiences and by working with different types of leaders and people in my different jobs. It is something that increases incrementally. You cannot ignore these fundamentals and principles in leadership. Over the years, you add on.

When I was with the Bakrie Brothers, I faced different challenges in the family business. I had to adapt myself and work to put the fundamentals and systems in place to make them more efficient.

Shifting from corporate to political position with the government is almost like entering a totally new territory. Here, you need to deliver quick wins to earn public respect.

Probably, the most challenging aspect of leadership is dealing with people. People all over the world have different cultures and habits. But, deep inside, they are all the same. They want to be respected and recognized. They want to understand you and they want you to understand them. What is crucial is communication.

Successful leaders are learners. They learn and they learn fast. I never pretend that I know everything. I am a learner. I learn from the different experiences and from anyone.

 Tell us about your experiences working with two presidents of Indonesia, President Suharto and President Habibe. What did you learn from them?

 Under former President Suharto, I learned to be decisive in decision-making. Once he had decided, he got things moving. And he was an excellent motivator with ample wisdom.

After my appointment as State-Owned Enterprises Minister, he instructed me to rescue Garuda and that I must not allow it to fail.

After studying the airline, I decided that I had to replace the CEO of Garuda, as there had been very serious mismanagement issues. Many of my friends warned me that I would lose my job if I asked for the removal of the CEO. I had also found the perfect man for the job, Robby Djohan, former CEO of Bank Niaga. He had retired and did not need a high salary. Most of all, he had a high level of integrity and would never succumb to corruption.

I went to President Suharto to inform him that I had to replace the CEO of Garuda with Robby Djohan. He sat quietly, leaned back on his chair, thought for a while gave me a nod and said, "Sure, why don't you retire the entire board as well?" After that, he asked me to drink my tea, which was a sign that it was time to leave.

So, I went to offer Robby the job. He agreed on two conditions: He would only report to me and he must have the authority to change the entire board, which he thought was impossible. This was because a number of the board members were the president's loyalists.

Unknown to him, I already got permission to replace the whole board from President Suharto. So, I said, "Sure. You've got a deal."

The ex-President Suharto was a true Javanese; he seldom got angry or showed his anger. Being brought up in a more Western and Sulawesi approach, I was more direct. In my meetings with him, even when I spoke very directly with him, he would listen.

He would teach people in a way without offending you. After my first few meetings with him, he must have thought that I was too Western and if I wanted to survive in my position as Minister, I needed to be more Javanese. So he sent me a book, *Butir Butir Javanese Culture*. I got the hint. I read the book and am still applying some of the useful principles about Javanese leadership even today.

That's what I learned from Suharto: Be decisive, get the job done, and teach but do not offend.

Under ex-President Habibe, I found him to be very intelligent and Western-trained in his thinking and leading. Once he said to me, "There is no one who lives forever, you got to die. What is eternal is the person's thinking and the system that he builds. That will last forever." He taught me to think and create systems.

 What is one memorable life-changing experience that has impacted and shaped the way you lead?

 I come from a small village on the Selayar island in South Sulawesi where there was no electricity. I studied for six years in the only elementary school there and then moved to the city of Makassar. The one year in the US with the American Field Service at the age of 19 years old was the most life-changing experience for me.

The biggest change was my perspective of life. When I was in a little village, I had wanted to become a teacher. The teacher was the most respected person in the village. I like to be respected. Then I went to US, and living with the Gibsons, an American family, I learned about being transparent and open.

When I was young, I don't question things. But in the US, they discuss things. You don't have to be a teacher to be respected. I was a student and I was respected. We should respect everyone and treat each person with respect.

Also, I learned that it's okay to be a business person. In my village, a business person was perceived to be a second-class citizen. I realize that you can be in business because you provide employment for people, you pay taxes, you contribute to the country. I can be a business person and be respected. That was how I started my career as a professional.

 What is the most crushing adversity you have ever faced in your leadership? How did you deal with it?

 Going into politics. Moving from the business to the political arena, I realized that there is no exactness. You need to compromise. In business, everything is based on logic. But in politics, it is opposite from my past training and behaviors. I am straightforward. I trust people and I want to be trusted. But in politics, I find that I cannot trust everybody. An ally can become an enemy. That was a real learning point for me. Perhaps, that is why I did not succeed in politics.

As a minister, I had to deal with political forces and work with 158 corporations with total assets of US$200 billion. I had to create value and I had to sell my vision. But, other interests came into play. People from different political parties prevented me and did not permit me to succeed. They had their lobbies. Because of my lack of experience in politics and my inability to compromise, that was the beginning of the demise of my political career. They were trying to get rid of me because they had other personal interests. I had to finally follow President Habibie when he decided not to be re-elected.

 How can you compromise without compromising your integrity?

 First, I have to learn what is crucial and what is not.

Among the 158 CEOs in the state-owned enterprises, 40 were crucial. There were people who had lobbies and friends who said, "I want this guy for this corporation." I said, "No".

I needed to choose what to sacrifice and what not to. Is this a critical industry or company? I needed to make some compromises without jeopardizing the big picture.

Second, I needed to ask, "Is this guy totally useless?" Can I work with him? I would need to find ways to work with and through him. I wanted to make him succeed. In other words, I needed to find creative solutions without compromising my own integrity.

Third, I needed to learn and understand and do things differently. I could not project myself as being too confident, and had to learn to get the people to work towards the best for the country.

How do I deal with the cronies and family members of the president? What if they want to 'buy' the assets? My solution to the president is to build the system so that at least we all play by the system. They have to comply with the system. Don't reject them directly or offend them. If they are rejected, it is the system that does it. I also try to help them and be competitive within the system. My advice to the president, "Do what is best for the nation." Create a system without offending the people. That is creative and wise leadership.

Science (System) and Art (Wisdom) — this is what leadership is all about!

 Over the years, it must have been very difficult for you to keep these values intact. How did you do it?

 Once you have accepted this philosophy of life — be honest and you don't have to be rich to live comfortably. Earn and do things honestly. People have called me stupid because I could have made a lot of money. They say that I will never be too successful and I am too moral. Morality is something I won't compromise. So, I cannot compromise.

If you keep changing, you are going to be very tired. You will meet with different situations, and if you keep changing your principles, you are going to be too tired. This is the only way to avoid temptation. It is by living out your conviction. The best way for me is to preach to my children.

Allow me to share an experience. On my 70th birthday celebration, March 2012, I wrote my first small book, *No Regrets*. My first son, Emil, who is now a member of parliament, shared, "My father is 70 years old tonight. I am proud that I have adopted his philosophy in life: live with no regrets — be honest, you don't have to be rich to live comfortably. In this way, you will have a lot of friends and no enemies."

I was extremely proud because my son has embraced my values. They have seen how I live and they have caught it!

 What is one legacy you have left behind in your organization?

 The legacy I want to leave behind is to know that YOU are not all powerful. The power is in the system. During my stint in all the organizations I lead, I leave behind a system. The power is not in Tanri Abeng but it is in the system.

 What is one advice you would give to emerging leaders?

 Never think that you are right all the time. You have to continue learning. You will accumulate wisdom. Leaders will survive when you have good people. You are only as good as the people around you. So, get good people.

OUR REFLECTIONS: LEADERSHIP LESSONS

Leadership is a journey of learning, unlearning and relearning. We count it a deep honor and privilege to have sat with these Asian leaders, as so much can be gleaned from these exclusive heart-to-heart conversations. Initially, many of them were reluctant to open their hearts to us. In fact, some of them even felt that they were not good enough.

These are the role-models of society. Why do they feel they are not good enough? Then, we begin to realize that they are authentic leaders who prefer not to harp on their achievements. They are not arrogant or boastful. They recognize that their journey can fail any time because they are human. Therefore, it will be foolish to be interviewed about their successes. They do not want to be wrongly perceived or misunderstood by friends, enemies or the media.

Finally, they recognize that whatever achievements they have accomplished are very little. All of them recognize that who they are today is the result of the contributions of their parents, mentors, peers, and many of them, their God.

Gratefully, after much prodding and assurance, they decided on these candid interviews.

In this final chapter, we hope to summarize the key characteristics of these leaders — Integrity, Humility, Recovery and Divine Intervention.

A. The Multi-faced Dimensions of Integrity

"The world has no shortage of creativity but it is short of integrity."

— *Edward Ong.*

To all these leaders, integrity is not merely a concept but a practice. It is through integrity that trust is built for the long haul. Be it with the leadership team, staff or clients, it is the corner stone of relationships and the galvanizing force of the organization. It is something so precious that money cannot buy. Primarily, integrity is being a genuine and authentic person, "walking the talk and talking the walk".

Some of them learned integrity from their parents. Lee Oi Hian, chairman of Kuala Lumpur Kepong, describes his father as a man of integrity, honesty and hard work. His father demonstrated these values through his dealings with people and taught him from young as Oi Hian observed his life and lifestyle while working for his dad after school.

Lim Guan Eng, Penang Chief Minister, has the same inspiration. His father, Lim Kit Siang's indomitable spirit and absolute integrity were a fine example for him to follow.

So did Edward Ong, the founder of Sutera Harbor Resort. His father Ong Chwee Kou told him, "*You can lose money, but you cannot lose integrity.*" It was his exemplary example that Edward had maintained and practiced in all his business dealings.

Ho Peng Kee, former Singapore Senior Minister of State for Home Affairs and Law, found his inspiration in his father, who started from scratch after the war to build a successful watch business. He was hardworking and determined, a man of integrity. Peng Kee confessed that he picked up those traits from him.

We find that integrity is multi-faceted.

1. Integrity means doing the right thing

Integrity is having the courage to do the right thing, being prepared to pay a personal price and being willing to face the consequences of their actions.

Jaruvan Maintaka, the former Auditor-General of Thailand, is a leader who is prepared to die for her convictions. Her fight against corruption had resulted in death threats to her and her family. For a year, when she was collecting evidence against corrupt leaders and practices in her country, she had to have five bodyguards armed with M-16s, revolvers and bullet proof vests. Her house was even burnt.

Another example of doing the right thing and paying the price is the family of Edwin Soeryadjaya, founding partner of Sarotoga Capital. Edwin belongs to the Astra Group, a household name known for their integrity and one of the best-run corporations in Indonesia.

As Kwik Kian Gie, the former Indonesia Minister of National Development Planning, writes, "*What impressed me most is not what they have done to Astra to make it successful, but rather what they did with Astra when the family's other investment in a financial institution was in need of funds to repay the creditors and depositors. The family's decision to voluntarily sell Astra to repay creditors and depositors in full, shows their integrity in business dealings.*"

Former Temasek Holdings chairman S. Dhanabalan was prepared to leave his cabinet position if he felt it went against principle and belief. He was also prepared to remove leaders who have moral defects. In his own words, "*Competence cannot trump moral defects in character.*"

Amnuay Tapingkae, former chairman of Payap University in Thailand, was willing to put his presidential position and faith on the line when the President of the Faculty Association and some faculty members insisted on putting a Buddha statue at Payap University. He refused because Payap is a Christian university. He challenged them, "*I am prepared to die for my faith for this cause. If you are prepared to do the same, then we can talk.*" They never came back with the same request.

United Overseas Bank chairman Hsieh Fu Hua recounted an incident whereby he had to pay the price for making an erroneous personal investment for which he could have hidden but chose to redress. He said: "*As a leader, we have a duty to uphold the rules of the game and the rules call for fairness and transparency. These rules must apply to you, even if it is hugely embarrassing. That is the right thing to do.*"

Paul Low, Minister for Integrity, Governance and Human Rights in the Malaysia Cabinet, has always championed integrity and fought against corruption. Recalling his call to become President of Transparency International (TI), many people complained and prayed against corruption and corrupt leaders, but very few wanted to stand up and speak against it. He finally served as president for five years, employing professionals and building it into a top TI chapter globally. He changed it from activism to constructive engagement, i.e. to deal with issues, solve problems, implement solutions in a practical way over time.

Lim Guan Eng is a champion of this. He keeps what he does in Penang simple: *"Do what is right. Don't steal people's money. Stick to the rules you set."*

2. Integrity means delivering results

Whether it is managing a hotel, restructuring a company, being a politician, or transforming communities, a leader with integrity has to be very good at what he does.

Idris Jala, chief executive of PEMANDU (Performance Management and Delivery Unit), is an exemplary leader in this aspect. He was personally chosen by the Malaysian Government to turn around loss-making Malaysian Airlines (MAS) based on his integrity and competence as a leader in Royal Dutch Shell. Within two years, he had turned around RM1.3 billion in losses into a RM260 million profit. He was then personally chosen by the Malaysia Prime Minister to be CEO of PEMANDU.

This was also the case for Sandra Lee, who became the CEO of Crabtree & Evelyn, and engineered its turn-around when it was undergoing Chapter 11 bankruptcy proceedings. She had to prove her integrity by transforming the company. To do this, she had to lead with passion at Crabtree, which she claimed was made easy because as she put it, *"The brand was my passion. My vocation was my vacation."* Even then, she had to galvanize her team with a clear vision and mission to rebuild the brand and turn it around. She made it profitable within three years.

Edwin Soeryadjaya rebuilt his career and business at Saratoga Group by recognizing that trust was something that money could not buy. He learned from his father by recruiting trusted, competent people who had a proven track record from Astra to manage his company. He ensured that his company reduced its borrowing cost.

In doing so, he rebuilt trust again by having good governance, executing discipline, and being fair to people. He said: *"If more people catch you being dishonest, the more they will not trust you. Trust breeds trust."*

Phillip Capital chairman Lim Hua Min described the twin 'Doing the Right Thing' and 'Delivering Result' as the two dimensions of trust — the 'Alignment of Value' and 'Ability to Deliver'. For trust to grow, there must be both these aspects. There must be a constant alignment of values on the one hand and the ability to deliver on the other hand. This trust relationship will grow and be sustained 'over time' rather than 'just a point in time'. This builds consistency and trust over time.

3. Integrity means not accepting or paying bribes

Jaruvan Maintaka has been tempted many times to take bribes. She confessed that each time she was tempted, she would often think about its impact on her family and felt strongly that she could never let her children down. She has this firm belief — *"Money is not everything. I have very good chances to get rich easily. I tell myself if I had taken the money, I would be in jail by now and that would have ruined my reputation."*

This aspect of integrity of not accepting or paying bribes is also seen in the example of fast food businessman George Ting's philosophy. For him, *"If you pay to one government department, the other departments will know and then it becomes a norm. So it's better not to start."*

Edward Ong believes that business leaders must take the lead in the fight against corruption and not wait for the government to eradicate it. He said: *"If there is no payment, there is no corruption! We cannot stop the solicitation but we can stop the manifestation."*

4. Integrity means being fair

OUE chairman Stephen Riady has to be fair when removing people who are not competent and not able to deliver results in their work, even though they may share the same faith.

Before he dismisses any staff, he ensures that there are enough evidence and facts. But, at the same time, he has to be sensitive to them and their family's needs. He will never embarrass the employees by disciplining them publicly. He will ensure that they are adequately compensated, even at times, dishing out his own money as well as ensuring that the company helps them find alternative jobs.

Springhill Management chairman Kim Tan believes that intelligence without integrity is certain failure. He cited the global finance meltdown of 2008 as a case in point. He hires people first by looking at their integrity record.

As a family business, Francis Yeoh, managing director of YTL Corporation, also ensures that his company practices meritocracy and healthy competition. Teaching his children a sense of stewardship and selflessness is an important part to ensure fairness and professionalism in the organization. The children of the Yeoh clan were placed in leadership positions out of merit and not entitlement. They have to work hard, perform well, deliver results and be measured accordingly.

5. **Integrity means upholding a higher standard of morality**

For Roosniati Salihin, deputy CEO of Panin Bank, integrity is the defining value of a banker, as *"trust is the biggest asset and reputation"*. This is the key criterion which she believes makes a banker successful in the long term. As she puts it, "banking knowledge can be taught and learned but integrity has to be earned".

To put this into practice, she refuses to accept any gift given to her by her clients and makes this practice part of the organizational culture. Whenever a gift is received, she would make all the employees return it to the client with a thank you letter, informing them that this is company policy, and mentioning that providing good service is part of their professional duty.

For Francis Yeoh, corruption is a choice. It is having the courage to walk away from lucrative business opportunities and from what we consider as expedient. It means the company has to work harder and be more transparent in all dealings. It also means making business smarter and better to create niches and blue ocean strategies.

Ngiam Tong Dow, former Permanent Secretary in the Singapore Ministry of Finance, remembers the words of his mentor, the late Goh Keng Swee, ex-Deputy Prime Minister of Singapore: *"Your job as permanent secretary is to raise the competence of your team to a higher plateau."* Since then, his mission in any ministry he has led is to raise the bar of the whole organization.

For George Ting, it even goes beyond the issue of bribery. It means doing everything to comply with the laws and the regulations and beyond. It also means paying suppliers with better payment terms and on time, so that that there is less chance for corruption. In the process, he obtains the best prices from the suppliers.

In the life of Hsieh Fu Hua, integrity means building trust between the chairman of the Board and the CEO. He opined: *"As the chairman, you help the CEO by showing understanding and listening well to the ground, not micromanaging or interfering. If both have any major disagreements, the issues must be raised directly and not through a third party. The CEO must be given the opportunity to execute and let him/her deliver the goals in his/her own way."*

Indeed, integrity is the most outstanding and definitive characteristic of the leaders we interviewed. Integrity is all of these: who they are, what they say and what they will do. This helps them build trust with all parties.

Integrity is the foundational trademark of their lives, families and businesses. It is what makes them tick. In a world of corruption and compromises, finding leaders with integrity is like unearthing a rare diamond. Thus, it is no wonder that they have been so successful and effective in their leadership.

B. The Transformative Power of Humility

"Pride comes when people treat you with great respect and you enjoy it so much that you refuse to let it go. Humility is the ability to accept humiliation and not be upset."

— S. Dhanabalan

Another consistent theme of these leaders is their humility. Some of these leaders have humility inculcated in them since young, having come from a humble background. George Ting's father was a fisherman and his mother was a rubber tapper. That was why he could feel for and understand the predicament of the poor. Kim Tan's father was a coolie and later became a vegetable-seller. They were so poor that he had to study under candlelight, next to a smelly outdoor toilet, where the 'night-soil man' removed the bucket.

Ngiam Tong Dow also had a humble beginning — his mother was illiterate and was a washerwoman. However, her indomitable spirit made her focus on educating her children because she believed, *"If you have one talent, and excel in it, you will never starve."* All of her children went to university on bursaries or scholarships. Tong Dow became one of the brightest scholars in the administrative system.

Tanri Abeng, former Indonesia Minister of State-Owned Enterprises in Suharto's cabinet, was born in a rural village on the island of Selayar in South Sulawasi, Indonesia. His parents were poor farmers but both were resilient and adaptable. He had to sell bananas to fellow students to buy books and material to go to school. At age 10, his parents died and he was sent to live in Makassar. To finish his education, he had to sell stenciled copies of school notes. He became one of the luminaries in corporate leadership in Indonesia.

Stephen Riady learned humility from his father Mochtar Riady, who likes to talk to people and listen to them regardless of their rank or importance. Everyone can have access to him. He never despised others.

Others learned humility through crisis, such as retired Malaysian businessman Roland Wong. His company Wong Heng and Wanga Hikmat was doing so well that it was going for a public listing.

He was living the high life — having special places at restaurants, privileged seats on important occasions, beautiful cars, and branded goods. All these came crashing down during the Asian Financial Crisis and he was completely devastated. His perseverance to clear his debts and his involvement with displaced migrants have kept him humble.

For Jocelyn Chng, it was going through tough times and learning to face shattering personal crises that made her humble and strong. She took over the family business Sin Hwa Dee Foodstuff when she was 21 while studying in the university. At 37, her grandmother and her husband died. She described them as the 'twinpillars' of her life. The loss made her even more determined to succeed as a single mother, oldest daughter and businesswoman. She not only survived but also overcame her adversity and the toughest of times to become a successful entrepreneur.

Tough times have a way of keeping them grounded and humble.

1. Humility means being honest of your own weakness

Humility comes from a deep self-awareness — recognizing who we are, where we come from, and what our strengths and weaknesses are.

Every one we interviewed is conscious of his or her weaknesses:

- Paul Chan — *"Tendency to criticize and seeing the negative aspect of people, not building enough bridges to people."*

- Jocelyn Chng — *"It is being too soft-hearted."*
- S. Dhanabalan — *"My biggest struggle is pride, when I am not treated with respect."*
- Chatree Duangnet — *"Not spending enough time with family."*
- Ho Peng Kee — *"It is being too assertive and demanding because of my passion and enthusiasm."*
- Hsieh Fu Hua — *"It is managing one's ego."*
- Idris Jala — *"Inability to make the trade-offs and who to listen to — the majority or the minority?"*
- Sandra Lee — *"Having a Type A personality, I am impatient and quick-tempered."*
- Lee Oi Hian — *"Being too superficial and not going into details enough."*
- Lim Guan Eng — *"Impatience."*
- Lim Siong Guan — *"My strength is my weakness."*
- Jaruvan Maintaka — *"Too demanding. When they can't do it, I rather do it myself."*
- Ngiam Tong Dow — *"My greatest handicap is to look at the bright side of people."*
- Edward Ong — *"It is impatience".*
- Stephen Riady — *"Not being tough enough".*
- Edwin Soeryadjaya — *"I was raised by indulgent parents, and must admit I in turn indulge my children. I find it very hard to say no to them."*
- Kim Tan — *"My biggest struggle is with materialism and all that comes with it, having designer-everything."*
- Amnuay Tapingkae — *"Being too quick to judge."*

For many, their strengths can also become their weakness. Kim Tan, who is passionate for the poor, finds that his biggest struggle is materialism. Edward's desire for excellence makes him impatient. Jaruvan's pursuit for justice makes her a very demanding boss.

However, they are able to go beyond their self-awareness to self-management. That marks them out as great leaders.

2. **Humility means serving the people and the poor**

The outworking of humility is to serve others. GIC group president Lim Siong Guan describes his servant-leadership model: *"A leader is to serve people, and help people to be the best that they can be, and do as much for them as he/she can."* His purpose in every place he has served is to *"leave behind a place where people want to be the best."*

Tan Cheng Bock, who came in a close second at the 2011 Singapore Presidential Election, is a great example of a people-focused leader. From his days of being a doctor in Ama Keng — a very poor village in Singapore at that time — to being a Member of Parliament (MP) in his constituency, his heart has always been for the poor. His clinic was a run-down shop house of half-zinc, half-attap roof. Some of them had to pay him in kind in the form of farm produce, eggs, and chickens. He felt that *whether that MP has a way with people is in the handshake. You will know the type of person you are going to deal with after a handshake. Some don't even look you in the eye when shaking your hands.* For him, people must come first and leaders must also be prepared to listen to their advice, because sometimes leaders may be wrong.

Paul Low is another example of humility. He is prepared to do menial tasks such as shifting chairs or even cleaning the toilet in church. His modus operandi is always to serve. Whether it was being chairman of the Malaysian Manufacturing Association, starting and providing counseling for the mentally sick, or being involved in Transparency International Malaysia or now serving in the Malaysia Cabinet, he is driven by one passion — a constructive engagement to serve the people. He said: *"The biggest part of their character should be humility. When you are humble, people will connect with you."*

This is the same stance of Ngiam Tong Dow, whose ability to be humble all the time is to be sensitive to people, have compassion for the poor, reminding himself where he came from and not lord over them.

In the case of Ho Peng Kee, he has always aimed to be a leader with a personal touch. When he was serving as Master of Kent Ridge Hall of Residence, he made it a point to know the students' names. He believes there is good in every person and sees to bring it out in him or her. He was also a leader and politician who was known as the 'second-chance' man, someone who pushed hard for rehabilitation.

3.   **Humility means shunning materialism and glamor**

Humility can be practically displayed in their daily routines and choices. For instance, Lim Siong Guan still takes public transport to work despite running a multi-billion dollar organization.

Dhanabalan's definition of humility is the ability to let go of privileges that hold you.

Kim Tan's multi-million dollar company has a policy of flying economy, renting modest cars, entertaining modestly and staying in four-star hotels. This is the result of learning from the late British stock investor and philanthropist John Templeton to live modestly, and he combats the cult of 'celebrity leadership' with 'servant leadership'. Yet, Kim Tan also accepts that everyone has their own set of indulgences. For him, it was owning the internationally acclaimed Saracen Rugby Club.

Lim Guan Eng still flies economy despite being the Penang Chief Minister. He was asked by the people: *"Why don't you take business class? Why fly economy? How much money can you save?"* He replied: *"I agree with you I can't save much money. But I want to send a strong message to my civil servants. I want to cut cost. If I can save, you can also save. If I can take economy, you better follow me by cutting costs…. That's the message I want to send: If we can save, we save. You are the custodian of people's funds. You must uphold the sacred trust."*

4.   Humility means adopting a learning posture

The person who epitomizes the above is James Chia. He has been learning at every phase of his life and from various people — from his cultural heritage, his National Service (Compulsory Military Service), his siblings, his customers, and from being a grandparent. He says, *"At different phases of my life, I was blessed to work with very capable people who became my mentors."* Most of all, he learns from his wife, who is a voracious reader like himself.

Ngiam Tong Dow practices humility by his willingness to listen to the *"people on the streets besides the Harvard graduates"*. He believes they have as much wisdom as the latter and have much to teach him.

During his stint at the Badminton Association of Malaysia, Roland Wong was one leader who galvanized his fellow leaders to come on board. To do this, he had to be a good learner. Being a good learner means being a good listener. He said: *"I allow people to go against my proposals. I don't insist on them following my way. Although at times I may feel hurt, I still go along and support their decision."*

Not surprising, humility is another characteristic of these great leaders. What stands out for us is that this value is consistently cultivated and lived out in practical ways through their learning posture, service to people, passion for the poor, shunning of glamor, and adoption of a modest lifestyle.

Most of all, they discipline themselves by keeping their egos in check, especially when they are at the pinnacle of their successes and positions. They do not allow their special status to enslave them and become victims of an entitlement mentality. It is this trait that their followers admire them the most for, because it impacts them the most.

C. The Comebacks of Recovery

"The night is always the darkest just before dawn. Things will get worse before they become better. When you are at your depths, it will pass. When you are at your heights, it will also pass."

— *Lim Guan Eng*

Crisis is a common experience for all. A number of these leaders experienced the trauma and pain of the Asian Financial Crisis in 1997, when the exchange rate of their local currencies moved sharply against them swiftly.

Many of them collapsed financially and went through emotional upheaval. They had sleepless nights when creditors were after them. Their emotions ranged from anger to despair. Their personal and family lives were affected. But they never allowed these multiple and mounting crises to cripple them. They persevered and bounced back remarkably.

1. Recovery means confronting realities squarely

For Hsieh Fu Hua, the leader should lead from the front in crisis. He feels that the leader must be more proactive, demonstrate control, galvanize the people and maintain his sense of perspective and make the final call. Leaders should not play the 'blame-game'. *"During such tough times, a leader should confront the problems head-on rather than confronting his people,"* he said.

Roland Wong's business almost became insolvent during the Asian Financial Crisis. He had to face up to the cruel realities of bankruptcy honestly. He had to meet up with his creditors and bankers one by one. Because he had a good credit history with them, they did not foreclose his company. For a long period, he had no peace — he could not sleep and had to be on tranquilizers.

But he came to terms with it. He met up with each creditor and promised that he would repay them slowly but surely. They trusted him and he eventually settled all his debts.

Similarly, when Stephen Riady faced a crisis, he confronted it and did not pretend there was no crisis. He learned to face each creditor and sought ways to repay each one because he believes that if you are sincere, people will trust you. The worst thing to do is to abscond.

Another aspect of facing realities is to assume responsibility as a corporate citizen. Lim Hua Min recalled the 1985 Pan-El stock market crisis in Singapore. Even though his company was badly affected like most others and remained solvent, every stock broking firm, including Phillip Capital, was made to bear corporate responsibility by signing a S$6 million guarantee. Although it seemed unfair to him, he realized that in crisis, there was a public responsibility he had to bear.

2.   **Recovery means learning from failures, forgiving and making comebacks**

Recovery also involves recognizing their own failures and being willing to correct them. During his first stint as CEO of Bangkok Hospital, Chatree Duangnet failed miserably as a change leader. He confessed that he wanted to push through the changes and found that no one was following him. He had a big ego and a big vision. He had to change. In making his comeback to Bangkok Hospital a few years later, he did things very differently. He intentionally ensured and enabled that his key leaders were with him in the vision and transformation. In short, they have *"to cross the river together with me"*, he said. *"A leader is successful only when his followers are successful."*

Lim Siong Guan's galvanizing perspective about adversity keeps him in check. He said as a matter-of-factly without sounding cocky: *"I don't have any crisis."* He explained: *"My frame is that if I fall, I change and learn from the opportunity. I keep a short memory. Even when people have fallen, I help them recover."*

Lim Guan Eng's two-term imprisonment never made him bitter and filled him with hatred. As he puts it, to become bitter will "satisfy his tormentors" and he "will be like his tormentors in [his] hate". He had to learn to forgive: *"If you don't forgive the person, you are not forgiving yourself and you will become the person that you hate. Forgiveness is not laced with vengeance but is laced with justice, tempered by mercy and compassion."*

Edwin Soeryadjaya describes himself as a 'Johnny-Come-Lately' leader. His family had to sell off the Astra Group, the largest conglomerate in Indonesia. In his own admission, he started work only at the age of 42. In fact, people despised him, *"You are a playboy, and you don't know how to run a company."* According to him, *"It was the biggest slap on my face. It was a wake up call. That was the turning point of my life."*

He had to relearn, recoup, recover and rebuild from the crisis. He could not save Astra. But he rose from the ashes of the family's loss in Astra to become one of the most respected and successful entrepreneurs in starting the Saratoga Group today.

3. Recovery means maintaining discipline

Maybank Kim Eng (Thailand) CEO Montree Sornpaisan recalled the Asian Financial Crisis in 1997 and how his company at that time — Jardine Fleming — had to work professionally, ethically and prudently with discipline. It was keeping these fundamentals in place before the crisis that saved the day during the crisis. From the business standpoint, for him it meant prudence (not being greedy, not over-leveraging and not under-capitalizing), ethics (not fake market signals, not fake accounts, not fake performance) and professionalism (loving your life, family, job, and country).

Edward Ong almost lost everything in the Sutera Harbor Resort. He lost US$125 million in one day because of the Asian Financial Crisis in 1997. At other times, there were the severe acute respiratory syndrome (SARS), Swine, and Avian Flu crises that almost derailed his resort business. Soon, his debt grew to US$2.2 billion. He wanted to do it right and not take the easy way out. He assured the bankers and kept slogging through day by day. Finally, he sold his stake and repaid his bankers.

Recovery is not just for themselves and their people. These leaders also help organizations prepare for the future by developing what Lim Siong Guan calls an *"organization's emotional resilience and perseverance, which is to prepare the organization for the future and prevent hemorrhages"*.

For Lim Hua Min, maintaining discipline means building when times are bad, and harvesting when times are good. He said: *"When times are bad, you can then use your spare resources to innovate or diversify for the next lap. When times are good, all your capacity is fully utilized. Therefore, you should be harvesting. You should take the opportunity to maximize your sales and profit."*

For Tanri Abeng during his stint as an Indonesia Minister, maintaining discipline involved knowing what was crucial and what was not. He had to choose between which company had to be sacrificed and which critical company could not be sacrificed, so that he did not jeopardize the big picture. His advice to President Suharto was to "do what is best for the nation" and not to please his cronies or relatives.

4. Recovery means having a support system and loved ones standing firmly with you

For most, their recovery had to do with their closest friends, spouses and families standing by them through thick and thin.

For Roland Wong, it was his wife and daughter, who saw him through the crisis. He acknowledges: *"I am deeply grateful to my wife, Amy, who stood by me throughout this crisis… I would not have survived without her. Amy and I prayed together often which constantly kept me at peace and brought clarity to my thinking."*

When dealing with crisis during the Atlanta Olympics in 1996 with the Badminton Association of Malaysia, he always reminded the team: *"Please help me to help you. If you punch one hole in the boat, another punches a second hole, we will sink together. So let's behave like a family."* It was this camaraderie perspective that he inculcated that helped pulled him through many challenges.

What kept Lim Guan Eng through his personal crises and failures as a politician were his "father, comrades and friends". He describes his father as *"holding the torch during the dark days"*. Despite the fact that his father had no power, the force of his ideas and the spirit of his courage really lifted many Malaysians. That was his motivation for recovery.

5. Recovery means preparing and charting the future

This mindset is most prominent in Lim Siong Guan. For him, leaders must anticipate change, welcome change, and execute the change. It has to do with the capacity to respond to unexpected situations. This means anticipating the future, expecting the crisis and preventing hemorrhages, without assuming the system will not break down.

This, in essence, is what he means by the future-oriented leader. It is a frame of mind of being No.1, which is learning as much as we can and the ability to create and innovate. His mantra is "Think Future, Think People, Think Excellence".

Chatree Duangnet prepares for the future by developing a pipeline of talent for succession planning. He meets up with a group of young doctors every week to learn, study and grow together.

From these stories of recovery, we find that making comebacks and dealing with crisis are part and parcel of every leader's journey.

Recovery involves preparation to ensure that their organizations are resilient enough to manage crisis. It means having the courage to define clearly their crushing realities and be unfazed by them. It is having the right perspective of seeing it as a learning opportunity. It is learning to forgive and not succumbing to the betrayal of bitterness and hatred. It also demands a disciplined perseverance to work through crisis. It is also the rallying of support from spouses, family members, friends and staff to see them through their emotional upheaval. Finally, it also requires the leader to galvanize the team to look beyond the crisis to a future not only full of hope but also one anchored in reality.

D. The Miracle of Divine Intervention

"You must always believe that there's an element of luck, and if you're a believer — God's grace."

— *Stephen Riady*

One significant aspect of the leaders' stories is witnessing divine intervention in their lives. For some, this is seen as luck or fate. To most, it is their belief in God.

Most found God in their crisis and also learned to trust Him during their crisis. A number of them had come to the end of their road , but they found God and released everything to Him. They recognized that there was a power beyond them. They were not God but mere mortals. They had no control of everything. In fact, everything had gone out of control. They learned the lesson of submission and released their crisis to a higher being.

When his debt grew from RM750 million to RM1.4 billion in 1998 and his wife left him, it was like a hangman's noose for Edward Ong. He became disillusioned and angry with God because it happened after he had become a Christian. His sleepless nights were haunted with nightmares, as he was so emotionally worn out. There were two options — either to walk away or submit totally to God. He said: *"I began to realize I had nothing to show, nothing to prove, nothing to hide."*

It was then that he resolved to own up to the bankers, who showed him favor and he had to repay his debts slowly. It was only in 2014, after 26 years, that he finally cleared his debt when he sold a 77.5% stake to a fellow Singaporean businessman. His perseverance paid off when he was given the 2014 Entrepreneurial Leaders Award by his fellow business leaders.

Another leader who found God during the Asian Financial Crisis was Roland Wong. He faced millions of dollars in debt and his company almost collapsed. There was no light at the end of the tunnel. He despaired: *"If there was any light, it was only the light from an oncoming train."*

Being a non-religious person, he was so desperate that he turned to any god who could help him. He prayed to Buddha. One Sunday, he felt the urge to go to church. One song touched him so deeply, *"God will make a way, where there seems no way."* He suddenly burst into tears, which had never happened to him. He confessed that he was a tough Chinese businessman who could shed blood but never tears. That morning, he wept like a baby but he felt a deep peace in him. It was as though a heavy burden had been lifted from him. That was the beginning of his redemption. Like Edward Ong, he began to confront his bankers and creditors. He paid them slowly and finally cleared off all his debts.

Edwin Soeryadjaya tried everything to save the Astra Group but he failed. His wife felt that selling Astra was the best thing that has happened to him. She was right because he was very proud and arrogant. Losing Astra humbled him. It was then that he found God.

During the Asian Financial Crisis, Stephen Riady confessed that his faith grew the most during that period. He said: *"During a crisis, outwardly you may be suffering, but inwardly you still have joy because you have the supply of hidden manna from God."*

For others, God has been a constant in their lives. Amnuay Tapingkae's turning point was his conversion to Christianity through his own miraculous healing of typhoid fever. Since then, his faith has been his guiding light, and he lives by the motto — *"The heart of education is the education of the heart".*

Another leader who outwardly proclaims and practices his faith is Francis Yeoh. He attributes all his successes to God: *"If we look back at the growth of YTL's businesses, we not only see God's fingerprints everywhere but also His footprints! They are simply miraculous. I give God all the glory!"* Also, he does not flinch in acknowledging his dependency on God. He recognizes that he has "millions of weaknesses" which he battles with every day.

Stephen Riady puts it most succinctly: *"You must always believe that there's an element of luck, and if you're a believer — God's grace."*

Printed in the United States
By Bookmasters